RESISTING INVISIBILITY

Detecting the Female Body in Spanish Crime Fiction

Resisting Invisibility

Detecting the Female Body in Spanish Crime Fiction

DIANA ARAMBURU

UNIVERSITY OF TORONTO PRESS
Toronto Buffalo London

Toronto Buffalo London
utorontopress.com

ISBN 978-1-4875-0459-5

Toronto Iberic

Library and Archives Canada Cataloguing in Publication

Title: Resisting invisibility : detecting the female body in Spanish crime fiction / Diana Aramburu.
Names: Aramburu, Diana, 1981–, author.
Series: Toronto Iberic.
Description: Series statement: Toronto Iberic | Includes bibliographical references and index.
Identifiers: Canadiana 20190050071 | ISBN 9781487504595 (hardcover)
Subjects: LCSH: Detective and mystery stories, Spanish – History and criticism. | LCSH: Suspense fiction, Spanish – History and criticism. | LCSH: Women in literature. | LCSH: Human body in literature. | LCSH: Femininity in literature.
Classification: LCC PQ6147.D47 A73 2019 | DDC 863/.0872093522 – dc23

This book has been published with the assistance of the Asociación de Estudios de Género y Sexualidades (AEGS) and the Office of Research and College of Letters & Science at the University of California, Davis.

University of Toronto Press acknowledges the financial assistance to its publishing program of the Canada Council for the Arts and the Ontario Arts Council, an agency of the Government of Ontario.

Canada Council for the Arts   Conseil des Arts du Canada

Funded by the Government of Canada   Financé par le gouvernement du Canada

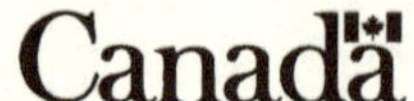

To Ana and Walter Snow

The detective story differs from every other story in this: that the reader is only happy if he feels a fool.

G.K. Chesterton, "The Ideal Detective Story"

Contents

Acknowledgments

Resisting Invisibility won the 2017 Premio de Monografía Crítica Victoria Urbano, an international prize awarded by the Asociación de Estudios de Género y Sexualidades (AEGS). I want to thank AEGS for their support of this project. An earlier version of a section of chapter 4 was published as "The Detective Turned Victim: The Victimization and the Visibility of the Female Body in Maria-Antònia Oliver's Lònia Guiu Series" in *Ámbitos Feministas*, vol. 6, 2016, pp. 79–91. Also, an abbreviated version of chapter 5's section on Isabel Franc's Emma García series first appeared as "Resisting Invisibility: Lesbianizing the Public Space in Isabel Franc's Emma García Stories" in *Hispanic Review*, vol. 85, no. 1, Winter 2017, pp. 47–67. (Copyright © 2017 University of Pennsylvania Press.) All rights reserved. Lastly, a few paragraphs from the introduction and from chapter 4 were included in "Revenge by Castration: Breaking the Narrative Thread of Rape in Maria-Antònia Oliver's Fiction" in *Studies in 20th & 21st Century Literature*, vol. 41, no. 1, Spring 2017, Article 17. I would like to thank Carmen Urioste, Linda Grabner, and Necia Chronister for their editorial guidance. I remain indebted to Mario Santana and Agnes Lugo-Ortiz for their support throughout the course of the research and writing of this book and for their continued mentorship. A very special thank you goes to Kathleen McNerney and to Nick Phillips for their feedback on the manuscript and to Melissa Stewart for her advice during the earlier stages of the process.

Thanks also go to my UC Davis colleagues, especially Robert Newcomb for his comments on the manuscript, as well as John Slater and Michael Subialka for their encouragement and advice throughout this process. I am grateful to my former research assistant, Alba Marcé García, and my current research assistant, Morgan Smith, both of whose editorial and translation help proved most useful during the later stages of the project, and to the graduate students at UC Davis who participated in my seminar on female crime fiction for our insightful discussions. I would also like to thank the University of Toronto Press, particularly Mark Thompson and Janice Evans, for supporting this project, and my external readers for their comments and recommendations.

Finally, I am most grateful to my family, especially Brian, Yolanda, Pedro Antonio, Juan Pablo, Pedro José and Nancy, Ken, Arlene, and my grandmother, Ana, and my friends, in particular Gretchen and Russell, who have offered their unconditional love and support as I completed this study.

RESISTING INVISIBILITY

Detecting the Female Body in Spanish Crime Fiction

Introduction

Detecting the Female Body in Gendered Mysteries

The year 2016 was a contentious one for the *novela negra* in Spain as crime fiction writers, critics, and readers debated how to define the genre and which works could still be categorized under this label. The problem, it seemed, was that the crime novels being published were not *noir* enough. Missing were psychopaths, serial killers, *mafiosos*, and sometimes even the detective and/or the crime itself. Taking their place were the everyman and everywoman – people you would probably cross paths with on a daily basis – and situations that you hear about in the news. The socioeconomic crisis that Spain has been suffering since 2007–8 also plays a prevalent role in these new articulations of the genre, since crimes are commonly born out of necessity and those who resort to violence sometimes make unlikely criminals. These revisions encouraged those with more traditional or conservative views on crime fiction to claim that these new generic formulations should not be considered or sold under the fashionable *novela negra* label.

Since Francisco Franco's death in 1975, the detective novel, in particular the *novela negra*, has been one of Spain's most popular types of fiction because, beyond its entertainment value, it functions as a critical and strategic literary space that problematizes the sociopolitical and cultural panorama of the time. Appropriated from the North American hard-boiled novel, made popular by authors such as Dashiell Hammett and Raymond Chandler, the *novela negra* served to uncover and denounce the continued violence and injustices and to represent the disillusionment people felt during the Transition in Spain, according to José Colmeiro's *La novela policiaca española* (*The Spanish Detective Novel* 213). Because the hard-boiled novel refuses "the sometimes constricting formulas of the formal detective novel," it takes on an urban documentary format, since the crimes investigated in these fictional representations are supposed to mirror those of the real world, using a more fast-paced, violent, and colloquial format (Grella 412). The *novela negra*'s sleuth, a solitary figure modelled after the hard-boiled detective who is able to infiltrate all social classes because of her/his marginalization, demonstrates and problematizes the system's faults, focusing less on the investigation and more on what has led to the violence and crimes committed (Lissorgues 179).

In speaking about the birth of the *novela negra*, Paul Preston has noted that the *serie negra*, which is fashioned after "American detective fiction [which] assumes that the political system is immutable and the detective puts right things the system cannot" without transforming "anything fundamental," is a "literature of passivity" ("Materialism" 11). Preston presents this as paradox: at a moment of significant political change after the fall of the regime, which should be pregnant with hope and activity, we find the emergence of a literature that seems to assume a political immutability. According to Preston, the *serie negra* attracted authors who were looking for "a genre which is popular and pays well, yet also permits them an oblique, deeply moralistic, albeit ultimately impotent, comment on the corruption and materialism of politics" (13). For Preston, the genre provides solutions to "imaginary problems" without engaging in the current sociopolitical and economic crises, and instead, functions as a form of escapism from the political context that is the reason for its popularity (15–16). As no new order is proposed in the *serie negra* because it is assumed that the political system will remain unaltered, "[t]he detective novel provides the illusion that there is an explanation and that there is justice" (15).

Whereas Preston characterizes the genre under the label of pulp and escapist fiction, which has no real intention of making changes (13), Colmeiro suggests that after the fall of the regime, the boom of this subgenre in the 1970s and 1980s was not only the result of the economic, political, and social crises during the Transition; a cultural necessity also arose after the dictatorship to represent the marginalized spaces and social classes, and the writers of the *novela negra* looked to fill this cultural void (*La novela policiaca española* 213). Authors like Manuel Vázquez Montalbán, Eduardo Mendoza, Andreu Martín, and Juan Madrid were able to adapt certain features of hard-boiled fiction to create an instrument for social critique that could also unmask corrupt power structures (213). Beyond chronicling the general disillusionment with the Transition, the *novela negra* also created a site for the recuperation of historical memory, what Caragh Wells refers to as "nostalgia as a critical tool against the culture of forgetting" (284). A trendsetter for other *novela negra* writers, Vázquez Montalbán formulated a series that "illustrates how the Transition, in overlooking the actions of the victors, forgot the hopes of the losers of the Spanish Civil War," according to Susana Bayó Belenguer ("Montalbán's Carvalho Series" 300). By showcasing Barcelona's marginalized peoples in his Pepe Carvalho novels, Vázquez Montalbán provides a window into what it means to have been on the losing side of the Civil War in addition to representing the working-class underbelly of Barcelona's urban neighborhoods (Wells 284). Mario Santana elucidates that "[i]n this sense, detective stories are less about self-recognition than discovery – or, more appropriately in Carvalho's case, re-discovery, as his inquiry is a process closely linked to the operation of memory" (542). Carvalho also undergoes a continuous process of self (re)discovery, suffering multiple crises of identity, where he is forced to confront others who question his function as a detective, but who also challenge how he relates to those around him, especially the women in the series.

The economic collapse of 2007–8 has produced this same sort of cultural necessity to represent the disillusionment felt towards a government that advocates for the interests of the upper echelons and towards a banking system that preys on the middle and lower classes. Newly marginalized and ignored social classes and peoples are claiming visibility and resisting invisibility, and crime fiction authors are responding by converting them into their protagonists. In fact, contemporary writers in Spain have felt the need to respond to the crisis in a manner similar to those of the Transition – by uncovering continued injustices, corruption, and violence and by giving visibility to those who are ignored or concealed by the system.

Recent crime fiction that is emerging after 2008 functions as a chronicle of the crisis, as literature that is born from the *gris asfalto* (grey asphalt), a term coined by writer Empar Fernández in a 2016 article titled "Lejos del negro absoluto" ("Far from True Noir"). Since authors like Fernández and Anna Maria Villalonga were publishing novels that did not follow the conventions of the traditional *novela negra*, with the lack of professional detectives and unconventional crimes and criminals, the debate over how to redefine the *novela negra* prompted them to declare the existence of an alternative crime fiction model, or subgenre – the *gris asfalto* novel.[1] In the *gris asfalto* narrative, Fernández clarifies, the crime committed "a menudo es fruto del azar o de la fatalidad; no es un propósito en sí mismo ni reside en la naturaleza de los protagonistas. El personaje que intenta descifrar el 'enigma' no es un profesional – funcionario o investigador privado – y no obedece ningún tipo de protocolo" ("is often the result of chance or misfortune; it is not an objective in itself nor does it reside in the nature of the protagonists.

The character trying to decipher the 'enigma' is not a professional – an official or private investigator – and does not obey any sort of protocol").[2] Furthermore, to represent the crisis, the *novela negra*'s formula had to change. According to Villalonga, the *gris asfalto* narrative employs antiheroic characters whose motives for committing these crimes, such as revenge, injustice, and guilt, are easily identifiable to readers ("Si no pot ser 'negra,'" "If It Can't Be 'Noir'"). By relating experiences and creating characters from our everyday reality, the *gris asfalto* novels force us to reconsider traditional conceptions of crime and criminality and reexamine our fixed definitions of delinquency.

These changes to the *novela negra*, however, did not start with the birth of the *gris asfalto*, but with the appearance of the modern female detective in crime literature. A boom of the last decade, but also with roots in the transitional years, the *detectivas* of the *novela negra* started populating a once-male-only genre, producing female detectives who break with traditional stereotypes and captivate a crime-fiction-hungry audience. In examining crime and violence from a woman's perspective, female crime fiction in Spain has opened the doors for the *gris aslfalto* subgenre because by feminizing the eye, regendering the eye and I of the detective, crucial changes and subversions to the genre have occurred, beginning with the genre's politics of visibility.[3] By politics of female visibility, I am referring to the textual practices that determine the perceptibility of women's bodies, including both exposure and erasure. What is at stake in the politics of visibility is the constitution of women as political subjects, subjects who can receive justice, as well as knowing subjects, like detectives, who can act in the interests of others. The politics of visibility take on a crucial role in crime fiction because they change the nature of the story, from a plot that hinges on the pain and death of a female body denied full political participation through various strategies of objectification, to a narrative where the female body functions as a critical tool of resistance to pinpoint the ineffectiveness of the legal system's response to gender violence.

Here I find it useful to invoke Monica J. Casper and Lisa Jean Moore's definition of the body's politics of visibility as "the conditions under which certain bodies become visible or remain hidden ... the dimensions of visibility depend, to some degree, on what category bodies fit into" (181). These authors point out that it is fundamental to identify "how we look" at these bodies, for that too will determine the "different degrees of visibility [that] emerge" (181). Although Casper and Moore explore in their sociological study how actual bodies are celebrated with exposure while others are denied visibility, Kath Woodward emphasizes the literary implications of these representations where "[v]isibility involves power relations ... An explanation of being there contributes to an understanding the specific nuances, connections and disconnections, which make up the politics of in/visibility and the processes which are implicated in seeing and being seen, or not seen, and looking and being looked at, or not" (8). Woodward proposes that these processes of being made visible or invisible, of "[b]eing there and being seen to be there are not innocent or neutral processes; their presence raises questions about responsibility and agency and about the nature of being visibly situated within a particular context. The operation of power involves the re-instatement of inequalities and challenges to them through the politics of visibility" (12).

In this book, I provide insight into how certain crime fiction authors engage readers with the politics of visibility of the female body by manipulating generic conventions involving the gaze, and how, in turn, the female body gains or resists visibility. Crime fiction is a site where the debate over the politics of female visibility becomes clear; since its inception in Spain, it has been motivated by how the delinquent female body is read and staged. As the eye/I of the gaze changes in crime fiction, however, so too does the generic formula because the female body and perspective gain a new visibility and voice in female crime literature, a crucial variant of which is lesbian crime fiction, when women detectives take a leading role. This new visibility in female crime fiction has opened an alternative discursive space, which promotes and creates awareness of women's vulnerability in the patriarchal system, but also functions as an effective site of resistance.

In little over a decade, female crime fiction has established itself in the Spanish literary market as a credible variety of the detective genre. It has captured the attention of scholars, the publishing industry, and the media, which labelled the phenomenon *femicrime* because crime and violence, but also issues of identity and gender, are now being explored from a woman-centred perspective.[4] Adopted from the Danish term *femikrimi*, which became popular in Denmark during the 2000s, the particularities of this phenomenon in Spain have been examined by the Centre Dona i Literatura (Centre for Women and Literature) at the University of Barcelona, creators of the Mujeres y Novela Criminal en España (Women and the Crime Novel in Spain) or MUNCE project in 2012.[5] Led by Elena Losada Soler, the MUNCE project established an online database and catalogue of crime fiction novels authored by women in Spain since 1975 in addition to the publication of critical anthologies that analyze these novels, television series, and films from a feminist and gender studies perspective. MUNCE's creation and success is not at all unexpected considering female crime fiction's current popularity.

The beginnings of this *femicrime* phenomenon in Spain, however, date back to 1979, when the first female hard-boiled detective, Bárbara Arenas, appears in Lourdes Ortiz's *Picadura mortal* (*Mortal Sting*). Though highly criticized for imitating the male models of the genre by well-known crime fiction scholars such as Colmeiro, Patricia Hart, and Robert C. Spires, among others, upon careful examination Ortiz's text exposes and parodies the *novela negra*'s gazing and policing function of the female body. This is not surprising because in order to problematize and invert the male models of the genre, the feminization of crime fiction will use parody in its imitation of the male generic forms, but will do so in a way that is both self-reflective and critical. Here, I am referring to Linda Hutcheon's definition of parody and its relation to irony:

> Parody, then, in its ironic "trans-contextualization" and inversion, is repetition with difference. A critical distance is implied between the backgrounded text being parodied and the new incorporating work, a distance usually signaled by irony. But this irony can be playful as well as belittling; it can be critically constructive as well as destructive. The pleasure of parody's irony comes not from humor in particular but from the degree of engagement of the reader in the intertextual "bouncing" (to use E.M. Forster's famous term) between complicity and distance. (32)

The feminization of the genre will initially rely on the imitation of male models, but this imitation is "characterized by ironic inversion" and "marks difference rather than similarity" to use Hutcheon's words (6). By inverting and replacing the male perspective with a female point of view, *Picadura mortal*, for example, recreates the gazing spectacle of the male-dominated *novela negra* to caricature it, hence subverting it. Margaret Rose has previously explained that "the use of parody may aim both at a comic effect and at the transmission of both complex and serious messages." (29). Ortiz's novel engages in this sort of critical exposition through targeted ridicule to signal the *machista* attitudes and the patriarchal system under which crime fiction operates to free itself from it. Although critics like Colmeiro, Hart, and Spires have considered her attempt to free the female detective from the male generic forms unsuccessful, *Picadura mortal* arguably sets the stage for a new politics of visibility of the female body for contemporary female crime fiction. The first modern female detective novel, therefore, could be read as an investigation of female gender roles.

Regarding early female detectives such as Albert Aiken's Mignon Warner or Mrs Julia Herlock Shomes who appears in "The Adventures of the Tomato on the Wall" (1894) and "The Identity of Miss Angelica Vespers" (1894) by Ka, Sally Munt has previously pointed out how it is important to "read into these early sleuths, in their fizzling irreverence, a strategy of disruption adjunctive to *and* moderating of the genre's conventional masculinity" because these first women-centred narratives "'feminized' the form by a process of intrepid infiltration" (*Murder* 5; italics in original). This initial infiltration and subsequent transgression of the masculine-centred form occurs through parody, for "parody was an inevitable response to their position as literary intruders" (5). Munt gives the example of Agatha Christie, whose detective heroes, whether they are the feminized Hercule Poirot or female sleuths like Tuppence Beresford or Miss Marple, disrupt male myths through parody, and consequently reject the masculine detective hero model (8). Both early twentieth-century female crime fiction authors and more contemporary women writers in Spain will use parody as a narrative strategy to destabilize male authority in the genre, in particular the notion of the valiant, confident, ethical, and intelligent detective, or to use Munt's term, "the Great Detective as an icon of Man" (204). Parody allows for the unmasking of myths surrounding the detective, which are satirized through humour and through the performance of female stereotypes (204). Since feminization occurs through parodic inversion, both the male and female myths are shown as what they are – performances that preserve a patriarchal ideology.

The masculinity of the canon is disrupted by not only rewriting the female role in the genre through this inversion of the private eye's perspective, but also by redefining the politics of visibility surrounding the female body. The management of the female body's visibility has clearly changed with the new modes of representation of women's bodies and perspectives in contemporary female crime fiction, but there are also certain elements that seem to remain. Understanding the body as both metaphor and presence and the site for differing discursive and cultural inscriptions, I investigate the gendering of crime fiction by juxtaposing how the female body is mobilized in the four phases of its feminization, exploring an alternative genealogy, with a particular emphasis on the modes of representation of the female body and perspective. The four main types of bodies that I will be emphasizing are delinquent, victimized, and eroticized female bodies as well as detective bodies. It is important to note that these types will intersect and create binaries, which means that the blurring of these categories must also be analyzed. By comparing how the female body is activated in the early phases of the genre through contemporary female detective fiction, I establish a type of genealogy of the different viewpoints regarding women's position in these narratives before and after the so-called feminization of the genre. While most scholars situate the feminization of the genre during the second wave of the feminist movement, even in the first models that we have of women delinquents in Pedro Antonio de Alarcón's *El clavo* (*The Nail,* 1853) and Emilia Pardo Bazán's *La gota de sangre* (*The Drop of Blood,* 1911) we can already observe how the genre has been reconceived because the female criminal is the central figure upon which the plot turns and unfolds. What this illustrates is that there is a simultaneous generic tradition that has not been taken into account when studying the contemporary female detective, which has been understood by some scholars as a mere replica of the male detective. Contemporary female detectives have their own tradition, a tradition that has precedents in the feminization of the picaresque, which has rejected the female body as an object of the male gaze.

Studying the body's staging is crucial precisely because we begin with the body in crime fiction. Sarah Dunant, the author of the Hannah Wolfe crime series, emphasizes that "[c]rime fiction, by its very nature, has an intimate relationship with the dead body" (11). The narrative of investigation begins once the dead body is uncovered, and the detective's first focus, as an "organ of perception," to use Fredric Jameson's terminology, must be on the body. The detective, who Jameson claims navigates through and links different parts of a fragmented society, also moves through bodies (131). The trail to uncovering how one body ceased to exist or was hurt and how another body made this possible is the base narrative upon which the genre is built. However, when "the narrative of investigation supersedes the narrative of crime," there is a generic movement from initial victim visibility to almost irrelevant invisibility, as Kathleen Gregory Klein affirms ("*Habeas Corpus*" 173). Put differently, the male-dominated genre routinely uses the female corpse as its foundation and later discards it, making it invisible (Godsland, *Killing Carmens* 85–90). According to Shelley Godsland, "The pages of many male-authored detective fictions are littered with women's lifeless bodies that have been sexually misused by male protagonists" (ibid., 89). Now, while the investigation is born from the victim's body, the criminal body is the one the detective conventionally moves towards. The end result is to make the delinquent visible, confirming the detective's power and success over the transgressive body. Whereas the victim's body undergoes erasure, the criminal body moves into the visual spotlight to be exposed.

To use a Foucauldian term, traditional crime fiction is very much entrenched in "bio-power," meaning it looks to subdue unruly bodies, those of criminals, and restore a disrupted patriarchal order (Foucault, *History* 139). Conventional hierarchies of power in crime literature follow the same format as social power hierarchies described by Michel Foucault as "centered on the body as a machine: its disciplining, the optimization of its capabilities, ... the parallel increase of its usefulness and its docility, [and] its integration into systems of efficient and economic controls." (139). Basing her argument on Foucault's *Discipline and Punish* and using the Lacanian idea of the Law-of-the-Father, Teresa L. Ebert makes the connection between the male sleuth and patriarchal authority by signalling that "the detective does the *work* of patriarchy" by implementing "the Law-of-the-Father (through violence if necessary) ensuring that individuals line up on the side of the phallic divide signaled by their anatomy, and he preserves and secures the system of privilege, labor, and exploitation based on gender, resolving its contradictions and restoring its hegemony and legitimacy" (8; italics in original). The male sleuth forms part of the normalizing narrative of detective fiction that looks to construct or exhibit what would be considered idealized and ordered norms of conduct. Furthermore, it is up to the male sleuth to exert his mastery and control over the delinquent body by bringing it into the visual realm. Because the female criminal poses a heightened danger in that she "refuse[s] to stay fixed in the place patriarchal ideology assigns," according to Ebert, the detective makes her visible to scrutinize, contain, and put her (back) in her place (7).

With the hard-boiled generic variety, sexuality becomes instrumental to the plot, although in earlier forms this is rarely the case (*Murder* 1–4). The moment where the display of the female character occurs in both literature and cinema depends upon what Laura Mulvey calls "the determining male gaze," so that the male spectator can experience "strong visual and erotic impact" ("Visual Pleasure" 837). From both Mulvey and Teresa de Lauretis, we ascertain that the gaze is identified as both masculine and active because it involves the looks of the camera and of the male characters, whereas the image, in turn, is feminine and passive because it is the body, the landscape (de Lauretis 144). In both literature and film, the narrative pauses to fixate on the female body and to view it in piecemeal fashion – containing it in the masculine "eye." Evidently, the tradition has been "[w]omen displayed as sexual object" because it "is the leit-motiff [*sic*] of erotic spectacle" according to Mulvey, and hard-boiled male crime fiction has not shied away from using female characters for this end (837). Mulvey's argument can also be used to explain how male crime fiction pauses not only to expose its female characters as erotic objects for the pleasure of the male detective, but presumably for the male reader (838). Though we do not have a camera in crime fiction, we do have a narrative voice that allows us to (re)explore the gazing and staging of the female body.

Containing the female threat to patriarchy, however, does not detract from the scopophilic pleasure of making the female body visible. Putting her back in her place also signifies being able to engage in what Annette Kuhn defines as "pleasurable looking," where the look "takes the form of voyeurism, in which the object of the look is outside of, and distanced from, the subject, and there is apparently no comeback for the spectator in the form either of a returned look or other response, or of punishment for looking" (*Women's Pictures* 57). It is, accentuates Kuhn, "a kind of 'lawless seeing,' and this is one of the major sources of its pleasure" (57). This lawless seeing, furthermore, combats any sort of threat that the female image entails because if she is fetishized, "the castratory aspects of the image" are neutralized (60). When female bodies are displayed in traditional crime fiction, it is this sort of lawless looking that occurs, which Godsland claims "is possibly an expression of a wish for control of the feminine, as is heterosexual pornography, which is of itself a violence visited on the female body" (*Killing Carmens* 89). Transformed into the object of the gaze, she is contained by the eye of the detective, and is traditionally not given the space to look back. This fetishization of the female image thus contributes to the pleasure of the sleuth and his reader. But what occurs when she does look back? What changes when the female character is given the opportunity to return the gaze, or when she is the owner of the "eye" that is doing the looking?

These instances of the feminizing of the gaze reformulate the conventional politics of visibility that we are used to encountering in the male-centred crime novel. This feminization of the eye or these instances of feminizing the look in the genre forces an opening and activates, while at the same time challenging, the act of reading by creating a plurality of meanings, as Kuhn argues regarding cinema (*Women's Pictures* 11–12). What this means, then, is that new "conditions of visibility" are established, to use de Lauretis's terminology, where the female body moves away from being the eroticized object of the male gaze and alternative inscriptions of women's bodies are created, where she is no longer contained (68). It is in this space of new visibility and redefinition where a blurring of boundaries can occur, and so the limits between victim and criminal, or, later, between detective and victim (or detective and criminal), are erased, freeing her from one classification or role. The gendering of the genre provokes these erasures and creates another set of binaries, which are present from the earliest examples we have of crime fiction in Spain.

In nineteenth- and early twentieth-century crime literature, we encounter female delinquent bodies that transgress moral and legal boundaries and that make a mockery of Spanish patriarchal institutions that were oppressive to women. Margaret E. Jones illustrates that until the 1980s, "[c]ivil law treated women as minors who passed from father to husband" (312). While this was true following the Spanish Civil War, Jones points out that some advances had been made during the Second Republic that were then overturned during the Franco regime (312). The first wave of the feminist movement, which had begun mobilizing at the end of the nineteenth century and advocated for women's right to work and to have an education, had achieved a number of reforms, such as voting rights in 1931 and the Ley del Divorcio (Divorce Law) in 1932. As Lidia Falcón makes clear,

> From 1931, when the Second Spanish Republic gave women the vote, until 1939, when the war ended with the defeat of democracy, Spanish women saw their suffering alleviated by the approval of civil marriage, divorce, equality in marriage, shared *patria potestad* (custody), removal of legal discriminations against unwed mothers, and the legislated right of a woman to administer her own property. ("Spain" 627)

According to Falcón, even abortion was briefly legalized in 1937 by "Federica Montseny, the first female Minister to the Department of Health, [who] approved the law that allowed women to exercise control over their bodies." (627). With Franco, however, there was a return to nineteenth-century civil codes that signalled the repression of women's rights, where women needed their husband's or father's permission to open a bank account, to acquire a passport, or even to obtain certain jobs (see Falcón's "Spain"; Jones; Levine). Like nineteenth-century women, women in Franco's Spain found themselves subjected to a "Spanish legal system [that] legislated morality with a modern equivalent of the Golden Age honor code" because these attitudes towards women "had roots in the traditional Spanish culture that had supported patriarchal norms and defined woman as a possession or an object rather than as an individual in her own right" (Jones 312).

Nineteenth-century women found themselves at the mercy of laws that placed husbands and fathers in a position of absolute power over the household, as signalled in the *Código penal de España* (Penal Code of Spain) of 1848 where, for example, female adultery would carry a prison sentence whereas a husband would be punished only if his adultery caused a scandal or if his lover was living under the same roof as his wife (91). Here, I want to specifically highlight the crime of adultery because at the same time the crime fiction genre begins to take shape in nineteenth-century Spain, the literary construct of the criminalized female body develops from the figure of the adulteress, a character that marks the Spanish obsession, from Golden Age literature onwards, with honour. Regarding this connection between the female body and the Spanish obsession with honour in seventeenth-century Spanish literature, Marcia L. Welles argues that "[r]hetoric and social practice locate a man's honor in the body and being of the female, whose responsibility it is not to besmirch a family's reputation" (29). Embodying the metaphor for the body politic, the female body was to be maintained pure and "kept free of the stain and dishonor of foreign intrusion" (26). Using Welles's terminology, the female body is to maintain "intact boundaries" (29), and thus, the literary construct of the female criminal presents an image of a woman whose intact boundaries have disappeared. The feminization of crime fiction, therefore, begins with the assault on the "intact boundaries" of the body.

In speaking about the idea of the body's frontiers, it is also worth emphasizing that the notion of intact boundaries is closely linked to the concept of women as other or the othering of women, which, according to Ruth El Saffar, begins with a unified Spain because it is then that "woman becomes the primary representative of otherness, and is therefore seen as a dangerous element that must be subdued" (35). This othering of women and the danger posed by an unsubdued woman is clearly noted in the gendering of the picaresque genre in Spanish literature. When the male rogue protagonist is replaced by a female delinquent, the *pícara*, the discourse surrounding the picaresque body is problematized because she is a clear agent not only of moral delinquency, but also of sexual delinquency. More than the *pícaro*, her body is fundamental to the plot of the female picaresque novel, not only because she is a victim of hunger, though this is still a recurring theme, but also because it is through the commerce of her body that she is able to survive. Anne Cruz has previously signalled that the *pícara's* role is restricted to what her body can do, "primarily to her sexual function" (136). Due to the sexual commerce of her body, the female rogue is also a source of venereal diseases, particularly syphilis, which heightens the significance of her body because of the danger it poses. In fact, the moment Justina, the protagonist of *La pícara Justina* (*The Rogue Justina*, 1605) by Francisco López de Úbeda, starts writing, one of her hairs gets stuck in her "pluma," making her unable to commence her autobiography because her hair is falling out due to her syphilitic condition. The first female variation of the picaresque and a parody of Mateo Alemán's *Aventuras y vida de Guzmán de Alfarache* (*The Life and Adventures of Guzmán de Alfarache* 1599, 1604), *La pícara Justina* uses the combination of the diseased and delinquent body as a springboard for fiction and for the creation of a female autobiographical voice in the genre. An agent of contagion for the body politic, the sick female rogue also symbolizes the dangers of allowing the uncontrolled transit of women. The female picaresque genre's interest in the prostitute and in prostitution exposes the polarized view prevalent in Early Modern Spain regarding women's morality as demonstrated by these male authors – they were either good and enclosed or bad and loose, public women who moved about uninhibited and needed to be contained and punished (Cruz 138–44).

The gendering of the picaresque novel through the diseased and delinquent female body provides insight into the feminization of nineteenth-century crime fiction. Speaking about the connection with the picaresque, Josefina Ludmer, in her study of crime as a foundational element in Argentine literature, proposes that, "la cadena de mujeres que matan cuenta que cada vez que un sujeto-posición diferente se abre camino entre los intersticios de los demás (entre los intersticios lingüísticos, sociales, nacionales, de sexo, de raza), es representado literariamente en ficción de delito o ante la ley" ("the chain of women who kill tells us that every time a different subject-position makes its way through the interstices of others (through linguistic, social, national, sex, and racial interstices), it is represented literarily in crime fiction or before the law") (369). A similar impulse to expose and contain dominates early crime literature, especially with nineteenth-century science and medicine consistently preoccupied with deviant female sexuality. Since sexuality came to be included in nineteenth-century medicine, the drive was to separate the normal from the abnormal according to Foucault because there was a "development of the juridical and medical control of perversions, for the sake of a general protection of society and the race" (*History* 122). Basing her argument on Foucault, Rebecca Stott explains that the classification anxieties of the period led to the "mapping" out of "the abnormal, pathological and alien" and the containment of everything outside or other (27). The idea was to identify the degenerate and the abnormal to expel it as part of what Stott calls the "degeneration anxieties" of the time, in particular during the latter half of the nineteenth century (22). By delimiting the other, the non-other would thus be safeguarded, and so the feminine other needed to be not only studied and classified, but also contained and tamed.[6]

During this period, an image of a more threatening female type also surfaces, the femme fatale, who encapsulates the fears of transgressive female sexuality and the moral degeneration of society. The 1890s, in particular, were "a period haunted by fears of cultural degeneration," and since fin-de-siècle Spain saw itself in decline, like other Western European powers, there was an emphasis on the need to protect morality by identifying and containing further threats, including the feminine threat in both fictional and nonfictional works (Stott 25). As Mary Ann Doane proposes,

> Her [the femme fatale's] appearance marks the confluence of modernity, urbanization, Freudian psychoanalysis and new technologies of production and reproduction (photography, the cinema) born of the Industrial Revolution. The femme fatale is a clear indication of the extent of the fears and anxieties prompted by shifts in the understanding of sexual difference in the late nineteenth century. (1–2)

Of course, the femme fatale is especially threatening to patriarchal authority and power, for she can use her body to satisfy her needs and desires, whether these be economic, social, or sexual (see Grossman 3). In her study of the mid-Victorian femme fatale, Jennifer Hedgecock describes this figure as one who "transgresses social boundaries and overtly – even mockingly – rebels against conformist attitudes" (1). Her transgression of these boundaries occurs through the exposure or erasure of her body because she expertly manages the politics of her body's visibility. For this reason, Doane draws attention to how "the femme fatale overrepresents the body" (2). This overrepresentation problematizes the intact (female) body's boundaries discussed previously because the femme fatale represents excess and "shapelessness" to use Stott's term (40). She cannot be contained, at least initially, because she rejects the limits imposed on women and signifies multiplicity and porousness, which is precisely what occurs to the narrative that attempts to confine her – it is forced open to allow a blurring of boundaries.[7]

With dreams of attaining an equal standing with men dashed after the Spanish Civil War, the women represented in male-dominated crime fiction during the early decades of the Franco dictatorship seem to either exemplify the angel in the house or the villainess, who, as a disruptive woman, had to be punished in line with the ideas propagated by the strict moral codes of the Catholic-oriented regime. The female body's sexualization would take place more towards the end of the regime and especially during the boom of the *novela negra* and with the influence of film noir.[8] For example, Manuel de Pedrolo, considered one of the founding fathers of the *novela negra* by numerous critics, such as Joan Ramon Resina, José Colmeiro, and Àlex Martín Escribà, among others, and who published before the genre's boom, uses the eroticized female body as a cautionary tale in *Joc brut* (*Playing Dirty*, 1965). In Pedrolo's novel, male criminalization is the result of the desperation produced in wanting to possess the femme fatale. Prior to the rise of the *novela negra*, we already see the narrative gazing mechanisms that sexualize the object of the male eye – the female body. Due to the censorship of sexual content, however, most of the pre-*novela negra* novels that emerged during the Franco dictatorship, modelled after the North American and British varieties of the 1920s and 1930s, might throw a spotlight on the attractive female body, as in Federico Mediante's detective novels of the 1940s for the Serie Wallace, but avoid the sort of eroticization that occurs in Pedrolo's *Joc brut*.[9] For example, in Mediante's *La señorita detective* (*The Lady Detective*, 1944), readers would encounter the first woman investigator in Spanish crime literature, and yet, though representing an innovation in the genre, the female sleuth acquiesces to the same patriarchal order that converts her into an object of the male gaze.

According to Salvador Vázquez de Parga, the detective novel had begun gaining popularity in the 1920s and throughout the 1930s with the translation of well-known authors such as Dashiell Hammett and Edgar Wallace. The 1940s, in turn, sparked a proliferation of crime fiction series collections by publishing houses like Editorial Molino, known for its Biblioteca de Oro series, and Editorial Clíper, which bought Editorial Cisne in 1945, that would come to include authors from Spain like Federico Mediante ("La novela policíaca" 28). As such, the context was ripe for the creation of "una novela policíaca española auténtica y verdadera" ("an authentic and true Spanish crime novel"), but due to censorship concerns, that never materialized (28). Instead, crime fiction authors in Spain closely imitated their North American and British predecessors, and yet they made sure to eliminate any female nudity and even sexually suggestive dialogues.

Despite the years of oppression under the Franco dictatorship, a few women writers, following in Pardo Bazán's footsteps, were producing crime fiction during this turbulent period in Spain's history. The female body, however, does not function as a site of resistance in these works, if it is represented at all. As Godsland signals in *Killing Carmens*, during the 1930s authors such as Mercè Rodoreda, Josefina de la Torre (using the pseudonym Laura de Cominges), and Mercedes Ballesteros Gaibrois, who was better known as Rocq Morris, would all publish crime literature (2).[10] Rodoreda's *Crim* (*Crime*, 1936) is particularly interesting because her only experiment with the crime novel is a parody of the genre and less of a crime fiction work itself, according to Resina and Godsland.[11] Even though it is titled *Crim*, there is no crime, for the murder is not of a person, but of a shoe. Instead of a crime story, *Crim* functions as a commentary on the corruption of those in power because the murder of the shoe "displays an absurdity to be found in the generic formula itself" ("Detective Formula" 121). What is important for our purposes, however, is that, through the parody of the genre, Rodoreda draws attention to what has been left out, "to the emptiness of the form, or, more exactly, to the gap between its intended function and its contemporary pragmatics" (120). Discussed in chapter 4, Maria-Antònia Oliver's Lònia Guiu series also employs the genre to pinpoint what has been left out – the female victim – and what has changed now that the leading detective is female. It could be argued that Rodoreda's critique of the genre during Britain's Golden Age of crime fiction is more radical than Oliver's because although Oliver critiques and attacks some of the features of the male-dominated form (first, by replacing a male detective with a female one), Rodoreda, in her parody of the genre, attacks the generic form itself.

Two other female authors who published crime fiction during the 1950s and 1960s were Isabel Calvo de Aguilar and Maria Aurèlia

Capmany, who, like Rodoreda, paved the way for contemporary women writers. Calvo de Aguilar's novels "can be read as fundamentally feminist texts that articulate the concerns of their author about the straitjacking of women, their intellects, and aspirations, under the Franco regime" (*Killing Carmens* 3).[12] In Calvo de Aguilar's *La isla de los siete pecados* (*The Island of the Seven Sins*), for example, the crime fiction model, in conjunction with the *novela rosa* (romance novel), is used to critique patriarchal models that stereotype and continue to categorize women into the same two categories of pure and untainted versus delinquent and scheming. Capmany, on the other hand, employed the genre to parody the North American hard-boiled novel as a way to avoid the censorship laws of the Franco regime. According to Godsland, Capmany's *Traduït de l'americà* (*Translated from the American*, 1959) "read as if it had been translated from English – another form of transcultural reinscription – in terms of plot, characters, and location" by setting it in the police state of Albania (160).[13] Similarly, Capmany's second detective novel, *El jaqué de la democràcia* (*The Morning Coat of Democracy*, 1972), is set in Salona, the industrial capital of a fictitious nation by the sea called Balvacària, an imaginary Barcelona where a corrupt legal system evokes the violence and the crimes committed against the Catalan people during the Franco regime (163–4). In this way, Capmany was a pioneer in her use of crime fiction. Her innovative use of the genre to reach out to a Catalan reading public set a precedent for female Catalan crime fiction authors like Oliver, who employ this type of popular fiction to articulate national, linguistic, ecological, and, most significantly, feminist concerns.

With the strengthening of the feminist movement in Spain following Franco's death in 1975, the female body as a site of resistance would come to be reworked in contemporary female crime fiction, signifying the de-eroticization of its women characters while also producing alternative conditions of visibility. Since women's subjugation occurs via the body, Susan Bordo highlights that feminism had to reinvent the body, reversing and altering "the old metaphor of the Body Politic, ... to a new metaphor: the politics of the body" (21). This new metaphor allowed feminism to reimagine "the human body as *itself* a politically inscribed entity, its physiology and morphology shaped by histories and practices of containment and control" (21; italics in original). By reading the body through this metaphoric lens, the site of subjugation becomes a site of resistance. In the crime fiction works studied, the female body acts as a site of resistance when it problematizes its own legibility or when the conditions for a new visibility are created. This is particularly true in contemporary female crime fiction that presents the female body in the form of a victimized body, one that is marked by gender and sexual violence.

Dunant explains that during a first stage of their incursion into crime fiction, women writers in the 1970s and especially in the 1980s "dealt with violence, and particularly violence towards women, differently from men. To start with we didn't revel in it. Often we didn't go into it at all ... Although most of us were interested in the dynamics of sexual politics, that was not the same thing as sexual violence" (18–19). Dunant suggests that women writers' use of violence signifies circumventing "the gratuitous, the voyeuristic" because, as she clarifies, "we wrote it in a way which meant we didn't get off on it, so neither could the reader" (19). The female crime novel emphasizes giving the female corpse or victim an identity to veer away from a more voyeuristic image, to avoid the narrative pleasure that Dunant alludes to above (see *Killing Carmens* 88). Seen through a feminist perspective, what is highlighted is the experience of violence upon the body – the body marked by pain and victimization narrated by the female sleuth. Using this opportunity, contemporary women authors, according to Dunant, who includes herself in this affirmation, "have got down and dirty when it comes to writing about sex and violence" to redefine the conditions of visibility (19). Still, it is worth repeating the questions that Saidiya Hartman poses when analyzing the function and role of spectatorship in discussing scenes of torture and victimization: "Are we witnesses who confirm the truth of what happened ... ? Or are we voyeurs fascinated with and repelled by exhibitions of terror and sufferance? What does the exposure of the violated body yield?" (3).

To answer these questions, we need to analyze the context in which the first female detective series in Spain emerged. In Spain, second-wave feminism advocated for victims of gender and sexual violence, and would continue to address a legal system that, despite the reforms passed in the 1978 Constitution (including the legalization of contraceptives and the decriminalization of adultery), and the divorce law of 1981, was still noticeably adverse to female victims of sexual violence. Falcón, in her 1991 book *Violencia contra la mujer* (*Violence Against Women*), estimated that between 200,000 and 2 million women are abused each year in Spain (36). Linda Gould Levine draws attention to a 1992 study published by the Institut Català de la Dona (Catalan Women's Institute) that indicated that at least 10 per cent of the Catalan female population (330,000 women) were habitual victims of gender violence (66). Levine underscores that despite feminist groups and women's associations insisting that legislation was needed to specifically address gender violence and abuse, it was not until 2004 that the Ley Orgánica 1/2004, de 28 de diciembre, de Medidas de Protección Integral Contra la Violencia de Género (Organic Law 1/2004, of 28 December, on Integral Protection Measures against Gender Violence) was approved (67).[14] According to Levine, these measures were passed "debido al aumento de casos de violencia contra la mujer o bien al aumento de la publicidad sobre esos casos" ("due to the increase in cases of gender violence or the increase in the publicity concerning these cases") (67). It was, then, the visibility afforded to victims of gender violence that would finally prompt changes in legislation. Thus, the framework for contemporary female crime fiction series during the 1980s and 1990s would be the feminist debates that were taking place during the Transition and into the Post-Transition, which, in addition to promoting increases in punishment for perpetrators of domestic and sexual violence, would also include the depenalization of abortion (1985) and pay equality, among other topics.

Female crime fiction in Spain would address this lack of victim visibility and make it a focal point because the autobiographical voice of the female sleuth now occupied a "position of subjectivity" that replaced the female corpse or the femme fatale, the objectified body, to advocate for the victimized (Walton and Jones 152). This new inscription of the body in the female detective novel marks a transition to de-eroticizing the woman character, whereby the victimized serves as proof that the legal system is adverse to women. These revisions to the genre would also rely on theories of rape and victimization from the 1970s and the 1980s that problematized the idea that "[r]ape is held to be a natural behavior, and not to rape must be learned," as stated by Susan Griffin in 1971 (27). Griffin, who would be one of the first in a long line of theorists who would come to redefine rape during these decades, argued that "it is rape itself that is learned" (27).[15] Defining rape as an "act of violence," Griffin also considers that "rape is a form of mass terrorism, for the victims of rape are chosen indiscriminately" (35). Susan Brownmiller would later add to this argument in 1975 by claiming that "[f]rom prehistoric times to the present, I believe, rape has played a critical function. It is nothing more or less than a conscious process of intimidation by which *all men* keep *all women* in a state of fear" (15; italics in original). While both Griffin and Brownmiller were highly influential in redefining rape as a crime of violence that subjugates all women, later theorists like Catharine MacKinnon would emphasize the sexual nature of rape: "If sexuality is central to women's definition and forced sex is central to sexuality, rape is indigenous, not exceptional, to women's social condition. In feminist analysis, a rape is not an isolated event or moral transgression or individual interchange gone wrong but an act of terrorism and torture within a systemic context of group subjection, like lynching" (172). What rape demonstrates, according to MacKinnon, is that women are not in control of their sexuality because male dominance depends on men's access to and domination of the female sex (127). For this reason, MacKinnon states that "[f]rom women's point of view, rape is not prohibited; it is regulated" by the state (179).

This idea that patriarchal institutions allow rape to happen is echoed by Nina Molinaro in her study of contemporary female crime fiction in Spain. She makes clear in her analysis of Maria-Antònia Oliver's *Estudi en lila* (1985) (*Study in Lilac*, 1987), the first installment of the Lònia Guiu trilogy, that "Oliver's novel participates in the feminocentric detection of deception, all the while characterizing rape as a crime of violence. Rape is a crime committed by men against women, because the former consider it their right and because they assume that they can get away with it" ("Writing" 113). Oliver's answer to this, discussed in chapter 4, is to allow the female body to tell the story of its victimization and violation, transforming any potential spectators into witnesses. As Eleni Coundouriotis underscores, "[w]itnessing, in fact, entails an emotional involvement in what one sees," for whereas the voyeuristic spectator "colonizes what it sees" by othering, the witness "yields testimony," and is forced to engage on a subjective level (125). The act of witnessing sexual violence in female crime fiction activates both an empathetic and a testimonial reaction, forcing an analysis of the reader's position and involvement. Though Suzanne Keen claims that "fictional worlds provide safe zones for readers' feeling empathy without experiencing a resultant demand on real-world action" (4), I am suggesting that female crime fiction's answer to this is to allow the victimized body to tell the story of its violation and create a space for an act of witnessing to occur. While the voyeuristic look seeks to control, the act of witness provokes awareness and compels a moral judgement. With these new conditions of visibility, power is returned to the victim's body, and its witnesses/readers are forced to reflect upon their complicity with a system that allows gender violence to occur.

Thanks to Isabel Franc's Emma García and the emergence of a few more lesbian detective protagonists that have appeared in serial form, such as Ixtaro Borda's Amaia Ezpeldoi, Javier Otaola's Felicidad Olaizola,

Clara Asunción García's Cate Maynes, and Susana Hernández's Rebeca Santana, lesbian crime fiction in Spain has also garnered an increasing amount of critical attention in the last few years, according to Inmaculada Pertusa Seva's "Nuevas detectives lesbianas" ("New Lesbian Detectives"). Although the lesbian subgenre also focuses on issues of victim invisibility and gender violence, the visibility of the lesbian community is also of crucial importance. Besides the investigative aspect of these works, the personal life of the lesbian detective takes centre stage, giving visibility to the lesbian experience of romance, love, and sex. Since the Franco regime oppressed the homosexual population into invisibility, lesbian literature of the Post-Transition rescues the lesbian subject by having lesbianness occupy generic spaces. What makes crime fiction attractive for this venture is that writers can use the detective's eye/I and the genre's working of the gaze to give voice and visibility to the lesbian experience, as exemplified in Isabel Franc's Lola Van Guardia trilogy and Emma García series and in Susana Hernández's police-procedural novels. Significantly, contemporary lesbian crime fiction explores the female body's doubling as a body that can be in pain, but also pleasure, thus contributing to redefining the politics of visibility and vulnerability in contemporary formulations of the genre.

To investigate how female crime fiction and the lesbian subgenre subvert the conditions of visibility in traditional male-centred crime fiction, chapter 1 explores how the image that we obtain of the female delinquent body in crime fiction is generated and mobilized in the nineteenth and early twentieth century. With the literary construct of the criminalized female body developing at the same time the crime genre begins to take shape in Spain, this produces the first manifestations of a protofeminist counterdiscourse that is critical of the patriarchal institutions that oppressed nineteenth- and twentieth-century women by subjecting them to laws that treated them unequally. For this reason, it is crucial to establish a genealogy of this protofeminist phenomenon in the earliest examples of the genre, Alarcón's *El clavo* and Pardo Bazán's *La gota de sangre*. Here, my analysis differs from that of other critics because I signal that the feminization of crime fiction does not begin in 1979 with Lourdes Ortiz's *Picadura mortal*, but has already taken form in the earliest crime fiction models produced in Spain, which question the mobilization of gender in the genre by centring the narrative on the female delinquent.

While chapter 1 focuses exclusively on the female criminal model, chapter 2 continues analyzing the feminization of the genre with the first female detective to spring forth in a detective novel, Federico Mediante's *La señorita detective,* in addition to studying Mediante's female criminal models in *Sombras siniestras* (*Sinister Shadows*) and *Fuerzas ocultas* (*Hidden Forces*). By putting these different female types into dialogue with one another, we note the influence of the delinquent woman model as a *femme moderne* in Mediante's development of his female detective. Following Mediante, the second half of the chapter examines the femme fatale model in Manuel de Pedrolo's *Joc brut,* an archetype that will be prominent during the boom of the male-centred *novela negra.* I explore how the gazing mechanisms work in these narratives, especially when the female body is the target of the male eye/I, and demonstrate how the female characters employ the male gaze against itself.

The reversal of the look in these crime fiction novels draws attention to the process by which the gaze is feminized in crime fiction, first through the act of misreading, which is underscored in chapter 2, and then through the parody of the male forms of the genre in chapter 3's analysis of Lourdes Ortiz's *Picadura mortal.* Ortiz's only female detective novel ridicules the male-dominated *novela negra* to investigate female gender roles in a Post-Francoist society in addition to signalling crime fiction's prevailing *machista* attitudes. The mechanism of subversion in *Picadura mortal* relies on a reformulation of the politics of visibility in the genre. It has a twofold approach: first, it refocalizes the attention away from the female body as an object by problematizing these moments of objectification; second, it recreates these scenes with male characters in a parodic form.

Unlike the representations of women's bodies in traditional crime fiction, which are displayed to be pleasurable for the reader, chapter 4 studies Maria-Antònia Oliver's crime series, where for the first time there is a real exploration of the female body as a victimized body. Oliver's Lònia Guiu novels, the first female detective series in Spain, are crucial to the development of female crime fiction because they constitute a radical shift in the genre's politics of visibility. Gaining visibility when viciously abused, the female body is now the site for a discussion of gender violence and for redefining victimhood and justice in the genre. More significantly, Oliver's female detective also doubles as a victim because she experiences sexual violence firsthand. Oliver confronts the traditionally masculine space of crime fiction by using the scenes where the female private eye is assaulted to guide her reader's gaze to this new representation of the female body in the genre – the victimized detective body. Although there is a movement towards the female body's de-eroticization, the inverse process entails heightening the moments of visibility where the victimization of the body occurs, since the current legal system fails to punish men who victimize women. It is, then, a new inscription of the body that tells the story of its victimization and violation.

Subversive bodies are the focus of chapter 5's analysis of Isabel Franc's Emma García stories as well as Susana Hernández's crime fiction because both authors employ the lesbian subgenre and its lesbian pulp base to redefine the conditions of visibility for lesbian women. Franc emphasizes resisting invisibility in her Emma García stories, where the focus is the protection of the lesbian community against a patriarchal system that endangers it by threatening the union of same-sex couples. Here, the detective becomes a protector of lesbian couples, defending them against *lo masculino* (the masculine) and a return to invisibility. Focusing on Hernández's police-procedural series, the second half of this chapter underscores how lesbian crime fiction changes the discourse on the body by staging it as a site of both narrative pleasure and of victimization. Put differently, while the victimized body is still given visibility, the eroticized female body also appears because women's bodies are resexualized in lesbian crime fiction, as exemplified in Hernández's novels. More significantly, with Hernández's lesbian inspector Rebeca Santana, and Miriam Vázquez, a heterosexual middle-aged veteran of the police force, I argue that instead of an objectified female body, the reader encounters women's bodies offering and experiencing sexual pleasure, where visibility is given to women's sexual experience, both lesbian and non-lesbian.

By establishing this genealogy of the different viewpoints of women's position in these narratives, I demonstrate that the feminized form of justice at work in female crime fiction has its roots in the first female delinquents, who uncover and denounce a social, moral, and legal system that is unfair in its (mis)reading of and stance towards women. This genealogy represents a departure from traditional forms of understanding female characters in crime fiction. These women do not fit into Ricardo Landeira's description of the typical evolution of the female character who starts out as a victim, matures into an accomplice, turns into a criminal, and finally becomes a detective (18). In fact, all the female delinquents skip the accomplice stage. They are the authors of their crimes without needing to become accomplices first. Even before the boom of female crime fiction in Spain, Mediante's female secret agent already anticipates certain characteristics of the modern woman investigator, for example her quick-wittedness, her bravery, her ability to read her rivals, and her use of her femininity as a tool of manipulation. In tracing the misreading of female deviance, I demonstrate that in the first crime fiction of the nineteenth century, the reasoning behind exteriorizing female delinquency was exercised in an effort to reach a level of control and ordering of these transgressive bodies. Starting with Pardo Bazán and continuing through to contemporary female crime fiction, certain forms of female criminality are vindicated in an effort to override the patriarchal legal system. A liberating discourse, therefore, will be born from misreading female deviance, where victimization is redefined and from which empowerment springs forth.

Chapter One

Reading the Female Delinquent in Early Spanish Crime Fiction

With nineteenth-century science and medicine consistently preoccupied with deviant female sexuality, it is no surprise that the image of the female delinquent, especially the femme fatale variation, would materialize with such force during this period, and consequently that genres such as crime fiction would attempt to disarm said threat. According to critics like Rebecca Stott and Virginia Allen, who study this archetype, the femme fatale emerges as a construction during the latter part of the nineteenth century to define a type of woman that posed a danger both to male power and to traditional female roles – a threat to both the masculine and the feminine. Stott clarifies that the femme fatale "is not unique to the nineteenth century, but she is fabricated, reconstructed in, and apparently necessary to, the cultural expressions of the closing years of the century" (viii). Like Stott, Allen, in her study of the femme fatale in the visual arts, associates her with mythical figures of antiquity such as "Siren, Circe, Salome, Cleopatra" because this distances her from everyday women (1). The femme fatale type transits between beauty and exoticism on the one hand and destruction and eroticism on the other. Significantly, the construction of the femme fatale accentuates her control over her sexuality, as a seducer of men who effectively "drained them of their 'vital powers,' in an exercise of eroticism" because "[s]he was – and is – the diametric opposite of the 'good' woman who passively accepted impregnation, motherhood, domesticity, the control and domination of her sexuality by men" (4). Moreover, Allen proposes that the femme fatale's dichotomy is explained by the construction of the "eternal feminine," which would be "reduced to two variations on a female theme: the mother on the one hand, the sex object on the other," an opposition present in the visual arts since antiquity (7). Stemming from the obsession with classification and categorization in fin-de-siècle Europe, in addition to the heightened threat that female sexuality seemed to pose, the nineteenth century saw a renewed fascination with this figure and both "an inundation of images now labelled femme fatales" and an "intensification of the imagery itself" or its effect (10). What was transmitted in the construction of the nineteenth-century archetype in both the verbal and visual arts was a woman whose fatality was far more erotic and deviant than before, according to these scholars. The same can be said to occur with the fictional works that incorporated the figure of the female criminal because the threat that the female delinquent presented was amplified by first framing her as a transgressor of sexual morality and patriarchal law and later, more threateningly, as a femme fatale.

In crime fiction, the female delinquent, her heightened form being that of the femme fatale, is not only threatening to male authority in the fictional works, but to the stability of the genre itself. She places the restoration of order that crime fiction traditionally promises in danger. Frank Kermode explains that the end of the nineteenth century was dominated by "a deal of apocalyptic feeling at that time," which translated into "the 'decadence' which became a literary category" (96–7). The femme fatale, part of the fabric of these apocalyptic images, as described by scholars like Stott, would also signify this end. Arguably, she carries a sense of finality – the culmination of a male-centred order, the conclusion to a power hierarchy. Alongside the degeneration discourses of the time, the femme fatale represents both the fear of the feminine, in particular the "dark continent" of the female mind and sexuality, to invoke a Freudian reference, and the threat to the masculine (see Stott 35).[1]

Female sexuality, one of the great unknowns during this period, would, like non-European cultures, come under "the theme of domination/subordination central both to nineteenth-century masculine identity and to the western sense of superiority," according to Joanna de Groot (91). The construction of an "us" relied on a definition of otherness shaped by the revamped disciplines of anthropology and medicine (92–3). In Western Europe, this process was necessary for demarcating difference and solidifying boundaries not only between men and women, but between different races and ethnic groups. The purpose was "grounding the 'Otherness' of femininity or ethnic identity in 'real' knowledge wielded by prestigious professionals (doctors, academics, 'experts')" (95). These experts possessed the sort of critical and clinical eye to establish and categorize difference. What this meant was that by understanding and accepting gender and race "as *essential*, 'naturally' fixed categories, they could not then be affected by *contingent* factors, whether history, social change, or demands for reform" (96; italics in original). Femininity and sexual discourse were used not only to relegate women to a position of inferiority, but also to confine them to a space of otherness, likewise inhabited by those who were racially or ethnically excluded from the "us." This demarcation, created to distance the self/the us from the "Other," invokes the use of the stereotype. Explained by Sander L. Gilman, "Stereotypes are a crude set of mental representations of the world ... They perpetuate a needed sense of difference between the 'self' and the 'object,' which becomes the 'Other'" (*Difference* 17–18). Stereotypes are necessary to deal with threats, and "the idea of the pathological is a central marker for difference" (23). For this reason, nineteenth-century medical and legal discourses would home in on female sexuality, so much so that Gilman has previously posited that "female genitalia came to define the female for the nineteenth century" ("Black Bodies" 216).[2]

In an era where the classification and categorization impulse dominated intellectual and scientific circles, the image of the femme fatale type becomes popular in that it threatens precisely these stable categories and even subverts the man/woman hierarchical dualism to a certain extent. Basing her argument on Toril Moi's interpretation that the femme fatale should be understood as a sign, Stott proposes that the archetype "signifies all that lies beyond the frontier or sign '/': the signifying frontier marking the distinction of the two elements of the binary opposition: the sign that marks the end of order and the beginning of Otherness" (39). Her seductiveness, I would argue, is that she sits on the border of what she should be, the ideal angel of the house, and what she should not be, the overtly sexual and independent woman who lies closer to the prostitute in the nineteenth-century imagination, a figure closely linked to images of contagion and disease. Sitting on this border is precisely why the femme fatale can remain unreadable and hence, is misread. She defies boundaries by rejecting the markers delimiting the space that she should reside in, but will not.[3] Along with other deviants, sexual and otherwise, the femme fatale is relegated to what Stott calls the "Dark Continent of Otherness" (50).

With an increased interest in protecting public morality against the threat of transgressive females and, more generally, social and moral degeneration, early Spanish crime fiction would also address the politics of visibility of the delinquent woman. This emphasis on recording delinquency, however, formed part of what Jo Labanyi signals as the nineteenth-century attempt to create a form of social medicine to treat and cure a nation characterized as a diseased body, which in turn required the expert attention of medical professionals (66–7). Criminal women, therefore, functioned as an effective literary trope to investigate the inner workings of a sick society. What is more, increased visibility becomes an answer to the threat posed by the feminine other – the criminal woman and her later heightened form, the femme fatale. In the analysis that follows, I examine how the female body is mobilized in the earliest examples of the genre with Pedro Antonio de Alarcón's *El clavo* and Emilia Pardo Bazán's *La gota de sangre*. Depicting the first female criminal in Spanish crime fiction, Alarcón's Gabriela Zahara does not neatly fit into the victim/villainess dichotomy that we find in the classic forms of the genre. Instead, Gabriela Zahara complicates this dichotomy and challenges the stereotype because she can only be understood as a criminal if she is also read as a victim of a society that forces her to stay married to a man that she does not love and who would punish her for committing adultery. Here, the politics of being a visible subject enable our reading of a hybrid character. Following Alarcón's model, in *La gota de sangre,* Pardo Bazán employs a version of the femme fatale with her character Chulita Ferna, whose heightened visibility is the result of her questionable morality. And yet, her increased visibility and legibility as a transgressive woman allows her to outwit the Holmesian amateur sleuth, Selva. There is a reversal in the function of the politics of women's visibility because female exposure works against the male pseudo-detective's reading of the crime. As I demonstrate, in both *El clavo* and *La gota de sangre,* female criminals are responsible for exposing the vulnerability of the patriarchal order and the legal system.

The Emplotment of the Female Body in Pedro Antonio de Alarcón's *El clavo*

From its beginnings, crime fiction manifests an interest in reading the body because the criminal narrative commences with the victimized or dead body. To solve the crime, however, the narrative of investigation focuses on reading the delinquent's body, the clues it has left behind, which in the mid- to late nineteenth century was influenced by the emerging field of criminal anthropology. The founder of criminal anthropology, Cesare Lombroso, would argue for a new focus on the body, relocating criminology's emphasis on crime to reading the delinquent body. Analyzing Lombroso's revolutionary approach to the study of crime and criminals, David Horn clarifies that "although the criminal body may have been constituted as a text to be read, it was frequently imagined to resist the exegesis of both lay and professional readers, or to be only partially legible ... the body was assumed to be actively involved in the production of anthropological knowledge; in particular, it was imagined to testify against itself" (*Criminal Body* 6). Lombroso's theories stress the body's habit of confessing, and so the reader of the delinquent body must be able to effectively read and interpret the body's signs.

Although his study of female delinquency would not be published until 1893, Lombroso's investigations would later demonstrate that reading the female body presents particular challenges in that no clear distinction could be made between the criminal and the normal woman ("This Norm" 115). Lombroso emphasized that "the female born criminal is ... doubly exceptional, first as a woman and then as a criminal ... As a double exception, then, the criminal woman is a true monster" (*Criminal Woman* 183–5). As Horn suggests, for Lombroso the female criminal body "was constituted as a particular kind of social text: an index of present and potential risks to the larger social organism" ("This Norm" 109). The potential threat posed by women meant that they were "suitable objects of ongoing surveillance and corrective interventions that, in an effort to restrict 'opportunities' for criminality, blurred the lines between penal practices and social work" (121). In the Spanish context, criminology functioned as a more precise discipline and instrument to record physical characteristics and intimate details that would mark certain bodies as potential social threats. According to Labanyi, in this way criminal anthropology resembled "the Inquisition's probing and recording of the most intimate details of private life" (77). Indeed, the anxieties surrounding the reading of the female body have long existed because if women's bodies are misread this puts male authority in danger, since the system of discerning "visible signs," to use Georgina Dopico Black's terminology, has failed. What this means is that as categories and classifications come under attack, the good virtuous woman and mother (Ave) cannot be told apart from the bad temptress and sinner (Eva). A topic already present in Early Modern Spanish literature, Dopico Black argues that the wife's body was understood "as a transcoder for interpretive anxieties, on one hand, and for cultural and political anxieties, on the other" (xix). Thus, misreading the female body has dire consequences for male honour and, more generally, for the patriarchal order.

Reading the female body turned into a national concern in nineteenth-century Spain as the reigning monarch, Isabel II, who governed from 1843 to 1868 and abdicated in 1870, became a contentious political symbol that represented feminine moral degeneration and delinquency. During her rule, the economic and social crises that debilitated Spain were, as Sarah White explicates, "linked to the person of the monarch, the private life of the queen became an eminently public issue; monarchical misbehavior led to national disrepair" (239). White comments that "[b]y describing the body politic as a female body, and linking the public life of the nation with the private life of the queen," her detractors were able to launch an attack against the queen and her supporters (235) because Isabel II became "the seditious symbol of sexual disorder" (243). Since Isabel did not encapsulate the ideal of the female monarch as the nurturer of the nation and its citizens, the national crises were attributed to a private life that was in disarray and that infected the nation's public life in the form of a delinquent body.[4] Reading the queen as a sexually deviant body became a rallying cry for the Glorious Revolution of 1868 that functioned to depose a queen who had endangered the country. What this meant was that "[a] degenerate Isabel represented the triad of feminine vices that had undermined the resuscitation of Spain: superstition, caprice, and ignorance. In their place, the revolutionaries championed the masculine virtues of reason, law, enlightenment, and the political formula which guaranteed them: popular sovereignty" (241). By converting the female body into a national threat and taking action against it, the moral integrity of Spain could be safeguarded against a queen who made the country vulnerable.

Published in 1853 but reworked in 1856 and again in 1880, Alarcón's *El clavo*, the first crime fiction story to be written in prose in Spain, responds to the dangers represented by the adulterous woman and emphasizes how the crimes of the body need to be made visible.[5] Put simply, it is a text that is concerned with female vices and moral degeneration and its effects on patriarchal institutions. *El clavo* is a tale that combines at least three main mysteries: 1) the investigation into the death of Alfonso Gutiérrez del Romeral, found with a nail sticking out of his skull eighteen months after he has been killed; 2) the identity of the young women with whom the narrator, Felipe, and his friend, the magistrate/investigator Joaquín Zarco, have fallen in love and who end up being the same woman, Gabriela Zahara; and 3) Gabriela's motive for murdering her husband, Alfonso. Most critics, such as José Colmeiro, argue that the amorous and melodramatic elements in *El clavo* take precedence over the criminal aspect of the story. Colmeiro claims that "[l]a intriga de la historia depende menos de la investigación que de la atmósfera en que ésta se desarrolla, en la que no faltan ninguno de los típicos ingredientes románticos" ("the plot of the story depends less on the investigation than on the atmosphere in which it develops, in which none of the typical novelistic ingredients is lacking") (*La novela policiaca española* 93). Taking this a step further, Salvador Vázquez de Parga contends that *El clavo* would have been the first detective story if Joaquín Zarco had been interested in the case and not in his amorous dilemmas (*La novela policiaca en España* 34). The inclusion of the two love stories, however, differentiates Alarcón's crime story from texts that would eventually be recognized as classic detective novels because, according to Ricardo Landeira, "[l]os detectives clásicos como Sherlock Holmes o Hercule Poirot son refractarios al amor, pues la dimensión erótica despista tanto al lector como al detective" ("classic detectives like Sherlock Holmes or Hercule Poirot are resistant to love, since the erotic dimension distracts both the reader and the detective") (68). I would propose that the amorous plot in *El clavo* functions not to distract the reader, but to underscore certain ideological, political, and moral concerns that were plaguing Spain at the time, the most central of which was the vulnerability of its patriarchal institutions, which were at the mercy of an adulterous and sexually deviant queen.

In my view, incorporating the amorous element serves the story's interest in uncovering the identity of the young widow that both men fall in love with and, more significantly, in revealing her motive for committing the crime, since Alarcón's Gabriela Zahara is the first model that we obtain of the female criminal in modern Spanish crime fiction. According to Landeira, "la mujer figura como parte íntegra, aunque no tanto como objeto amoroso sino como símbolo del pecado de la carne – el adulterio – y el subsiguiente crimen al que conduce – el parricidio – " ("the woman plays a key role, although not so much as a love object, but as a symbol of the sin of the flesh – adultery – and the crime that results from it – parricide –") (68). By referring to Gabriela as a symbol, Landeira subtracts agency from the female character's motives and actions for committing the crime. Landeira bases his reading of Gabriela Zahara on his argument that in crime fiction women begin as victims, turn into accomplices, later become the guilty party, and finally obtain the role of female detectives (18). Gabriela Zahara, however, is both a victim of an unhappy and failed marriage and a criminal without needing to pass through the stage of an accomplice to commit murder. As I demonstrate, this combination complicates the reading of Gabriela; throughout the narrative she is the object of the male gaze, which attempts to decipher her body and soul. Although she initially gains visibility due to her attractiveness, the narrative emphasizes her illegibility, her suitors' inability to read her. Furthermore, I argue that the politics of visibility in *El clavo* functions to accentuate the hybridity of this character, who cannot be understood as a criminal unless she is read as a victim. Straddling the line between husband-killer and victim, Alarcón's Gabriela Zahara is unmasked to become a visible example of moral degeneration, and yet she is also given the space to denounce the patriarchal system of laws that criminalize her. I claim that misreading the delinquent woman exposes the vulnerability not only of the moral codes of the patriarchal system, but also the particular susceptibility of the law in addressing female criminality.

El clavo begins with our narrator and protagonist Felipe's meeting of an enigmatic young widow, who does not reveal her name, in a stagecoach, as they journey from Granada to Málaga on a fall night in 1844. From the moment that he sets eyes on his female companion, he feels attracted to this woman that he describes as "una hermosísima mujer, joven, elegante, pálida, sola, vestida de luto ... era la viuda de mis esperanzas; era la realización del sueño que apenas había osado conceder; era el *non plus ultra* de mis ilusiones de viajero ... ¡Era *ella*!" (29) ("a supremely beautiful woman – young, graceful, pale, alone, and dressed in mourning ... the widow of my hopes, the fulfillment of the dream that I hadn't dared to entertain; it was the *ne plus ultra* of my illusions as a traveler; it was she!") (*The Nail* 29).[6] Despite not being able to see her in the dark of the night, Felipe feels drawn to this woman, and begins obsessing about knowing more about her. When he is better able to see her the next morning, he adds to this first portrayal by commenting on her display of sadness: "Pero, ¡qué sello de dolor sobre su frente! ¡Qué lúgubre oscuridad en sus bellos ojos! ¡Qué trágica expresión en todo su semblante! Algo muy triste había en el fondo de su alma" (30) ("But what grief was knitted on her brow! What dreadful gloom emanated from her lovely eyes! What a tragic expression stamped the whole of her face! There had to be something very sorrowful in the depths of her soul") (31). Although the case of "el clavo" has yet to begin, the cause of the widow's sorrow and despair will be one of the focal points for the detective tale. From its beginning, *El clavo* is concerned with reading, with deciphering the signs of the female character. Though Felipe emphasizes his trip companion's beauty, it is more than just the female body that is of interest here. The young widow's aloofness or haughtiness seduces Felipe to the point that he confesses his love to her, to which she responds by saying that she will never love again (31). The young widow's exclamation provides the first clue to uncovering her inner turmoil of feeling betrayed after having loved, and starts setting the scene for her multiple confessions, which we witness throughout the novel.

Coincidentally, a young widow possessing the same aloofness and tragic expression had enamoured his friend, Joaquín Zarco, a year earlier, as he tells Felipe when the two friends meet. It is the enigmatic quality surrounding this woman, and the inability to decipher her, which makes her enticing to both men. We learn from Zarco, who takes over as our narrator during chapter 5, that his love affair with this young widow from Madrid, whose name is Blanca, had taken place in an inn where they both stayed in Sevilla for three months. About three weeks into their relationship and after Zarco proclaims his love for her, Blanca, in turn, confesses that "me casé sin amor a mi marido. Poco tiempo después ... lo odiaba. Hoy ha muerto. ¡Sólo Dios sabe cuánto he sufrido! Yo comprendo el amor de esta suerte: es la gloria o es el infierno. Y para mí, hasta ahora, ¡siempre ha sido el infierno!" (35) ("'I married my husband without loving him,' she said one evening. 'A short time later ... I hated him. He's dead now. Only God knows how much I've suffered. Here's how I understand love: it's heaven or it's hell. And for me, up to now, it has always been hell'") (37–8). Here, Blanca's confession puts forth her condition as a victim of a loveless marriage and of a husband that she despised. With both suitors, she authors a narrative about herself that highlights her vulnerable state.

After learning that Blanca is pregnant and realizing that their relationship would be deemed sinful, Zarco, a magistrate and public prosecutor, proposes to Blanca:

> Además, tú conoces mi carácter, sabes que nunca transijo en materias de honra ... Pues bien: la sociedad en que vivimos llama *crimen* a nuestra dicha ... ¿Por qué no hemos de rendirnos al pie del altar? ¡Te quiero pura, te quiero noble, te quiero santa! ¡Te amaré entonces más que hoy! ... ¡Acepta mi mano! (36–7; italics in original)

> Besides, you know my character, you know that I never compromise on matters of honor. Well then, the society in which we live labels our happiness a sin. Why shouldn't we consecrate it at the foot of the altar? I want

> you pure, I want you noble, I want you saintly. I'll love you then more than now. Accept my hand. (39)

Understanding that Blanca has become a reflection of his moral state, Zarco is intent on protecting his honour from a female body that could be considered transgressive. Although they agree to meet at the same inn a month later on 15 May 1843, Zarco returns two weeks earlier than they had planned and learns that Blanca has left without informing him of her whereabouts. Zarco assumes that she has deceived him, and leaves Sevilla on 4 May, a date that will acquire greater significance when the widow's true story comes to light. Without knowing that they are talking about the same woman, both Felipe and Zarco are attracted by the difficulty that the young widow poses in their readings of her. In Zarco's case, however, he is seduced by an illegibility that puts his honour at stake.

What is more, Zarco recounts his love story to Felipe while they walk around the cemetery, foreshadowing the mysterious widow's connection to fatality and death. In speaking about this woman's enigma, the men happen upon a skull with a nail stuck in its forehead, which signals how the victimized body emerges to expose a crime. Believing that Providence is urging him to investigate this case, Zarco feels called upon as a magistrate to restore order by holding someone accountable for a crime that would otherwise have been left unpunished. We come to find out that the skull belongs to Alfonso Gutiérrez del Romeral, said to have died of a stroke on 3 May 1843 and buried 4 May, a date that becomes key to solving Zarco's love story because Blanca/Gabriela buries her husband the same day that Zarco leaves Sevilla, believing that she has deceived him. With the victimized body surfacing to testify against the criminal, the connection between the murder and the enigmatic woman/women in this story starts taking shape. Told that the only one present during Alfonso's death was his wife, Gabriela, those investigating now suspect that she is the one responsible for her husband's death, by driving a nail into his head and causing a cerebral haemorrhage.

With the investigation stalled because Gabriela is nowhere to be found, Felipe decides to spend that winter in Granada and re-encounters the young widow he met on the trip that opens the novel.[7] Told at a party that her name is Mercedes de Méridanueva, Felipe visits her the next day, and unknowingly sets in motion Gabriela's capture by recounting Zarco's love and betrayal story. Felipe functions as the narrative bridge between Zarco's love affair and the ongoing criminal investigation because he is also present when Zarco learns that Blanca is in town and has summoned him to meet her at a nearby inn and moments after Zarco returns, when they are told that Gabriela has been arrested. Though Felipe suspects that Gabriela and Blanca are likely the same person, he remains silent to allow divine justice to take its course, and instead, as a lawyer, reminds the magistrate that his duty is to uphold the law by compelling him to forget his role as a lover.

When Felipe finally looks at the accused, he recognizes Gabriela as the female companion of his travels. The woman that he has come to know as Mercedes is also Zarco's Blanca and the husband-murderer Gabriela: "Todas aquellas fantásticas mujeres se resumían en una sola, en una indudable, en una real y positiva, en una sobre quien pesaba la acusación de haber matado a su marido, en una que estaba condenada a muerte en rebeldía" (50) ("All those fantastic women combined into one, an indisputable one, a real and tangible one, upon whom weighed the accusation of having murdered her husband, one who was condemned to death by default") (55). The deceptive narratives that the enigmatic widow has authored about herself finally break down in this episode because the three women are reduced to the murdering wife. More than just the link that brings these three women together (Gabriela, Blanca, and Mercedes), Felipe's function is to strengthen the existing order. For this reason, the chapter titled "El juicio" ("The Trial"), opens with a quote from Montesquieu, "El Juez es una ley que habla y la ley un Juez mudo. La ley debe ser como la muerte, que no perdona a nadie" (50) ("The Judge is a law who speaks and the law a mute Judge. The law should be like death, which forgives no one") (55). Given his function within the narrative, Filipe's concern lies with Zarco's vulnerability as a representative of patriarchal law and the moral codes of his society. With this in mind, Felipe creates a contrast during this episode between Gabriela, the criminal mastermind, and a weakened male legal system, represented by a jilted and deceived lover.

Significantly, the narrative emphasizes how all those present at the hearing had gathered excitedly to see the accused (49). All await the spectacle of the unveiling of the female felon, and once Gabriela enters and becomes the object of the collective look, Felipe joins in on the communal gazing, closely examining Gabriela in hopes of uncovering her innocence or her guilt. The moment the narrative homes in on her, the text pauses, and Felipe paints the following picture:

> Gabriela – llamémosla, al fin, por su verdadero nombre – estaba sumamente pálida; pero también muy tranquila. Aquella calma, ¿era señal de su inocencia, o comprobaba la insensibilidad propia de los grandes criminales? ¿Confiaba la viuda de D. Alfonso en la fuerza de su derecho, o en la debilidad de su Juez? ...
>
> Entonces me vio a mí, y una llamarada de rubor, que me pareció de buen agüero, tiñó de escarlata su semblante.
>
> Pero muy luego se repuso, y tornó a su palidez y tranquilidad ... todos tenían fija la vista en Gabriela, cuya singular hermosura y suave y apacible voz considerábanse como indicios de inculpabilidad. ¡Hasta el sencillo traje negro que llevaba parecía declarar en su defensa! (50–1)

> Gabriela – let's call her, at last, by her real name – was exceedingly pale, but also very tranquil. Was that calm a sign of her innocence or did it confirm the insensitivity typical of hardened criminals? Was Don Alfonso's widow trusting in the righteousness of her position or in the weakness of her judge? ...
>
> Then she saw me, and a sudden blush, which seemed propitious, tinged her face scarlet.
>
> But she recovered at once and reverted to her paleness and calm ... they all had their eyes fixed on Gabriela, whose singular beauty and soft, gentle voice were regarded as signs of inculpability. Even the simple black dress that she wore seemed to speak in her defense. (55–6)

Even as the female criminal body is made visible during this moment, Felipe is unable to differentiate the signs that would testify to her innocence or her guilt. For this reason, he turns to survey the rest of Gabriela's spectators, and emphasizes how Gabriela's audience also studies her body for evidence of her true nature and for a language that will certify her culpability. The narrative calls for the unveiling of the signs of female delinquency and compels the female body to make its own transgression and corruption visible and legible. To solve the problem of the illegible female body, Zarco tests Gabriela by forcing her to look at her husband's nail-driven skull. It has the desired effect: she screams in horror as she tears at her hair and pronounces the name of the murdered Alfonso.

Once her body testifies against her, Gabriela is then given the space to speak during her confession scene. Taking on the role of the criminal in Spain's first crime fiction story, Gabriela is more than just the perpetrator of her crime; she is also its narrator. Gabriela justifies the act of killing her husband by explaining that she did it out of the love that she feels for Zarco:

> ¡Me declaro, pues, autora de tan horrendo crimen! ... Pero sabed que un hombre me obligó a cometerlo ...
>
> Gabriela miró al Juez con fanática adoración, como una madre a su atribulado hijo, y añadió con melancólico acento:
>
> – ¡Podría con una sola palabra, arrastrarlo al abismo en que me ha hecho caer! ¡Podría arrastrarlo al cadalso, a fin de que no se quedase en el mundo, para maldecirme tal vez al casarse con otra! ... ¡Pero no quiero! ¡Callaré su nombre, porque me ha amado y le amo! ¡Y le amo, aunque sé que no hará nada para impedir mi muerte! (52)

> So I do plead guilty to this gruesome crime, but it behooves you to know that a man forced me to commit it ...
>
> Gabriela stared at the judge with boundless worship, like a mother at her suffering child, and added in a melancholy voice:
>
> "I could with a single word, drag him down to the abyss into which he caused me to fall. I could drag him to the scaffold so that he wouldn't remain in this world and perhaps curse me upon marrying another woman. But I refuse to do that. I will not reveal his name because he loved me and I love him. And I love him although I know he will do nothing to prevent my death." (57)

By invoking Zarco during her confession, Gabriela converts him into her accomplice, criminalizing him through her testimony. In line with this idea, Patricia Hart remarks, "It is in this theme that the story is most modern as it examines, albeit crudely, the fine line between the criminal and the detective who pursues him, a theme played to perfection by Patricia Highsmith and others much later" (*The Spanish Sleuth* 18). Allowing the female criminal to deliver her own confession adds a further dimension to this scene because the narrative pauses to link deviancy with the female body. And yet, Gabriela's confession highlights that she too has been a victim not only of a loveless marriage, but also of needing to protect Zarco from her truth. The narrative draws attention to the maternal look that she bestows upon Zarco, suggesting that her confession is meant both to conceal and shield him. Invoking a mother narrative framework during this episode, we are reminded of Caron

Gentry and Laura Sjoberg's definition of the mother narratives, which "describe women's violence as a need to belong, a need to nurture, and a way of taking care of and being loyal to men; motherhood gone awry" (13). The mother narrative is invoked in this instance because Gabriela proves her loyalty to Zarco by remaining silent regarding his role. Even the murder of her husband connects back to safeguarding him from the threat of dishonour. Gabriela's actions during this scene, however, are more purposeful and agential than protecting Zarco, since there is also a degree of defiance in her confession that requires further examination.

Given a space to argue who the true criminal is in this scenario, Gabriela underscores that her crime is one born out of a previous offence because she was forced to marry a man she abhorred: "[M]i mano estaba vinculada a la vida de un hombre ruin, y entre matarlo a él o causar la desventura de mi hijo, la del hombre que adoraba y la mía propia, opté por arrancar su inútil y miserable vida al que era nuestro verdugo. Maté, pues, a mi marido ..., creyendo ejecutar un acto de justicia en el criminal que me había engañado infamemente al casarse conmigo" (53) ("I was already married and bound to a contemptible man, and between killing him or causing the misfortune of my child, that of the man I adored, and my own, I opted for snuffing out the useless, miserable life of the one who was our scourge. And so ... I killed my husband, believing that I was discharging an act of justice on a criminal who had deceived me horribly when he married me") (58). In her confession, Gabriela shifts the responsibility for the crime. The criminal is Alfonso, whose deception has prevented her from marrying a man who truly loves her and whose child she is carrying though we assume she later has a miscarriage. She assigns Alfonso the responsibility for making her relationship with Zarco a crime, and so when she is obliged to choose between both men because of Zarco's need to legitimize their union, she chooses to end Alfonso's life. Her love for Zarco criminalizes her, suggesting that female delinquency is born from this amorous relationship, and yet, her husband's murder is the result of this previous injustice. This same amorous affair, however, also serves to reveal the judicial system's weaknesses.

The politics of visibility that position Gabriela as a delinquent also provide her with the space to speak as a victim. The trial's confessional space allows Gabriela to give visibility to her status as a victim of the moral and legal codes that force her to stay married. For a woman living in nineteenth-century Spain, divorce would not have been an option. It was only a viable alternative for a man if female adultery occurred, according to the *Código penal* of 1848.[8] Had Gabriela's adultery been discovered, she would have been imprisoned, and Zarco could have been punished even if he had been unaware of her marital status. Since Alfonso's crime would not have been punished otherwise, Gabriela enacts her own version of justice, transforming Zarco into her accomplice because he supplied her with the motive. Although we have obtained glimpses of Gabriela prior to this moment, she now comes into full view for her spectators. The elusiveness and timidity that she exhibited before are replaced with a certain brazenness that Felipe illustrates the moment that she is taken away to her cell: "Gabriela se alejó con paso firme, no sin dirigirme antes una mirada espantosa, en que había más orgullo que arrepentimiento" (53) ("Gabriela left with a firm step, not without first giving me a frightful look, in which there was more pride than remorse") (59). Unlike the previous portrayals of Gabriela, she no longer appears vulnerable at the end of this episode. She has justified her crime, and returning the gaze, she looks back, satisfied that she has blurred the line between innocence and guilt for her audience.

As in the female picaresque novel that became popular in Early Modern Spanish literature because it showcases women's criminality via a corporeal discourse, there is a need to control and display the female delinquent body in Alarcón's *El clavo*. Gabriela, similar to female rogues like Francisco López de Úbeda's Justina, acts as an agent of chaos and disruption, and therefore must be silenced, contained, or eliminated. Despite killing her husband to be with Zarco, as her judge he condemns her to death, but disappears soon after to seek her pardon as her lover. Leaving us with Felipe's perspective during the final scene of her execution, it is through him that we get a final depiction of Gabriela:

> Al verla aparecer, costóme trabajo reconocerla. Había enflaquecido horriblemente, y apenas tenía fuerzas para llevar a sus labios el Crucifijo, que besaba a cada momento ...
>
> y cuando me hubo reconocido, exclamó: ...
>
> – ¡Hágalo Dios muy feliz! Dígale, cuando lo vea, que me perdone, para que me perdone Dios. Dígale que todavía le amo ..., aunque el amarle es causa de mi muerte. (54)

> When Gabriela appeared, I scarcely recognized her. She had become horribly emaciated and barely had the strength to raise to her lips the crucifix that she kissed time and again ...
>
> and when she recognized me, exclaimed: ...

> "May God make him happy. When you see him, tell him to forgive me so that God will. Tell him that I still love him, even though my love for him is the cause of my death." (60)

Standing in for the moral order of his society, Felipe asks to see Gabriela resign herself and accept her fate to authenticate the restorative gesture of her punishment. Her death should (re)legitimize and reestablish the moral codes that she has trespassed. Once Gabriela accepts her punishment as redemption, Zarco reenters the scene with her pardon. Though she has a chance to look at him and exclaim "¡Bendito seas!" (55) ("God bless you!") (61), the pardon arrives too late because she then loses consciousness and dies. In Landeira's view, she is punished because she acted from her passion, and had to die according to the moral codes of nineteenth-century Spain (69). Agreeing with Landeira's assertion, Joan Ramon Resina proposes in *El cadáver en la cocina* (*The Cadaver in the Kitchen*) that *El clavo* celebrates the triumph of justice and law over passion, and ends this way to detract from the romantic overtones of the novel (25). Although I agree that justice triumphs over passion at the end, I would argue that the narrative links Gabriela's death to her exposition of the vulnerabilities of the legal system and its representatives. Because she represents a threat to the male order and articulates a protofeminist ideology during her confession scene, eliminating Gabriela serves as a restorative gesture that reasserts patriarchal control over the disruptive female body. The last chapter of the novel, "Moraleja" ("Moral"), demonstrates that this order has indeed been reinstated because Zarco is now happily married, a magistrate, and a father in La Habana (55). Abiding by the moral codes of his society, Zarco is given the chance to start a new family because, according to the narrator, he has no reason to feel guilty. The "Moraleja" reveals the narrator's patriarchal philosophy and his ideological position on female delinquency. At the end of *El clavo*, Gabriela's condition as a victim is negated, and while she must perish at the end, Zarco can live happily ever after.

Using Peter Brook's terminology, I claim that Alarcón stages the female body in a way that is similar to later realist novels that present a woman's body, particularly the adulterous body, as "the site on which the aspirations, anxieties and contradictions, of a whole society are played out" (33). In *El clavo*, Gabriela encapsulates both the fears and desires of two men, but, more significantly, she represents a more generalized social anxiety regarding the disruption caused by transgressive female sexuality in addition to the unreadability of the female criminal.

Gabriela's illegibility, however, could be explained by the fact that she is also a victim in this story, that she straddles the line between innocence and guilt. The confession scene where Gabriela defends herself would appear to make her legible, and yet, she turns the table on her spectators/readers by placing the blame for her crime on both Alfonso and Zarco. Consequently, Gabriela cannot be read and understood as a criminal unless she is revealed and interpreted as a victim.

Though Lombroso's study on delinquent women would come much later, the character of Gabriela Zahara already addresses the concerns put forth by Lombroso in his study regarding the blurring of boundaries or limits between the delinquent and the non-delinquent woman. These preoccupations were particularly intensified when female delinquency was associated with transgressive female sexuality, according to Akiko Tsuchiya, who claims that "[f]emale deviance and sexuality were typically conflated in the nineteenth century through a linkage between deviance and the female body ... female deviance was automatically translated into sexual deviance, assumed to manifest itself in the materiality of the body" (14). It is no surprise, then, that "it is a female disorder – of a sexual nature, no less – that was blamed for the political, social, and economic woes that plagued the nation during the Isabelline period and beyond, well into the Restoration" (15–16). Moreover, the interest in reading the signs of the disruptive female body would translate into the later literary representation of the femme fatale as a powerful symbol of danger, which, according to Maryellen Bieder, would continue to dominate twentieth-century Spanish fiction. Bieder proposes that "the female body was frequently refigured as a textual space on which the male protagonist inscribed his obsessions. The body as a sign within a signifying community gave way to the woman's body as the linguistic projection of a male character" (5). We have already seen in *El clavo* that the preoccupation with "disruptive females" and the restoration of a male order would translate into Gabriela's condemnation at the end of the story despite the fact that she confesses to her crime by demonstrating that she is the victim of two men and the patriarchal system that protects them and punishes her. Even though Zarco obtains a pardon for Gabriela, the pardon becomes irrelevant because she is still condemned, and punished by God.

What is truly novel about Alarcón's *El clavo*, as Myung N. Choi has previously pointed out, is that it emphasizes Gabriela's perspective, "quien denuncia su situación de mujer que vive en el patriarcado sin ninguna posibilidad de escapar del sistema imperante" ("who speaks to her situation as a woman who lives in the patriarchy without any possibility of escaping from the prevailing social order") (28). Knowing that she will lose the legal battle at the end of the novel, she nevertheless puts on display the injustice that Alfonso has committed against her. Gabriela anticipates the fight for an equal system of justice that will constitute one of the major themes in the gendered version of the genre. Since the legal institution will not allow Gabriela to get divorced, she must provide her own form of justice – a personal form of justice, the likes of which we will see carried out in Emilia Pardo Bazán's *La gota de sangre* and in contemporary female crime fiction.

Before Femicrime: Emilia Pardo Bazán's *La gota de sangre*

The year 2016 witnessed a rise in protests against femicide and gender violence in countries around the world, with feminist organizations mobilizing to form part of the *Ni una menos* (*Not One Less*) movement and its demonstrations. As we watched these protests unfold, Emilia Pardo Bazán's words from 1915 in her column "La vida contemporánea" ("Contemporary Life"), about how the legal system treats female victims, continued to ring true: "Con razón decía un célebre jurisconsulto que la vida no está protegida; pero debió añadir 'en especial, la de la mujer.' Todo español cree tener sobre la mujer derecho de vida o muerte. Lo mismo da que se trate de su novia, de su amante, de su esposa" ("No wonder a renowned judge was correct when he said that life is not protected; but he should have added 'especially that of a woman.' Every Spanish man believes he has the power of life or death over women. It does not matter if she is his girlfriend, his lover, his wife") (1.740, 302).[9] The topic of gender violence and the status of women before the law would form part of Pardo Bazán's journalistic repertoire during the years that she regularly contributed to *La Ilustración Artística* between 1895 and 1916. Although she had published with the newspaper prior to 1895, she became a regular collaborator for the section "La vida contemporánea" starting that year (Ruiz Ocaña 179). Violence against women was a focal point for some of Pardo Bazón's columns, crimes that were being tried by the judicial system and in which men would end up not being convicted.[10] Two early examples in *La Ilustración Artística* are "Ensaladilla" ("Russian Salad," 1901), where she maintains that husbands who kill their wives are not harshly chastised by the legal system, and "Como en las cavernas" ("As in the Caverns," 1901), where the topic of rape surfaces as she recounts the story of a dressmaker who was sexually assaulted by two men and the punishment that she believes would suit them – lynching. Noting the difference in the sexes when it came to how they were treated by the judicial system in Spain, Pardo Bazán also spoke out against capital punishment, in particular when the one being tried was a woman. The inequality between men and women came to fuel her work on understanding female criminalization, and would later encourage her to produce a crime fiction novel, *La gota de sangre*, that, if published today, could be labelled female crime fiction, crime fiction written with a female-oriented perspective.

Although most crime fiction critics identify Pardo Bazán as a literary precursor, they consider that female crime fiction in Spain began in 1979 with Lourdes Ortiz's *Picadura mortal*, overlooking the female criminal mastermind, Chulita Ferna, at work in Pardo Bazán's *La gota de sangre*. I am arguing that *La gota de sangre* was born from Pardo Bazán's interest both in female delinquency and the legal system's treatment of women, evidence of which we find in her journalistic corpus. One particular national crime that she was profoundly affected by was none other than "el crimen de la calle de Fuencarral" ("the crime on Fuencarral Street"), an 1888 murder in Madrid that she referenced in her journalism pieces at the time and that would later inform her novel *La piedra angular* (*The Cornerstone*, 1891) because of her interest in criminology and capital punishment (Pattinson 74–5). The Fuencarral murder captured the attention of the Spanish press and fascinated authors like Pío Baroja, who would reference the crime in his *Mala Hierba* (*Bad Weeds*, 1904) and *La sensualidad pervertida* (*Perverted Sensuality*, 1920), and Benito Pérez Galdós, who covered the trial in a series of six columns for the Argentinian newspaper *La Prensa* (*The Press*) from 19 July 1888 to 30 May 1889, articles that were later published together as *El crimen de la calle de Fuencarral*.[11] The Fuencarral crime was the story of a maid, Higinia Balaguer, who was accused and later tried and executed for the brutal murder of her boss, Luciana Borcino, who was repeatedly stabbed, robbed of a considerable sum of money, and her lifeless body burned in an effort to erase any evidence. Though it may have contributed to the plot and themes of Pardo Bazán's *La piedra angular*, I am suggesting that the Fuencarral murder also informed her first crime fiction piece, *La gota de sangre*. Here, Pardo Bazán employs the detective genre to revisit the theme of female criminality through an amateur investigator who is, in many respects, a Holmesian wannabe. A parody of Arthur Conan Doyle's famous detective, Pardo Bazán's Selva becomes a sleuth out of boredom and for entertainment, but also to clear his name of a crime, the murder of Francisco Grijalba, which he did not commit. Selva's investigations lead him to discover that a couple, Andrés Ariza and Chulita Ferna, are the ones responsible for the murder, but what he does not expect is to be outwitted by the transgressive Chulita, who convinces him to finance her escape to France instead of alerting the authorities. With Selva's criminalization complete, Chulita eludes punishment for her crime whereas her male partner suffers an unfortunate ending because Selva convinces him to commit suicide to protect his honour.

I demonstrate that Chulita Ferna's evasion of the law is made possible through parody because Pardo Bazán sets the stage for the unmasking of the male detective myth. In *La gota de sangre*, the "Great Detective as an icon of Man," to use Sally Munt's phrase, is revealed for what he is – an amateur sleuth manipulated by the femme fatale to become her accomplice (*Murder* 204). A woman whose multiple indiscretions have been exposed, Chulita Ferna's heightened visibility favours her during her encounter with Selva, who believes that he can outsmart her into confessing because she has already been labelled a transgressive woman. And yet I am arguing that the politics of female visibility are reworked in Pardo Bazán's novel to allow Chulita Ferna to escape prosecution for her part in Grijalba's murder by transforming Selva into a willing accomplice who finances her defiance of the law. Since the transgressive woman triumphs over the male amateur sleuth, I propose that Pardo Bazán mobilizes justice in favour of the female criminal as part of her condemnation of Higinia Balaguer's death sentence in the Fuencarral case and in response to her interest in arguing for more female-friendly forms of justice.

Pardo Bazán's analysis of Higinia Balaguer's trial is well-documented both in journalistic pieces for *El Imparcial* (*The Impartial*), but also in one of the letters included in *Al pie de la Torre Eiffel* (*At the Foot of the Eiffel Tower*) during the Universal Exposition of 1889 in Paris. The nineteen letters that she wrote between 7 April and 14 July 1889 were later grouped together in this volume, and first published in October of that same year. She discusses the murder of Luciana Borcino in her Carta III (Letter III) of *Al pie de la Torre Eiffel*, which was written from Bordeaux on 2 May of that year. She begins by emphasizing that the crime, while serious, is also trivial, noting that "el célebre *crimen* es la cosa más vulgar del mundo, la menos digna de fijar la atención, no ya de las personas ilustradas, pero ni siquiera de la muchedumbre" ("the famous *crime* is the least noteworthy thing in the world, the least worthy of attention, not only from intellectuals, but also from the masses") (63; italics in original). Pardo Bazán even highlights that the crime merited no more than two days' attention for gossiping in the neighbourhood, and a twenty-four-hour news cycle to discuss it (63). The author recognizes, however, that there is something particular about this crime, "hay en él *algo* mucho más grave que los hechos aparentes; *algo* tan grave, tan serio, tan trascendental, que si el rumor público lo indica y la maledicencia lo subraya, la razón lo repugna y lo condena la verosimilitud" ("there is *something* about it much more serious than the obvious facts; *something* so severe, so serious, so momentous, that public outcry reflects it, slander emphasizes it, reason rejects it, and plausibility condemns it") (63; italics in original). Although the crime appears to be both vulgar and superficial, Pardo Bazán concludes that this crime touches on certain sensibilities that are not immediately apparent.

For Pardo Bazán, the Fuencarral crime elicited this response not because a maid killed and robbed her boss, but because Luciana's son, José Varela, was also a criminal, and during the time of her death was imprisoned in Madrid's infamous Cárcel Modelo. Pardo Bazán describes Varela as someone with "canallescos instintos, de estragadas costumbres, de propensiones feroces, siempre mezclado y confundido con la hez del populacho y entregado á escandalosas *juergas*" ("villainous instincts, corrupt habits, violent tendencies, always mixed up and involved with the dregs of society and devoted to scandalous *revelries*") (64; italics in original). The public wanted to believe that Varela, nicknamed *"el marquesito"* (*"little marquis"*), played a role in his mother's murder with the help of the prison director, thus confirming the public's suspicion that their penal and legal systems were both corrupt and flawed (ibid.). Here, Pardo Bazán claims that the trial demonstrates "la poca confianza que inspiran al pueblo español sus instituciones seculares, la que ya todo el mundo llama *justicia histórica*, la organización de los establecimientos penales, y el sistema político á cuyo amparo supone que tamaños abusos pueden ocurrir" ("the lack of confidence that the Spanish people feel towards their traditional institutions, *historical justice*, as everyone now calls it, the organization of penal establishments, and the political system under whose protection abuses so severe as this one can occur") (65; italics in original).

Critical of how the press handled the case and the resulting public opinion, Pardo Bazán divided them into two groups – the *insensatos* (*irrational or foolish*), who blame the son and the prison director, and the *sensatos* (*rational or wise*), who find Higinia to be the only guilty party with the help of some unfavourable characters (66). Pardo Bazán clarifies that the *insensatos* see in Luciana's murder "un parricidio nefando, fundándose en que quien hace tiempo abofeteó, hirió, maltrató y probó á abrasar con petróleo á su madre, y le deseó la muerte en voz alta, no se habrá descuidado en rematarla cuando tuvo favorable ocasión" ("a heinous case of parricide, given that the one who had long ago slapped, hurt, abused and tried to burn his mother with oil, and also wished her death aloud, would not have neglected the opportunity to off her when the circumstances were right") (66).[12] While she refers to this portion of the press and public as *insensatos*, there is something of note here – the fact that Luciana's son was her abuser. Pardo Bazán emphasizes this in her Carta III, giving visibility to Varela's crimes against his mother, which Galdós had already stressed in his columns for *La Prensa*, where he describes how Varela assaulted his mother with a knife, inflicting severe wounds (5). With respect to who is the guilty party, Pardo Bazán argues the following:

> Quien abofetea á su madre hasta arrancarla los dientes; quien esgrime contra ella la navaja y sepulta el hierro en las entrañas donde fue concebido, podrá (mediante el absurdo de las circunstancias fortuitas) no haber sido parricida material: moralmente lo es; inspira el horror consecuente al más nefando de los crímenes, á aquel que las leyes de Moisés y Solón no castigan, porque no admiten ni que pueda existir; á aquel que más ultraja las sacras leyes de la naturaleza. Pero repito que si esto pienso *como novelista*, como magistrado sólo pensaría que el crimen ha de estar más claro que la luz del sol para que la justicia humana pueda castigarlo sin recelo. (67; italics in original)

> He, who beats his mother to the extent of pulling out her teeth; he, who wields the knife against her and buries the blade in the womb where he was conceived, may (by means of the absurdity of unforeseen circumstances) not be the one who in a material sense committed the parricide: but morally, he is; he inspires the same horror as is inspired by the most heinous of crimes, a crime not punished by the laws of Moses and Solon, because they could not even imagine that it could exist; a crime that violates the most sacred laws of nature. But I repeat that I think this *as a novelist*; as a magistrate I would only think that the crime must be as clear as the light of day so that human justice can punish it without hesitation.

What is noteworthy is that Pardo Bazán uses this moment in her letter not to incriminate Higinia, but to draw attention to the physical abuse suffered by Luciana at the hands of her son, a crime that in her view makes him morally responsible. According to Marisol Donis, Varela had been suspected of physically abusing his mother, but, to protect her son, Luciana never admitted or confirmed this, and so Varela was never punished. And yet, the violence towards his mother had been aptly documented: "Violento con su madre, las discusiones entre ellos eran constantes y en más de una ocasión la golpeó brutalmente dejando las señales de su violencia en el rostro de la madre, que nunca quiso denunciarle" ("He was violent towards his mother, the arguments between them were constant and on more than one occasion he brutally beat her, leaving the marks of his violence on his mother's face, though she never wanted to accuse him") (Donis 132). In a still more violent episode, Varela fired a gun at her and while he did not hit her, they had to move from their house to a new home on Barquillo Street, where he then attacked her with a knife because she did not want to give him money to buy a horse (ibid.). Although the police were called, since Luciana's screams were heard by the neighbours, no action was taken to protect Luciana against her son even though she confessed that he had threatened to burn her alive (133). Learning of Varela's violence towards his mother, Pardo Bazán makes sure to expose it in her letter, giving visibility to an otherwise silenced offence. Here, Pardo Bazán anticipates her later journalistic writings on gender violence and how many of the crimes committed against women remain unpunished before the law.

Considered a suspect in his mother's murder due to one of Higinia Balaguer's initial statements, the focus would soon shift from Varela to Higinia and her friend Dolores as the authors of the crime. In his columns about the Fuencarral murder, Galdós accentuates how Higinia masterfully changes the direction of the hearings and the subsequent trial by providing six different and contradictory declarations – each of which modifies the part that she played in the crime. From victim to mastermind to Dolores's accomplice, Galdós's reading of Higinia emphasizes how she rewrites her role and acts out what she believes will satisfy not only the court officials, but also the press and public opinion:

> No vacila un momento en lo que dice: lleva muy estudiado su papel, contesta con extraordinaria seguridad a las preguntas, cuya intención penetra al instante; no se turba jamás; todo lo prevé y a todos los argumentos tiene un argumento que oponer; sabe manifestar aflicción cuando la aflicción le conviene, y la frialdad cuando esta es útil a su defensa. Se expresa con exactitud de frase, impropia de su condición social, pues debe advertirse, para que se juzgue de su educación, que no sabe leer ni escribir. (39)

> She does not hesitate for a moment in what she says: she has studied her role very carefully, she answers the questions with extraordinary confidence, perceiving the intention behind them instantly; she is never

> disturbed; she has foreseen everything, and has a counterargument to oppose any argument; she knows how to appear upset when this suits her, and to appear cold when this is useful to her defense. She expresses herself precisely, which is uncharacteristic of her social class, for it must be noted, based on her education, that she can neither read nor write.

Galdós draws attention to his perception of Higinia's contradictory nature, establishing how a woman unable to read or write can dictate how others read her – by initially presenting herself as the criminal/victim when she claims that the widow's insults drove her to commit the murder, later confessing to being the sole author of the crime, and finally testifying to being an accomplice first of Luciana's son and later, of Dolores, in one of her final accounts of the crime. Galdós's praise of Higinia is founded upon his interpretation of her ability to stage herself appropriately. According to Galdós, all of her performances have been astutely calculated to create multiple readings of her self, remaining a blank slate upon which a new story can be formulated.

Tried before both the criminal court and the court of public opinion, Higinia is found guilty and sentenced to be executed whereas the silent Dolores, who Higinia claims towards the end of her trial was the true mastermind and not just an accomplice to the murder, is sentenced to eighteen years. Once the sentences are handed down, Galdós highlights in his final article not only the injustice of rewarding the silent Dolores while punishing the person who has confessed, but also signals the bias in the verdict that condemns Higinia: "He aquí un veredicto que no satisface a nadie, pues los que negaban veracidad al relato de Higinia, llevan a mal que esta sea condenada, y los que creían en él no hallan justo que la iniciadora del crimen quede sin castigo mientras lo tiene tan cruel la que fue a él sugestionada por su compañera" ("Here is a verdict that does not satisfy anyone, for those who denied truthfulness to Higinia's account think it is wrong for her to be condemned, and those who believed in her account do not find it right that the author of the crime goes unpunished while the one who was drawn to the crime by her companion has such a cruel sentence") (54). From Donis's research on the case, we learn that Higinia Balaguer met with Emilia Pardo Bazán before her execution (159). According to Donis, Pardo Bazán had demonstrated a certain fondness towards Higinia, and for this reason,

> Siguió recordándola y años después escribiría: "su ceño tenía la trágica severidad de la Melpómene griega. Hay en su ser algo no vulgar, superior

a su historia entera, a sus hechos. Hay hombres y mujeres que valen más que su destino y que sus actos. La relación entre lo pensado, lo sentido y lo hecho no es siempre lógica." (165)

She continued to remember her, and years later she would write: "Her frown had the tragic severity of the Greek Melpomene. There is something about her which is not vulgar, which is superior to her entire story, to her deeds. There are men and women who are worth more than their fate and their actions. The relationship between what is thought, what is felt, and what is done is not always logical."

Pardo Bazán reads Higinia in a literary vein similar to Galdós, emphasizing an image of the female criminal that surpasses the vulgarity of her crime, but also of her social standing. Like Galdós, Pardo Bazán endows Higinia with a certain literary value, and her character description elevates the woman delinquent above her condition as a convict. For Galdós and Pardo Bazán, what makes Higinia truly fascinating is her ability to use her criminal wit to attempt to outmanoeuvre everyone associated with the trial even though she is executed in the end. Still, this ability to outsmart a patriarchal system is one that Pardo Bazán will develop in her fictional version of female delinquency in *La gota de sangre*.

Pardo Bazán would also be staunchly opposed to Higinia's death sentence; she would regularly argue against capital punishment, especially when it concerned female criminals, in her journalistic endeavours and even in her novels such as *La piedra angular*. In "Impresiones y sentimientos del día diecinueve" ("Perceptions and Feelings on the Nineteenth Day"), an article that she wrote for *El Imparcial* the day after Higinia's execution on 19 July, she concludes the following: "La sociedad que necesita matar prueba su debilidad para la represión activa, constante, severa, terrible. Es como el padre que pega y maltrata á sus hijos porque no acertó á educarles y á hacerse obedecer con solo el mandato categórico" ("A society that needs to kill demonstrates its weakness in terms of active, constant, severe, terrible repression. It is like the father who beats and abuses his children because he failed to educate them and to have them obey him with only his categorical command"). While describing Higinia's final moments, the author condemns a society that punishes its citizens in this way:

La claridad del sol, cruda y enemiga, abrasando los ojos enrojecidos por las lágrimas y alumbrando la vergüenza de las pálidas mejillas; la fatiga de la ascensión de un cuerpo exhausto, enervado y dolorido; la perspectiva del gentío curioso, de la viva ola que muge antes de escupir á la playa el cadáver; el instinto animal que aconseja la desesperada resistencia ó la fuga y los grillos que no consienten ni alzar las manos implorando á Dios; el sudor de la agonía al tocar el suelo del tablado; el velo de sombra en las pupilas al divisar el instrumento del suplicio.

The brightness of the sun, raw and hostile, burns the eyes reddened by tears, and illuminates the shame of the pale cheeks; the fatigue of the ascension of an exhausted, agitated, and sore body; the perspective of the curious crowd, of the living wave that moans before spitting the corpse onto the beach; the animal instinct that advises desperate resistance or flight, and the crickets that do not even consent to raise their hands to implore God; the sweat of the agony felt upon touching the stage floor; the veil of shadow in the pupils upon seeing the instrument of torture.

The execution of Higinia Balaguer on 19 July 1890 outside of the Cárcel Modelo would be the last public execution to take place in Madrid, sealing her importance as the last criminal whose death would be staged in this way (Donis 162–3).[13] Pardo Bazán makes this moment of the execution come to life for her readers, demonstrating Higinia's agony and desperation. But before providing her readers with this final image of Higinia, the author has already posed the following problem: "Si hay tal debilidad en la mujer, ¿puede en conciencia subir al patíbulo? Si es un ser que vive en perpetua minoría, ¿cómo no le aplica la sociedad el criterio protector á que los menores tienen derecho?" ("If women suffer from such weakness, can they in good conscience climb the gallows? If a woman is a being that lives as a perpetual minor, how does society not assign them the same protective status to which minors are entitled?"). In this article, Pardo Bazán remains critical of a society that is uneven in its treatment of men and women because it denotes females as an inferior minority, but insists on punishing men and women equally and just as harshly.

Protesting the capital punishment of women, Pardo Bazán leaves us with this final picture of Higinia's cadaver on stage before an audience that has just watched her be killed: "[Y] queda solo el reo, sentado, con la faz descubierta, la cabellera agitada por el aire, dominando con su trágica silueta el gentío estupefacto" ("And the only one left is the convict, sitting, with her face uncovered, her hair blown by the wind, dominating the stunned crowd with her tragic silhouette"). Pardo Bazán, however, also signals the importance of being able to make the female criminal legible. Higinia's multiple performances or declarations, according to Galdós's columns, contribute to her unreadability and the anxiety that this creates in the public that watches and reads her. It is on this final stage, where she is put to death, that she becomes decipherable and visible for her audience.

Pardo Bazán will revisit the theme of the female criminal's (un)readability and the visibility of female delinquency in *La gota de sangre*. Pardo Bazán allows her woman delinquent to succeed, to escape punishment by rewarding her ability to create misreadings, to remain, as Higinia has done, illegible. With her multiple declarations, however, Higinia ends up losing control over her image whereas Chulita Ferna is allowed to retake control, using her heightened visibility as a transgressive woman to create a series of misreadings. Employing the femme fatale type, Pardo Bazán appears to follow the formula set by the classic English detective novel, but instead produces a parody of the form by having her female criminal go head-to-head with the detective, modelled after Sherlock Holmes. Pardo Bazán's parodic experiment has not convinced some crime fiction critics like Vázquez de Parga and Colmeiro, who, while admiring her contribution, claim that Pardo Bazán simply wanted to experiment with the form, and imitate the structure and style of the British enigma by simply relocating the action to Madrid (*La novela policiaca en España* 37–8; *La novela policiaca española* 115). Although Vázquez de Parga and Colmeiro seem to overlook Pardo Bazán's parodic intentions in her employment of imported generic conventions, Resina argues that her use of British models converts *La gota de sangre* into "una narración poco elaborada y dependiente de modelos que no domina (fundamentalmente Conan Doyle)" ("a not-too-elaborate narration and one dependent on models that she does not dominate (fundamentally Conan Doyle)") (*El cadáver* 27). For Resina, Pardo Bazán's parodic intentions fall short with this work because "la parodia supone algo más que una conciencia de género" ("parody amounts to something more than an awareness of genre") (27). I disagree with Resina's argument here because I think that it is clear that Pardo Bazán's novel is a parody of Conan Doyle's works. She uses Sherlock Holmes as the inspiration for Selva and then has the female criminal outsmart him. It is because Selva is a reader and enthusiast of British detective fiction (and we assume an admirer of Sherlock Holmes) that he believes that he is the one who will be able to solve the case, outwitting the police. Instead, the Holmesian Selva falls victim to the female delinquent.

Critical of the genre's formulaic rigidness and its lack of authenticity when it came to portraying the human soul, Pardo Bazán explains the following when mentioning the works of Conan Doyle in a 1909 article for *La Ilustración Artística*:

> En las novelas de Conan Doyle el fondo, los tipos, los personajes, las decoraciones, lugares, muebles, armas (¡qué de armería!) son genuinos y castizos de Albión, y sin embargo, al acabar de leer, no ha penetrado en nosotros ni un átomo del sentido íntimo del alma inglesa ... Sherlock Holmes sólo observa lo material, y lo material cien veces observado. Nunca saca consecuencias del estudio de un espíritu, ó sea de la psicología. ("La vida contemporánea" 1.416, 122)

> In the novels of Conan Doyle the background, types, characters, decorations, places, furniture, weapons (what an armoury!) are genuinely and authentically English, and yet, after finishing reading, not even an atom of the English soul's inner sense has penetrated us ... Sherlock Holmes only observes the material, and he observes the material a hundred times over. He never draws conclusions from the study of a spirit, that is, from psychology.

Responding to this in *La gota de sangre*, Pardo Bazán's Selva manifests a particular interest in examining Chulita's character, revealing her motives for participating in Grijalba's murder. Consequently, the staging of Chulita Ferna is significant because she seduces Selva by appearing completely legible as a marginalized, delinquent woman, who accepts the role of Ariza's accomplice. Since she has already been rejected and ostracized by her neighbours and her social class, Selva's reading of Chulita is based on this social branding and the transgressive woman's stigmatization. Selva misreads her and is unable to see through the manufactured scene, the trap to seduce him that she has prepared when he goes to interview her.

The detective story commences with Selva's visit to the doctor, who recommends that the bored dandy should engage in activities that provide a certain stimulus to his life, diagnosing him with sluggishness and indifference (35). With this in mind, the doctor makes the following recommendation: "[E]xplore almas. No hay vida humana sin misterio. La curiosidad puede ascender a pasión. Para una persona como usted, que posee elementos de investigación psicológica" ("[E]xplore souls. There is no human life without mystery. Curiosity can rise to the level of passion. For a person like you, who possesses elements of psychological research") (36). The use of psychology in an investigation is precisely what Pardo Bazán considers that Conan Doyle's Sherlock Holmes lacks. What this implies is that the doctor's advice, in addition to what he says about Selva possessing the skills to carry out a character assessment, confirms *La gota de sangre*'s generic self-consciousness. Towards the end of the investigation and in another episode where the story affirms its self-conscious character, Selva reflects upon how his psychological inductions allowed him to solve the case despite facilitating Chulita's escape (97). Selva believes that he has acquired the adequate skills to become a fulltime investigator, and using an instance of targeted ridicule, Pardo Bazán ends her novel with Selva's decision to move to England and study under the masters of the trade.

The same day he is given this diagnosis Selva attends the theatre, where he encounters Andrés Ariza, who causes what Selva suspects from the beginning is a staged scene when he feigns anger at Selva for having tripped him as he heads towards his seat (37). Selva immediately suspects something is amiss with Ariza, and looks to uncover the motives behind his actions, employing his doctor's recommendation. Instead of focusing on what is occurring on stage, Selva describes "en la pechera de la camisa de Andrés, y casi cubierta por el chaleco – una diminuta manchita roja, viva como labio encendido por el amor; una reciente gotica de sangre" ("on the front of Andrés's shirt, and almost covered by the vest – a tiny red stain, as intensely red as lips emboldened by love; a recent little drop of blood") (38). Selva's case begins the moment he observes the drop of blood on Ariza's shirt because it is at that instant that he stops feeling bored, and starts creating a fiction of what he imagines has happened (38). When he discovers a cadaver on his way home from the theatre, he makes the instant connection between Ariza and the victim, later identified as Francisco Grijalba, evoked by Grijalba's moustache (41). Since he is the one who first finds the dead man in an undeveloped plot of land next to his home and because he has no verifiable alibi, Selva becomes the police enquiry's prime suspect. Selva convinces the judge not to incarcerate him by claiming that he is the only one who will be able to solve the case and discover the identity of the true felon: "[S]e me figura que solo yo lo he de lograr. Quizá me ha sugerido tal propósito la lectura de esas novelas inglesas que ahora están de moda, y en que hay policías de afición, o sea *detectives* por *sport*" ("I figure that only I will achieve it. Perhaps such an objective has been suggested to me by reading those English novels that are now in vogue, and that have amateur police officers, that is to say *detectives* for *sport*") (48; italics in original).[14] Using his reading of British detective fiction, the narrator justifies his own incursion into the genre – he too can become a detective for sport. Wondering what a professional detective would do when confronted with similar circumstances, Selva employs Holmes as a direct model. When preparing to visit Chulita, for example, he disguises himself as an "inglés elegante" ("elegant Englishman"), a clear reference to Sherlock Holmes, who was also fond of using disguises (78). This intertextual element highlights the parodic and self-conscious character of the story, for it reflects upon its own narrative process by invoking its British antecedents.

Diverging from the authorities' theories on the murder, Selva's investigation into Grijalba's death quickly leads him to suspect that a woman has been involved because the victim was killed while lying on a bed and the package containing his personal effects has been neatly wrapped: "Ese paquetito fue liado por una mujer. El pedazo de lustrina que lo envolvía no es cosa que tenga en su casa ningún hombre; solo las mujeres conservan retales así en sus armarios" ("That little package was wrapped by a woman. The piece of fabric that envelops it isn't something that a man would have in his house; only women keep such fabrics in their closets") (60). What is more, Selva has already posited an additional claim about the female delinquent when he explains to the police: "'Mujer anda por medio siempre,' afirmé, 'pero a veces se queda entre bastidores. Aquí, me atrevo a jurar que tomó parte activa'" ("'A woman is always involved,' I affirmed, 'but sometimes she stays behind the scenes. In this case, I bet she took an active part'") (60). Once Selva realizes that the only woman in the neighbourhood who could be an active accomplice to such a crime is Chulita, the narrative pauses to recount the story of Julia Fernandina:

> Era hermana de la actual condesa de la Tolvanera; pertenecía a familia virtuosa, muy grave, muy ilustre ... ¿Cómo Julita, la niña de la mejor sociedad, se había convertido en la Chulita Ferna, astro de la galantería equívoca? Como sucede en estos casos: empezando por el amor juvenil loco pero sagrado y acabando por el vicio y la decadencia ... A los veintitantos años, escandalizando a la *high-life* andaluza, la aristocrática joven se fugaba con un maestro de francés. (73)

> She was the sister of the current Countess of Tolvanera; she belonged to a virtuous family, very serious, very illustrious ... How did Julita, the

young girl from the best society, become Chulita Ferna, the star of errant gallantry? As it happens in these cases: it started with crazy but platonic young love and it ended with vice and decadence ... In her twenties, the aristocratic young woman scandalized Andalusian high-life when she ran away with a French teacher.

The combination of young love and degradation is to blame for the transformation of the high-society Julia Fernandina into the marginalized and delinquent Chulita Ferna. Once criminalized, she is renamed, and only women like her, "caídas y expulsadas de la sociedad" ("fallen and expelled from society") will attend her "tertulias" ("gatherings") and be seen with her (74). One of the problems that Selva will encounter in his reading of Chulita is that he is already biased. Her social branding determines how he studies and understands her. In other words, this social reading taints his examination of Chulita, and she will use this preconceived bias to her advantage during her encounter with the amateur sleuth.

In his interpretation of this passage, Landeira suggests that "[l]a caída moral de esta mujer la pinta Pardo Bazán como si fuera la de una sirena tentadora que cae en sus propias redes. Es la necesidad lo que empuja a una mujer de aquellos tiempos a usar su cuerpo deseado para prosperar, corriendo el riesgo de perderse a sí misma" ("the moral downfall of this woman is painted by Pardo Bazán as if it were that of a tempting siren who falls into her own net. It is necessity that pushes a woman of those times to use her lusted-after body for her own benefit, at the risk of losing herself") (116). For Landeira, there is no real imputation of guilt here, and Chulita's actions appear justified. To this effect, Colmeiro argues that "[e]l verdadero interés de la historia radica en el desarrollo moral del protagonista, en averiguar los motivos que impulsaron a los criminales a cometer el delito, en conocer la caída moral y social de Chulita y Ariza" ("the real interest of the story lies in the moral development of the protagonist, in learning the motives that prompted the criminals to commit the crime, in understanding the moral and social downfall of Chulita and Ariza") (120). Despite his curiosity regarding Chulita's downfall, however, the amateur detective shows no real interest in understanding her male criminal counterpart, and there is no moral component to his decision to undertake this investigation – he seeks to be entertained while clearing his name. Unlike the background information we obtain on Chulita, we know very little about Ariza beyond his initial appearance at the theatre and his involvement with Chulita. It is the female criminal mind that attracts Selva, and the investigation will hinge on his ability to make the woman delinquent legible, a skill that is questioned in the text.

As the narrative prepares the reader for what will be Selva's encounter with the femme fatale, the amateur detective brings into focus a physical portrayal of Chulita from memory:

> [C]uerpo de una gracia serpentina, cabecita pequeña, género Goya, del que ahora se llama "inquietante." Sus ojos eran flechadores y ojerosos, y al ensalzar sus encantos más o menos íntimos, se solía detallar su pie, muy arqueado y estrecho. Lo que tenía yo presente era la boca, cruenta en el rostro descolorido. Aquella boquillita bermeja me había sugerido, en ocasiones, ideas no muy santas. Actualmente, la semejanza de la boca con una herida fresca me recordó las dos del cadáver de Grijalba, el pecho blanco juvenil con agujeros lívidos. (74)

> A body of serpentine grace, small head, of the Goyaesque type, of the sort now called "disturbing." Her eyes were captivating and haggard, and when extolling her more or less intimate charms, her feet, very arched and narrow, would often be featured. What I remembered was her mouth, blood-red on her colorless face. On occasion that tiny red mouth suggested to me some quite improper ideas. At that moment, her mouth's resemblance to a fresh wound reminded me of the two wounds on Grijalba's corpse, his youthful white chest with livid holes.

Constituting a narrative pause, the passage demonstrates that Selva experiences both desire and repulsion towards the Goyaesque seductress. Linking her body to Grijalba's cadaver, the depiction of her mouth overshadows the rest of her image because it evokes the wounds found on the dead body. Violence and sexual desire are intertwined in this description because Selva is unable to picture Chulita without Grijalba's cadaver forming part of her portrayal. Channelling his memories of Chulita, his portrait of the temptress connects her to the crime, which, in turn, starts paving the way for his own seduction. Already, Chulita, who exemplifies the enigmatic qualities of the femme fatale and the archetype's connection to fatality and death, enraptures the amateur sleuth even before she appears in the narrative.

Deciding to find out more about Chulita's current lovers, Selva goes to La Peña, a gentleman's social club, and listens while three of his friends talk about Chulita. Speaking from experience, one of them comments on how he broke off his affair with her because he started fearing her, "Yo me entiendo ... Es temible. Derrite el dinero y derrite el tuétano" ("I know what I mean ... She's frightening. She melts money and marrow") (76). The men also emphasize how she is physically deceptive because she appears to be twenty-five when she is closer to forty. Significantly, the narrative posits that Chulita is illusory and menacing, someone to be wary and fearful of, who has the power to seduce and outsmart you. We are reminded, moreover, that Selva has previously described the woman who is involved in Grijalba's murder as one who actively participates in the crime. With the information gathered from this conversation, we begin to suspect that Chulita is more than just Ariza's accomplice and that perhaps she is the intellect behind the crime. Selva, however, ignores the warning and the threat that Chulita presents, and decides to interview her after learning that Chulita and Ariza are a couple. Essentially, he underestimates Chulita, and this miscalculation will prove costly.

Thinking he can easily outwit the female criminal, Selva's preparation to go and confront Chulita consists of masquerading as an elegant Englishman, which once again reaffirms Pardo Bazán's parody and critique of Sherlock Holmes, whose favourite tactic is disguising himself to outsmart his adversaries to obtain information. Upon entering Chulita's house, Selva walks into Chulita's trap, and finds himself immediately intrigued by the aromas of the house: "Desde la puerta, un perfume insinuante se me coló por las narices, dominándome el sentido. Era el aroma trastornador de la blanca y carnosa gardenia" ("From the door, an overpowering perfume slipped through my nostrils, dominating my senses. It was the maddening scent of the fleshy white gardenia") (79). The smell of Chulita's house creates an aroma of excitement for Selva, and he connects it to the smell emanating from Andrés Ariza at the theatre, which also reminds him of the image of the drop of blood – the drop of blood that he saw on Ariza's shirt at the theatre which now links him to both Chulita and the murder of Grijalba. Waiting for the femme fatale's appearance, the portrait of Chulita that decorates the living room also takes part in seducing Selva, and the narrative halts to describe its effect:

> El artista, muerto muy joven, había traducido fielmente aquella expresión enigmática de los oscuros ojos, aquella sangrante frescura de la boca y, además, el modelado exquisito de un busto perfecto, diminuto como el de una niña, diabólicamente virginal, que señalaba el ceñido traje, de forma Imperio, de gasa rojiza, realzado por cinturón y bordados de plata oxidada. (81–2)

> The artist, who died very young, had faithfully depicted the enigmatic expression of the dark eyes, that bleeding freshness of the mouth, and also, the exquisite modelling of a perfect bust, tiny like that of a girl and fiendishly virginal, which was emphasized by the tight dress, empire-style, reddish in color, topped off by a belt and oxidized silver embroidery.

Like the first description of Chulita, this portrait once again positions the female suspect as an object for contemplation, but does so to accentuate the power that Chulita will ultimately exert over the amateur detective. Selva enters the erotic and decadent space of the femme fatale, and unknowingly sets in motion his own criminalization. When she finally appears on scene, Selva draws attention, as the painting has already done, to her juvenile nature and to how misleadingly girlish she looks: "risueña, infantil, divinamente ataviada con un traje de interior, de crespones y cintas fofas; representaba los venticinco a lo sumo" ("cheerful, childlike, divinely outfitted in a house dress, with crepes and fluffy ribbons; she looked twenty-five at the oldest") (82). In contrast with Chulita's first portrayal, the following two depictions appear to highlight her vulnerability, her childlike looks and nature, even though there is still something diabolical, devilish about her. The narrative pauses throughout the scene to emphasize the femme fatale's dual nature – the feigned vulnerability or seeming purity that still persists versus the real sumptuousness of her body. The duality of Pardo Bazán's Chulita underscores the fluidity of the femme fatale archetype because Chulita transits between the erotic and the virginal, sitting on the border of the two sides of the eternal feminine – Ave/Eva.

Selva scares Chulita into believing that everyone knows that the couple is guilty of Grijalba's murder and that Ariza has gotten away, leaving her to take the blame. In response, Chulita pretends to faint in Selva's arms, and forces him to lay her down on the same bed upon which Grijalba has been killed. His description of the bed as a "nefando altar de galantería y depravación" ("heinous altar of gallantry and depravity") adds to the scene's diabolical character, since Selva remarks that Grijalba has been sacrificed here (84). Attempting to wake her up, he undresses her:

> [B]usqué la complicada abertura de su corpiño y desabroché y arranqué cintas, y desvié telas para que respirase, y de una mesilla con chismes de plata tomé, precipitadamente, un pulverizador. Del pulverizador salió un agua impregnada de aquel mismo capcioso, embriagador perfume que se

> respiraba en torno y cuyo vaho jaquecoso vino a mí en el teatro, saliendo de las ropas del asesino ... Yo perdí la razón y me entregué a la sugestión del perfume. (85)

> I searched for the complicated opening of her bodice and unbuttoned and untied ribbons, and removed layers of clothing for her to breathe, and I hastily took a perfume bottle from a small table with silver trinkets. The perfume bottle contained water that was saturated with that same devious, captious, exhilarating perfume that was in the air and whose dizzying mist came to me in the theater, wafting up from the murderer's clothes ... I lost my senses and gave myself over to the suggestion of the perfume.

Selva has now been caught in Chulita's trap by treating her as a damsel in distress. The smell of the crime, of depravity and transgression, envelops him in this moment, and he loses his senses to the femme fatale's enigma. Continuing with her act and feigning to wake up at that precise moment, he then falls prey to the diabolical temptress who both scares and attracts him, focusing on her "sonrisa silenciosa [que] florecía en el rojo cáliz de su boca sangrienta y en el negro abismo de sus pupilas un reflejo infernal" ("silent smile [that] bloomed in the red chalice of her bloody mouth and in the infernal reflection of the black abyss of her pupils") (85). Drawing him into her abyss, Selva explains that his fascination with Chulita is due not only to her physical appearance, but also because "aquella boca estaba macerada en el amargo licor del crimen" ("that mouth was soaked in the bitter liquor of the crime") (85). He is attracted to what he fears in her – the violence and death that her body projects. Once again, we return to the image of her mouth, a mouth that even before meeting her in person has evoked Grijalba's wounds and that has the colour of blood, which stands in for murder. Chulita represents Eve in this moment because she tempts him to take a bite of "la manzana fatal" ("the fatal apple"), a figurative bite of the female criminal body that he wishes to possess (85). Asking to be saved by Selva as she proclaims her love for him, Selva is caught "entre el nudo serpentino de sus brazos y el embrujamiento de sus labios" ("between the serpentine knot of her arms and the bewitchment of her lips"), which in addition to the aromas of her perfume completes his seduction: "Y la promesa me fue arrancada: – No tengas miedo; te salvaré" ("And the promise was torn from me: – Don't be afraid; I'll save you") (86). Taking a bite of "la manzana fatal," there is no going back for Selva because Chulita lures him into taking on the role of her accomplice.

Here, we are reminded that the femme fatale's allure can be found in how she fuses "feminine beauty and masculine power" according to Jess Sully, but this is taken one step further with Chulita, since she also signifies death (57). Her fatality, the *fatale* portion of this character is that she is Selva's connection to death, to Grijalba's cadaver, to sin – she is, effectively, his perdition. There is, then, something quite sinister about Chulita, quite deadly, in this scene where Selva is seduced and feels intoxicated by the fatal woman's allure and power. The femme fatale succeeds in ensnaring Selva, who remarks, "Una parte del pecado me correspondía ya. La horrible manzana había crujido entre mis dientes y su ceniza me obturaba la garganta, me cegaba los ojos" ("A part of the sin was mine already. The horrible apple had crunched between my teeth and its ash sealed my throat shut, blinded my eyes") (86). Tasting Chulita's transgression, the crime and the female body are intertwined in this scene, becoming one and the same in Selva's mind. Consequently, Selva reveals feeling penetrated by the crime itself: "[S]u crimen me entraba por los poros, me subía al cerebro, serpenteaba por mis nervios, cuya vibración sensual duraba aún y me envolvía en un aire de insensatez" ("[T]heir crime entered my pores, rose to my brain, twisted its way through my nerves, whose sensual vibration continued still and enveloped me in an air of folly") (86). Chulita serves as the medium to affectively connect him with the feeling surrounding the murderous act. He becomes infected with it and with her because she puts him in touch with his potential criminal nature. For Colmeiro, what this signifies is that "Selva va evolucionando en su conducta moral a través del desarrollo de la historia en una dirección irreconciliable con el orden establecido" ("Selva's moral conduct evolves through the development of the story in a direction that is irreconcilable with the established order") (121). Colmeiro's claim, however, overlooks the fact that Selva embarks on this investigation not due to moral concerns, but because he is in need of entertainment. More significantly, this argument disregards how Chulita has successfully entrapped the amateur sleuth. At the end of this scene, Selva describes how "me sonreía victoriosa, alegre con un triunfo más" ("she smiled victoriously, happy with another triumph") (87). Indeed, Chulita has outmanoeuvred the Holmesian wannabe.

A crucial aspect of Pardo Bazán's parody is having Chulita appear completely legible both as a seductress and as Ariza's sidekick when it is entirely possible that she is the criminal mastermind. During their encounter, Chulita directs Selva's reading of her by invoking how society has branded her as a lost and sinful woman. She stages this act of desperation, of begging for his merciful salvation, so that Selva can act out the role of the English gentleman investigator and saviour. Chulita plays to his arrogance, and Selva misreads her or only attempts a superficial reading – a Holmesian reading, if we are to follow Pardo Bazán's logic. Thinking that Chulita is in love with him and that he is coming up with this strategy on his own when, in effect, he is following Chulita's plan, Selva finances her escape to France. Consequently, the Holmesian intellect does not prosper during this confrontation because Chulita is smarter than Selva, who falls victim to his own arrogance.

What is more, we are reminded that Sherlock Holmes has also been outwitted by a woman, Irene Adler in "A Scandal in Bohemia" (1891). Both Holmes and Selva make the crucial mistake of underestimating their female rivals, which results in both women's escape. Although Irene lacks a confession scene, she leaves a photograph of herself with a letter addressed to Holmes at the end of the story, where she reveals that his disguises did not ultimately fool her but that he was a worthy adversary nonetheless. She also discloses that she has been the victim of the king of Bohemia's betrayal, and for this reason, she not only escapes, but also takes the key evidence with her – a photograph of herself with the king, which she does not plan to use unless forced to do so. It could be said that Holmes realizes that Irene was indeed the king's victim, and for this reason, he seeks no reward beyond asking to keep her photograph. According to Doctor Watson's revelation at the end of the novel, "And that was how a great scandal threatened to affect the kingdom of Bohemia, and how the best plans of Mr. Sherlock Holmes were beaten by a woman's wit. He used to make merry over the cleverness of women, but I have not heard him do it of late. And when he speaks of Irene Adler, or when he refers to her photograph, it is always under the honorable title of *the* woman" (28; italics in original). While he is able to solve the case, Holmes acknowledges that Irene has bested him, and her photograph is a constant reminder of this. What is more, the novel opens with Watson emphasizing, "To Sherlock Holmes she is always *the* woman. I have seldom heard him mention her under any other name. In his eyes she eclipses and predominates the whole of her sex" (3; italics in original). Both women are the detectives' intellectual peers, if not superior to them, but Pardo Bazán complicates this further by having Selva finance Chulita's exile to France, converting him into her accomplice. The key to Pardo Bazán's parody is that the criminal fools the detective, and by fooling him, criminalizes him.

Throughout the story, female criminality is made visible in the multiple portrayals of Chulita in which Selva finds evidence time and again of her transgressions, and yet, he is still enticed by her. According to Choi, "Esta visión negativa de la mujer en la novela de Pardo Bazán es producto de la actitud despectiva hacia el sexo femenino propia de la sociedad patriarcal, siendo la novela detectivesca una vía para exponer dicho pensamiento y costumbres sociales" ("This negative view of women in Pardo Bazán's novel is a product of the contemptuous attitude towards the female sex that is characteristic of patriarchal society, with the detective novel being a way to showcase such thinking and these social norms") (29). Choi's argument, however, ignores how Chulita becomes the tool for Pardo Bazán's parody, how she fools the detective using this negative image that her society has branded her with, and so her portrayal signifies more than assigning her a negative or positive role. It is true that Pardo Bazán's parody challenges negative female stereotypes, and as the first model of the femme fatale in modern Spanish crime fiction, Chulita Ferna is given a backstory that explains her transformation. Although the amorous element plays an integral part in *El clavo*'s plot, Chulita, like Gabriela, was also once a victim of love. Instead of positioning her as a fallen woman, Pardo Bazán provides her female delinquent with the tools to not only outwit her male counterparts, but also to triumph over the patriarchal system that condemned Higinia Balaguer. A provocateur, Chulita uses how she is read by her society – as a marginalized, transgressive woman – to her advantage, and thus, she is able to fool the detective into overriding a male system of justice that would otherwise condemn her. Selva's self-aggrandizing statement at the end of the novel substantiates this claim: "He descubierto el crimen; y como me repugnaba enviar al patíbulo, o siquiera al presidio, a una mujer, yo he asegurado la fuga de Chulita" ("I have solved the crime; and as I was disgusted at the prospect of sending a woman to the gallows, or even to prison, I have secured Chulita's escape") (99). In a way, this reminds us of Pardo Bazán's argument in "Impresiones y sentimientos del día diecinueve" following Higinia Balaguer's execution, where she condemns capital punishment, especially of the female variety. The philosophy governing Pardo Bazán's novel builds on her own condemnation of the verdict in Higinia Balaguer's case because she opens the doors for a female-friendly form of justice to prevail here, anticipating, in this way, the feminized sense of justice at work in contemporary female crime fiction.

This perspective of Gabriela Zahara and Chulita Ferna represents a departure from traditional forms of understanding female characters in crime fiction. They do not fit into the evolution of the female character that Landeira proposes, where she starts out as a victim and matures into an accomplice to then become a criminal. Both women skip the accomplice stage because they are the authors of their crimes without needing to become accomplices first. Additionally, Alarcón's Gabriela Zahara combines two roles – she is both an offender and a victim, and cannot be read as a criminal without being understood as a victim of the moral codes of patriarchal society. In the earliest model of the female delinquent in crime fiction in Spain, we already have a character who denounces the injustices suffered at the hands of a patriarchal system of law. A response to both Conan Doyle and Alarcón, Pardo Bazán refashions her female character into the femme fatale who takes on the male detective to parody Sherlock Holmes. Pardo Bazán also challenges Alarcón's surveillance reading practices by having Chulita, who knows how she is branded and that she is being watched, appear legible in this way and direct Selva's misreading, reminding us of how Higinia Balaguer staged (mis)readings of herself according to Galdós's columns. In the uncovering and denunciation of a sociopolitical system that is unfair in its reading of and position towards women, we can observe the first steps in the gendering of the genre.

Chapter Two

Investigating the "Eye" in Twentieth-Century Spanish Crime Novels

Combining Sigmund Freud's concept of scopophilia and Jacques Lacan's mirror stage to reflect upon the audience's identification with the male protagonist in cinematography, Laura Mulvey's "Visual Pleasure and Narrative Cinema" discusses both the construction of the image of women in film, and the implications of the pleasure of looking at the images of these women in mainstream cinema. In studying the function of the gaze in film, Mulvey asserts that the "pleasure in looking" has been traditionally divided between the passive female gaze and the active male gaze because while the male character's role is to move the action forward, the female character puts a stop to the action ("Visual Pleasure" 837). Something similar occurs in hard-boiled crime fiction, where it rests upon the male detective to advance the story, whereas the female character brings the action to a halt, so that she can be gazed at by her male counterparts. Raymond Chandler's *The Long Goodbye* (1953) exemplifies the heightened sexualization of the private eye's gaze:

> Right then a dream walked in. It seemed to me for an instant that there was no sound in the bar, that the sharpies stopped sharping and the drunk on the stool stopped burbling away, and it was like just after the conductor taps on his music stand and raises his aims and holds them poised.
>
> She was slim and quite tall in a white linen tailor-made with a black and white polka-dotted scarf around her throat. Her hair was the pale gold of a fairy princess. There was a small hat on it into which the pale gold hair nestled like a bird in its nest. Her eyes were cornflower blue, a rare color, and the lashes were long and almost too pale ...
>
> I stared. She caught me staring. She lifted her glance half an inch and I wasn't there any more. But wherever I was I was holding my breath. (74)

This episode, though clearly exaggerated, nonetheless illustrates the pause in the narrative action when the beautiful blonde enters the bar. The narrator observes that there is no noise, demonstrating how the sounds of the bar have deadened as she walks in and sits down. While everything else in the background dissipates, the narrator zooms in on the female character like a camera lens, and the reader is now in a privileged position to share in the narrator's stare. Without a doubt, the female body, depicted in piecemeal fashion, becomes the site of narrative pleasure.

In discussing cinematic representations of the female body, Teresa de Lauretis expounds upon Mulvey's claims by suggesting that the narrative comes together in the female image because "the female character [position] may be all along, throughout the film, representing and literally marking out the place (to) which the hero will cross" (139). The gaze is characterized as male and active because it involves the male eye behind the camera and that of the male characters whereas the body is identified as female and passive, an obstacle and space through which the protagonist advances the plot (de Lauretis 144). It is important to emphasize, according to Mulvey, that "the woman displayed has functioned on two levels: as erotic object for the characters within the screen story, and as erotic object for the spectator within the auditorium, with a shifting tension between the looks on either side of the screen" ("Visual Pleasure" 838). The staging of this interaction of looks can also take place in literature where the difference between the female versus the male gaze can be explored. This proves useful in analyzing how the female body is both exposed and gazed upon in varying genres, specifically the one that interests us – crime fiction.

Annette Kuhn's study of pornography's representation of women proposes that female sexuality is put on display and scrutinized with a male spectator in mind, "[t]he image, soliciting his gaze, draws him into what is happening, a position confirmed by revelations of 'the action' which set themselves up as authentic while at the same time operating as a display directed precisely at him" (*The Power* 33). These "softcore female pinup[s]" put forth the "promise that femininity may be investigated, even understood, by scrutinising its visible marks" (38). This is precisely what takes place in traditional male crime fiction when the attractive female body is staged – it is scrutinized, investigated, and sometimes contained. For Priscilla Walton and Manina Jones, "[i]n traditional private eye stories, as in traditional voyeuristic paradigms, the object of the gaze is typically female or feminized. The detective's scrutiny of the female form seems to literalize the voyeuristic nature of the private eye's inquiry" (157). What is more, the eye of the investigator captures and dominates the female body through what Walton and Jones maintain is a "violent gaze," which is continually striving to exert its authority over women characters (158).

Pardo Bazán's *La gota de sangre*, however, subverts this model by illustrating that though Chulita Ferna is scrutinized and investigated, she is never contained by the male gaze. Here, the femme fatale is used to expose the detective's and the genre's weakness in its reading of the female criminal body, critiquing how the legal system fails women, a theme in Pardo Bazán's journalistic and literary corpus. In the end, the female criminal, a modern woman looking for economic stability and independence, is able to outwit the Holmesian sleuth, making him into her accomplice and thus ensuring her escape from prosecution. Meanwhile, Chulita's predecessor, Alarcón's Gabriela Zahara, is also scrutinized by her suitors and by those present during her confession scene, but she is only contained at the end of the novel when she is imprisoned, and later, when she must perish to restore a sense of order. Some of the examples that we will be looking at in this chapter further challenge the power of the male gaze by complicating the workings of the "eye."

In the middle decades of the twentieth century, Federico Mediante and Manuel de Pedrolo wrote crime fiction in which female detectives' and criminals' success is made possible through a politics of visibility that aligns the female body with male vulnerability. Forcing the voyeuristic male eye to turn on itself, women prevail, even if momentarily, over a repressive system that seeks to objectify and subjugate them. While chapter 1 focuses exclusively on the female criminal model, Federico Mediante's *La señorita detective* is significant because it provides the first example of a female detective in Spanish crime fiction. Drawing on Mediante's work, including not only *La señorita detective* but also *Sombras siniestras* (*Sinister Shadows*) and *Fuerzas ocultas* (*Occult Forces*), I demonstrate that the politics of female visibility works to undermine the male gaze. By putting the woman criminal into dialogue with the female detective, I draw attention to the influence of the delinquent woman model as a *femme moderne* in Mediante's development of his sleuth. By *femmes modernes*, I am referring to Julie Grossman's new label for femmes fatales, which redefines them as "modern women struggling for independence" (38). Grossman's research on film noir underlines a certain flexibility to the femme fatale type that is routinely ignored in favour of more fixed representations because these simplify "the complexity of her represented experience, which almost always involves a woman trapped by the narrow categories on offer for understanding female social and sexual lives" (23). What becomes apparent is that these early challenges to the male gaze set the scene for the gendered substitution of the male I/eye in later examples of the genre. The conventional gazing mechanisms that are prevalent in crime fiction are now interrupted by how the male gaze is used against itself.

Following Mediante, the femme fatale model in Manuel de Pedrolo's *Joc brut*, an archetype that would become prominent during the boom of the male-centred *novela negra*, is responsible for the male protagonist's criminalization. Here, criminalization occurs through victimization because the protagonist, Xavier, is forced to see himself through the femme fatale, Juna, who uses his story and condition as a victim to corrupt him. Because Juna's body is mistaken as a site of erotic male pleasure, I contend that the politics that govern the female body effectively victimize the male onlooker, and compel the protagonist to double as both a victim and a murderer. Even though the female characters in both Mediante and Pedrolo's novels stage misreadings of themselves to manipulate the men around them, in the end their challenge to the patriarchal structure is negated to uphold the moral and legal order that is in place.

Using the Male Look against Itself: Federico Mediante's Crime Fiction

While the tendency to show female characters as erotic objects for the pleasure of the male detective and his reader is a trait adopted by the hard-boiled novelists in Spain during the 1970s, we can already see that the gazing mechanisms function in a similar manner in 1940s crime fiction. These pre-*novela negra* crime novels are seldom studied because, though written and published in Spain, they have nothing authentically Spanish about them, according to Joan Ramon Resina. What Resina means by this is that due to the literary and ideological censorship that occurred during Franco's regime, the tendency was to create works that were largely imitations of British and North American detective fiction produced during the same decades (*El cadáver* 25). For this reason, crime authors in Spain would sign their novels with anglicized pseudonyms to place their works alongside foreign texts to increase sales and combat the critical disregard with which these novels were judged (Valles Calatrava 143; "La novela policíaca" 29). Realizing the profitability of mass-producing crime fiction in serial form instead of only providing translations of British and North American detective fiction, publishing houses in Spain did just that in the 1940s – gather a host of writers to publish detective fiction within the same series.[1] An example of one such profitable series was the Serie Wallace by the publishing house Cisne, where the first female detective appears in Federico Mediante's *La señorita detective* in 1944.

In 1940s Spain, the Serie Wallace, named after the British crime novelist Edgar Wallace due to the popularity of his works in Spain, was the first collection of this sort to publish detective novels written by authors in Spain ("La novela policíaca" 29). Some of the pseudonyms found in the list of the Serie Wallace's published works, which include Jack Forbes, Gary Wells, Cecil Hodge, and Oscar Montgomery among others, initially confirm Salvador Vázquez de Parga's and José Valles Calatrava's claims that Spanish authors were adopting Anglo-Saxon sounding pseudonyms to increase their marketability. The publishing house, however, did allow authors like Federico Mediante, Manuel Vallvé, and Adelardo Fernández (A.F.) Arias to publish some of their works under their own name though they were also known to publish under various pseudonyms in the same series (29). A possible reason for this exception could be that these authors were somewhat better established in literary circles. Mediante, for example, had worked as a journalist for the Galician newspaper, *Las Riberas del Eo* (*The Banks of Eo*), and was a prolific writer of over one hundred works, experimenting with generic forms like the western, the adventure, and the travel novel.[2] Manuel Vallvé was well known as a translator, translating everything from Edgar Allen Poe's short stories to *The Knights of the Round Table* and *Grimm's Fairy Tales*. Quite prolific as a mystery and adventure novel writer, Adelardo Fernández Arias wrote for this particular series between the years of 1943 and 1945, and also published under various pseudonyms, including Jack Forbes, Gary Wells, and A. Warrer (Valles Calatrava 143).[3] The popularity of the Serie Wallace and other collections like it, however, would not continue into the next decade, and the emergence of crime fiction writers like Mario Lacruz and Tomás Salvador would signal the advent of a new type of formula for the genre, where the imitation of foreign models no longer predominated and the characters were more carefully developed and psychologically complex ("La novela policíaca" 32–3).[4]

Mediante, who is credited with creating the first female detective in Spanish literature with *La señorita detective*, also contributed to the development of the woman delinquent character during the 1940s.[5] In the Serie Wallace's *Sombras siniestras* and *Fuerzas ocultas*, Mediante expounds upon the female delinquent character as an unsuccessful robber in the former and as the author of the crime of murder in the latter. An *explicador* (film explainer) from 1900 to 1904 in Madrid, Mediante used his knowledge of cinema to aid in his formulation of the woman criminal, but also in his deployment of narrative framing techniques. Daniel Sánchez Salas demonstrates that the *explicador*'s function was to interpret the movie for the audience, commenting on the silent film while it was being projected (82–4). Sánchez Salas characterizes the *explicador* as "[a] mitad de camino entre el empleado de sala y el artista, su misión es conseguir que los espectadores, no sólo entiendan, sino que disfruten con un espectáculo cambiante" ("halfway between an usher and an artist, his mission is to get the spectators not only to understand, but also to enjoy a changing spectacle") (84). The *explicador* would also answer and reply to remarks made by the audience, establishing a dialogue with the spectators while the movie was taking place and adding sound effects using varying instruments (84). In his crime fiction, Mediante's familiarity with cinema and his former job as an *explicador* informs his use of narrative pauses, reminiscent of cinematic pauses, to frame his female characters. More significantly, Mediante reproduces characteristics of the film noir females to alter and subvert them to develop a particular version of the woman delinquent that will share some traits with his female investigator.

Grossman has previously theorized that bad women in film noir "are very often shown to be victims: first, of the social rules that dictate gender roles and, second, of reading practices that overidentify with and overinvest in the idea of the 'femme fatale'" (2). The problem, according to Grossman, has been too narrow a focus when studying the femme fatale and forgetting what makes her appealing beyond the sexual. The femme fatale's allure relies on her ambition to satisfy her needs and desires, whether these are economic, political, or social in nature (3). Her ambition simultaneously seduces both her male and female spectators because men cannot dominate her and she represents a departure from ordinary women. Consequently, femme fatales should be understood as a cross between a tough woman and a victim. This is particularly evident in "[f]ilm noir movies [that] work to identify their tough women as victims whose strength, perverse by conventional standards, keeps them from submitting to the gendered social institutions that oppress them. It is the dialogue between their perversity and their power and these films' illumination of modern women, *femmes modernes* ... that fascinates film viewers" (3). Expounding on Grossman's argument, the femme fatale type needs to be reimagined in more flexible or hybrid terms. If she is understood simplistically as a bad, sexy woman, this portrayal detracts from her agency by either trying to create an aura or mystique about her, or, in other cases, degrade her – in both cases, still objectifying her.

Studying Mediante's and, later, Pedrolo's female criminal models, I demonstrate how their women characters share similarities with how Grossman delineates film noir's femme fatales as "lawless agents of female desire, rebelling against the patriarchal relegation of women to the domestic sphere where they are deemed passive and valued only in relation to their maternal and wifely vocation" (4). Grossman's suggestion is to recategorize the rebellious and ambitious femme fatale as a *femme moderne*, an independent, modern woman attempting to survive economically (38). While some are more subversive than others, I argue that Mediante does take advantage of the femme fatale archetype's flexibility, and complicates the portrayal of women in the genre in the three separate manifestations studied here, with his female criminal models in *Sombras siniestras* and *Fuerzas ocultas* and with the first female investigator, Diana Fletcher, in *La señorita detective*.

In *Sombras siniestras*, Alfonso Phillys, a reporter for "El Cometa" ("The Comet"), travels on a train to Montfrey, a fictional town, to meet with the notary who is the executor for his dead aunt's estate. During this train trip, Alfonso is charged with inventing some sort of sensational crime to report back to his newspaper, but instead, upon meeting Ruth Geofrey, he becomes entangled in two very real crimes – the first involving the death of Ruth's travel companion, Esther Sulima, and the second having to do with the robbery of his briefcase, which contained some blueprints that Ruth had asked him to keep for her since they would not be safe in her possession. We come to learn that Esther's murder is directly linked to these blueprints, which had been drawn up by Ruth's father, for a new airplane model. The same men that Ruth suspects killed her father were now after her to obtain the blueprints for this invention, but instead of hurting her, they murder her travel companion, Esther, because the two women had switched beds. Staging a ruse with fake documents, Ruth returns home only to find that she is not safe there, since the man that has been following her on the train reappears in her bedroom to steal the coveted blueprints. In the end, we find out that Alfonso's notary has been responsible for both crimes.

During the trip, Alfonso makes note of all those travelling with him, but pays particular attention to the three female travellers. Though he professes an attraction to Ruth early on, Ágata Bellcome also catches his attention because this solitary fifty-something woman "que aparenta una sencillez desconcertante, tiene conocimientos dignos de una profesora de Historia Natural" ("who looks disconcertingly simple, has knowledge worthy of a professor of natural history") (13). The first sign we have that Ágata is somehow criminally involved is that she observes Ruth handing some documents over to Alfonso, who puts them in his briefcase. When they are not paying attention, she then switches his briefcase with hers (19). Later, Plácido Saranac, who has also been hired to steal the blueprints, exchanges his briefcase with Ágata's before departing the train. When she realizes this, she feigns surprise before Inspector Dorrington, who has come to investigate Esther's murder (22). Finding her behaviour odd, Dorrington questions Ágata, emphasizing that he does not believe that she was unaware of the switch in the briefcases. As she tries to come up with some justification for her actions, Dorrington remains suspicious, and orders his men to have her followed because "[m]e está pareciendo que esa mujer no es trigo limpio" ("it seems to me that this woman is a bit fishy") (24). Dorrington and Ágata meet only a second time in the novel, which will also be the female criminal's final scene, titled, "Una extraña visita" ("A Strange Visit"). Here, Mediante employs the formula of the face-off between the detective and the femme fatale, common both in the hard-boiled genre of Dashiell Hammett and Raymond Chandler and in the popular film noir of the 1940s. Regarding the femme fatale in cinema, E. Ann Kaplan claims that "film noir offers a space for the playing out of *various* gender fantasies," one of which is her encounter with the detective, which has both a sexual and a frustrating component for the investigator as her sexuality proves to be her most effective weapon ("Introduction" 10; italics in original). The femme fatale invokes her femininity and performs her sexuality to disarm and prevent the male sleuth from succeeding at his task of solving the case. Mediante reproduces a similar episode in *Sombras siniestras,* but he deemphasizes the sexual component even though the change in Ágata's appearance is also underscored: "Cualquier cosa esperaba el detective menos ver aparecer a la señora Ágata Bellcome, que ya había cambiado de ropa y se había peinado y retocado. Ahora parecía mucho más joven" ("The detective was ready for anything except the arrival of Mrs Ágata Bellcome, who had changed clothes, had combed her hair, and spruced up. Now she looked much younger")

(32). Instead, what ensues is a battle of wits. From the moment that she enters Dorrington's office, we witness the power play that unfolds:

> – Usted mandó que me siguieran.
>
> – ¿Cómo lo sabe?
>
> – ¿Qué importa eso? La cuestión es que lo sé.
>
> – En efecto, no tengo por qué negarlo. La mandé seguir porque me resultó sospechosa su declaración. Eso de los maletines no estaba muy claro.
>
> – Pues para hablar de eso he venido.
>
> El detective la miró, terminando por decir:
>
> – La inocencia tiene un enorme parecido con la culpabilidad, pero es muy difícil engañarme a mí en ninguno de los dos casos. ¿Quiere usted explicarse de una vez para que yo sepa si debo considerarla todavía como sospechosa?
>
> Ágata no pestañeó siquiera, limitándose a mirar al detective con una sonrisita de superioridad verdaderamente mortificante. (32)

> – You ordered them to follow me.
>
> – How do you know?
>
> – Does it matter? The fact is that I know.
>
> – Indeed, I have no reason to deny it. I ordered you followed because I found your statement suspicious. That thing with the briefcases didn't add up.
>
> – Well, that's what I'm here to talk about.
>
> The detective looked at her, and said:
>
> – Innocence very closely resembles guilt, but it's very difficult to fool me in either case. Will you explain yourself once and for all so that I can know if I should still consider you a suspect?
>
> Ágata didn't even blink, but looked at the detective with a truly mortifying smirk of superiority.

Knowing that the inspector ordered his men to have her followed, Ágata considers it advantageous to confess to the crime of switching the briefcases, explaining that she has been hired to steal the blueprints for a foreign factory. Initially, she attempts to seek Dorington's understanding by justifying coming forward to clear her conscience, but as he first feigns indifference to what she has to say and then claims that he knew she was guilty all along, she quickly modifies her approach. First, she confronts him with what he does not know and then draws attention to his ineffective handling of the case thus far. A frustrated

Dorrington threatens Ágata with imprisonment, to which she retorts, "[U]sted fracasaría en el descubrimiento del misterio. Es bueno que lo sepa de una vez, que usted sólo puede triunfar con mi ayuda" ("You wouldn't succeed in discovering the mystery. It's best that you realize that you can only succeed with my help") (33). During this exchange, we get the most detailed picture of Mediante's Ágata, who up until this point appears to be winning the face-off with the detective. Although she does not employ her sexuality or feminine wiles against him, she establishes herself as the one in power during this exchange because she has access to the criminal world that is off-limits to Dorrington.

Her sense of superiority over the detective, however, is derailed when he informs her that he is aware of her true identity: "El inspector abrió el cuaderno por una página que estaba marcada y levantándose se fue a enseñárselo a la señora Ágata. Ésta, al verlo, lanzó un grito de asombro y por poco se desmaya. Lo que estaba viendo era un retrato suyo hecho algunos años atrás, debajo del cual había un letrero que decía: 'Carole Pierlat, conocida estafadora que acaba de ser detenida'" ("The inspector opened the notebook to a page that was marked and got up to show it to Ms Ágata. When she saw it, she cried out in amazement and almost fainted. What she saw was a photo of herself taken some years earlier, below which was a caption that read: 'Carole Pierlat, a known swindler who has just been arrested'") (33). To further humiliate her and solidify his control over her, Dorrington stresses that her deception, her role-playing, has come to an end. Though Ágata/Carole screams in surprise upon first seeing the picture, she proves to be a master of composure, not allowing Dorrington's power play to overcome her. Instead, she assures him that "[a]quellos tiempos han pasado para no volver. Ya llovió desde entonces. Mis errores de otra época ya los he pagado. No debo nada. Emprendí vida nueva y estoy dispuesta a demostrarlo" ("those times have passed and won't return. That ship sailed long ago. I've paid for my mistakes from that time. I don't owe anything. I started a new life, and I'm willing to prove it") (33). Realizing that her act as Ágata has come to an end, she decides to reaffirm her commitment to help the police capture the true criminal responsible for Esther's murder (33). Despite Dorrington's big reveal, she successfully negotiates her freedom, convincing the detective that she is of more use to him as an ally. She promises to lead him to the real criminal, "el hombre de la hopalanda" ("the man wearing a houppelande"), who, as we will find out at the end of the novel, is the one who killed Esther and managed to steal the blueprints.

Despite Ágata's potential as a sidekick, Dorrington still wants to imprison and contain Ágata/Carole, but decides that because she can be useful, he will take advantage of her offer instead (34). The episode, however, does not end with the inspector having the final word. Instead, Ágata/Carole offers a final suggestion for the detective: "[D]ebe saber adivinar hasta los pensamientos. Dígale a su gente que no se moleste en seguirme, porque es inútil. También yo sé hacerme invisible cuando hace falta" ("You must know how to read minds. Tell your people not to bother following me, because it would be useless. I too know how to become invisible when necessary") (34). Slamming the door behind her, she leaves the detective in such a state that "[e]l inspector mascó con tal fuerza el puro, que lo partió por la mitad" ("the inspector chomped down on the cigar with such force that he broke it in half") (34). Ágata/Carole's play for her freedom and power has paid off, and she has bested the inspector, as evidenced by his final act in this scene. Emasculating the detective by making him feel inadequate about his investigative skills, Ágata/Carole ensures that she will remain free for the entire narrative by convincing him that she is his only link to the real criminals.

Although Ágata is an interesting contrast to the more traditional female character role of Ruth, Alfonso's love interest and a robbery victim, Mediante does not further develop the woman delinquent in this narrative. We only witness her brief reappearance when Ruth and Alfonso see her pass by on the street, and Alfonso remarks, "En el tren iba vestida casi como una pordiosera y ahora parece una princesa. Abrigo de pieles, zapatos de moda, sombrero ... y hasta parece que se ha pintado" ("On the train she was dressed almost like a beggar and now she looks like a princess. The fur coat, the stylish shoes, the hat ... and it even seems like she put makeup on") (39). Like Inspector Dorrington, Alfonso is surprised by the changes in Ágata's appearance. Here, the emphasis is on her lavish princess-like attire, which confirms the role-playing that occurred on the train and heightens any suspicion regarding her criminal activities. She is brought up a final time at the end of the novel by Alfonso, who recounts, "Esta mañana estuve hablando con Ágata Bellcome, ¿se acuerda usted?, y me ha dado valiosos pormenores de cosas que ignoraba" ("This morning I was talking to Ágata Bellcome, do you remember her? And she shared with me some valuable details about things that I didn't know") (58). Ágata, who was supposed to remain in touch with Dorrington, helps Alfonso in the end, clarifying each passenger's involvement with Esther's murder and the robbery of the blueprints. Thanks to her, Alfonso is able to zero in on his notary as the true criminal, and emerges a hero to Dorrington and to Ruth, who, thanks to this resolution, he can now marry. Ágata, who does not reappear after the sighting on the street, holds the key to solving the case because she bridges the criminal and the non-criminal worlds. Unlike the femme fatale of hard-boiled crime fiction and film noir, Ágata/Carole's weapon is not her sexuality, it is her ability to outwit those she encounters by authoring successful misreadings of herself. Her role-playing skills allow her to fulfill her financial ambition and avert any potential incarceration. By misdirecting those who try to read or expose her true self, Ágata/Carole transgresses patriarchal institutions, and while she appears only briefly in Mediante's *Sombras siniestras*, her character seems to be more in tune with the *femme moderne* because she refuses to submit to Dorrington, the novel's representative of law and order. Using her criminal past in her favour, she convinces Dorrington that she can be of use to him, and makes sure she reaffirms her value, a value not determined by her seductiveness but by her intelligence and manipulation of the situation.

Mediante follows a similar model in *Fuerzas ocultas*, where once again, a battle of wits between the woman delinquent and the male detective ensues. Unlike *Sombras siniestras*, both the detective and his sidekick find themselves seduced by the female criminal, and yet, like Ágata, the woman delinquent again follows the *femme moderne* model more closely than that of the femme fatale. Setting the action in Lima to add an element of the exotic, Mediante combines the murder of Mario Randolff, director of the Museo Arqueológico (Archaeological Museum), with a series of robberies of Inca artefacts. The gravity of the crimes forces the Lima police to request the help of Roque Drake, the famous Californian detective, and his sidekick, Robert Walter, who happen to be in Lima vacationing. At the beginning of the narrative, a woman is suspected of having participated in Mario Randolff's murder, which Drake uncovers when first investigating the scene and speaking to one of Randolff's servants, Pietro, who offers an initial description of the mysterious woman: "Alta y morena. Bien vestida. Guapa, guapa de verdad. Llevaba un vestido muy elegante y zapatos a la moda y hasta el sombrero era muy bonito" ("A tall brunette. Well dressed. Good looking, really good looking. She wore a very elegant dress and fashionable shoes and even her hat was very nice") (15). This elegantly dressed woman, who Drake calls the "mujer misteriosa" ("mysterious woman") and who Robert dreams about as the "reina de 'Los Esclavos del Sol'" ("Queen of 'the Slaves of the Sun'"), proves to be one of the leaders of this mysterious gang of Inca artefact robbers. In fact, the first narrative pause that includes this mysterious woman takes place during an odd dream sequence, adding to the element of the exotic of this particular femme fatale type. Robert, who is left in charge of watching Mario Randolff's house following their initial investigation, falls asleep and his dreams include a vision of "[l]a reina de 'Los esclavos del Sol'" (21). Mesmerized by this woman, the narrative accentuates how "Robert vió la criatura más bella que jamás pudo imaginar. Era una mujer joven cubierta por un manto de pieles orlado de pedrería. En la cintura, una faja formada por tres cadenetas de oro con broche jaspeado y en la cabeza, un casquete primoroso" ("Robert saw the most beautiful creature he could have ever imagined. She was a young woman covered with a fur cloak rimmed with jewels. Around her waist, she wore a belt composed of three gold chains with a marbled brooch, and on her head, a gorgeous hat") (21). In something of a veiled threat, the so-called queen, whose name, she reveals, is Hokama Akapy, emphasizes that it is time for Robert and Roque Drake to return to the United States because they will fail in their investigation (22). She admits, however, to being the same woman that Pietro described as having met with Mario Randolff the day he was murdered, and to being the daughter of Randolff's cook, Agatónica Paredones, all of which in the end will prove true. Although it is only a dream, this narrative sequence provides the first clues about this enigmatic woman, who has already enthralled the detective's sidekick.

Seeing that Robert and Drake continue to work the case, the mysterious woman/queen asks for a meeting with Drake at a cabaret club, to which he consents, realizing that she is somehow involved in Randolff's murder. A second narrative pause ensues as the female body is staged during Drake's examination of the mysterious woman:

> Era de regular estatura, y sin ser una belleza, había algo en ella que atraía desde el primer momento. Su rostro ovalado, un puro moreno, tenía rasgos enérgicos, firmes, y tal vez un poco irregulares, pero la pureza de líneas se confundía en el conjunto como algo impreciso y borroso. A Drake le pareció que estaba contemplando el rostro de una figura de madera, pero los ojos, aquellos ojos vivaces y de mirada penetrante, desmentían tal ilusión. (27)

> She was of average height, and without being a knockout, there was something about her that was attractive from the first glance. Her oval face,

> evenly tanned, had energetic, firm features, though perhaps a little irregular, but the exactness of her facial features seemed to come together to make an imprecise and inexact whole. It seemed to Drake that he was looking at the face of a wooden figurine, but her eyes, those lively, piercing eyes, belied that illusion.

With this narrative pause, the reader shares in Drake's pleasure in gazing at this enigmatic woman, and a complete sketch is provided, characterizing her as exotic, magnetic, and enchanting. Thinking that she can use her feminine wiles and bribe Drake into relinquishing the case, she is surprised to find that he will not relent. She then warns him that this complicated case can cost him his life (28). In response, Drake threatens to detain her, but decides against it because, as he explains, "Soy enemigo de victorias fáciles y me gusta la lucha; además es usted una mujer y eso me impide obrar con demasiada dureza" ("I'm the enemy of easy victories and I like a challenge; you're also a woman and that prevents me from acting too harshly") (28). The power play between the *dama misteriosa* and Drake, reminiscent of the detective versus femme fatale confrontations in film noir, ends with her disappearance from the club when he is about to arrest her, but not before warning the detective of the dangers that await him. This curious scene with the *dama misteriosa* results in the detective's later capture and imprisonment by the Esclavos del Sol, and a voice claiming to be that of the enigmatic woman informs him that he will not be set free until their mission to recuperate all the Inca relics and artefacts is complete.

Of course, Roque Drake escapes the makeshift prison, and we do not reencounter the female criminal until we see her at the circus as Esther "La Gladiadora" ("The Woman Gladiator") during her final show. After her knife-throwing performance, Mario Randolff's son publicly accuses her of killing his father, but before they can capture her, she flees once again. Mediante's female criminal in *Fuerzas ocultas* is more complex because she performs various roles that will intersect at the end when Drake discovers that the *dama misteriosa*, La Gladiadora, and the queen from Robert's dream are all Malva Apiyu, the daughter of an Inca chief seeking vengeance against Mario Randolff for stealing Atahualpa's knife from her father. Fueled by her need for revenge, Malva, with the help of her adopted mother, Agatónica Paredones or Hokama Apiyú (her Indian name), killed Mario Randolff, took Atahualpa's knife, and created a makeshift organization to steal back other Inca artefacts. At the end, Drake is able to confront the female criminal and prove her guilt during the trial:

> Usted asesinó a Mario Randolff por un antagonismo ancestral que no tiene explicación. Durante diez años, fué preparando el terreno y almacenando rencores en su alma perversa. Auxiliada por su ex nodriza, cometió el crimen por vengar algo que no merecía venganza. Mario Randolff, compró a su padre, que era el jefe de la tribu de los omapas, el puñal de Atahualpa. (64)
>
> You murdered Mario Randolff because of an ancestral feud that has no logical explanation. For ten years you paved the way [for this crime] and held grudges in your perverse soul. With the help of your ex-wetnurse, you committed the crime to avenge something that didn't deserve to be avenged. Mario Randolff bought Atahualpa's dagger from your father, the head of the tribe of the Omapas.

Drake is able to defeat the female criminal and restore order because once he exposes her vengeance as unfounded, he provides evidence that demonstrates that she killed Mario Randolff. Realizing that Drake has outsmarted her and tied her to the crime by seeing through her multiple personas, she surrenders: "Cuenta usted las cosas como si las estuviese viendo. Hagan de mí lo que quieran, yo no niego nada" ("You tell things as if you were seeing them. Do whatever you want with me. I don't deny anything") (64). After demonstrating her power over men and her leadership skills in addition to acting out the different roles that she has created for herself throughout the narrative, Malva concedes quite easily at the end of *Fuerzas ocultas*, seemingly paralyzed as Roque Drake recounts her story. Eliminating her ability to recreate herself when needed, Drake leaves her punishment up to the law because, he reaffirms to Robert, that "ese justo castigo servirá de ejemplo. Es necesario que sepan de una vez todos, que con la Ley no se juega" ("this just punishment will serve as an example. It's necessary that everyone learn that you cannot play games with the law") (64). It is worth underscoring, however, that Malva's desire for vengeance stems from more of a victim role, avenging what she believes has been a crime against her father. In this way, the female criminal positions herself as a victim of a patriarchal system that also treats Indigenous tribes as others even though Drake proves that her father obtained money from the transaction.

Unlike *Sombras siniestras*'s Ágata, who remains unpunished for her crime, Malva must submit to a patriarchal system of law and order that seeks to make an example out of her. Still, her initial resistance and rebellion suggests that this character represents more of a hybrid type in continuous transformation – beginning with a type more closely related to the femme fatale, born out of what she believes is a previous victimization, and even becoming something of a *femme moderne* until she relinquishes her agency and power at the end of the novel. With his female criminals, Mediante borrows from the film noir model, but also complicates these characters in such a way that they fail to fully encapsulate the femme fatale or even the *femme moderne* model – they remain incomplete hybrid versions of both because while they initially challenge a patriarchal order, they end up submitting to it. Mediante's female delinquent model informs or shares close similarities with the first female detective in Spanish crime literature with his *La señorita detective*. No longer a victim/criminal or a femme fatale, Mediante's secret agent is now responsible for helping to restore order and making sure that the criminals are apprehended and punished. *La señorita detective* presents us with another interesting type that differs from the female delinquents represented in Alarcón and Pardo Bazán and even in Mediante's novels.

Following the formula of the detective novels published in the 1940s in Spain, the cities that appear in Mediante's *La señorita detective* are either foreign or fictional and most of the characters' names are anglicized.[6] Primarily set in the imaginary city of Geolandia, the case in *La señorita detective* involves locating an experimental formula stolen from the National Chemical Laboratory that can be used to produce fake diamonds. The secret agent number 12, whose name, we later find out, is Diana Fletcher, is assigned to recover the formula and find the men responsible for stealing it. Passing herself off as a secretary, the secret agent quickly and easily infiltrates the business where the formula is being held and retrieves it after flirting with the guard and getting him intoxicated. Upon realizing that she is being followed on a train ride back to the capital and is in grave danger, Diana hands the formula, which we later find out is a fake copy, to a reporter, Leslie Bird. At this point in the narrative, the focus is no longer on the female agent, but on the reporter, who is instructed to hand the formula over to the agent's boss, Marcos Dubois. Diana, meanwhile, is thrown off the train after being injected, we later learn, with a paralytic drug. After miraculously surviving, she is hospitalized with some severe injuries. The story ends with the female agent's recovery and the apprehension of the criminals because the woman detective has intelligently mailed the formula to herself, and is able to hand over the formula to a government minister at the end. With the case resolved, the female secret agent is happily married off to the reporter, Leslie Bird.

Although the title of the work is *La señorita detective*, at least half of the narrative concentrates on following the adventures of the reporter. Still, Mediante should be credited for having introduced the first woman sleuth in Spanish crime fiction during a time when literary works were strictly censored.[7] The narrative portrays Diana as both captivating and beautiful, but also emphasizes her intelligence, her bravery, and the fact that a man would not have been successful in his investigation of this particular case. Diana Fletcher's success in solving the case reminds us of a skill that she shares with Gabriela Zahara, Chulita Ferna, and Mediante's Ágata and Malva – the ability to use the male gaze against itself to create and direct a series of misreadings. Like her predecessors, I argue that Diana Fletcher plays with her legibility as a text, making her body applicable to various readings. By doing so, I claim that this character further exposes, more than Mediante's criminal models, the connection between female visibility and the vulnerability of the voyeuristic male eye.

Diana Fletcher first appears on the scene during a meeting with four high-ranking policemen. Her boss, Dubois, does not prepare the three other men, or the reader for that matter, by saying that they are about to meet a young woman. He only refers to her as "the agent," and so the men are caught off-guard when "[e]n el dintel de la puerta apareció una mujer" ("a woman appeared in the doorway") (5). Dubois introduces her as secret agent number 12, and the narrative halts to display the young woman. All eyes are set on her during this first narrative pause:

> Aquella mujer, que no tendría más de veinte años, era de una belleza maravillosa. Compendio fiel de todas las perfecciones, tenía un rostro de un óvalo correcto; ojos negros, boca pequeña y cabellera renegrida cortada en melena. Su mirar era sereno, pero profundo. Una sonrisa que parecía estereotipada en su semblante daba a éste un reflejo de gracia. (5)

> The woman, scarcely older than twenty, was marvelously attractive. She was a perfect compendium of female beauty and had a symmetrically oval face; black eyes, a small mouth and a head of very black loose hair. Her gaze was serene, but profound. A smile that seemed firmly planted gave her face a touch of grace.

The narrative brings the female character into focus, and consequently the male characters, together with the reader, share in the pleasure of looking at this woman.[8] After serving as momentary eye candy, however, the narrative provides Diana with the space to speak, the opportunity to express how she views her profession and highlight her sense of responsibility and her bravery. When asked if she understands that she is putting her life in danger, she answers, "Mentiría si dijese que la muerte no me asusta, porque a los veinte años la vida siempre es estimada, pero los peligros no han de ser causa para que yo abandone jamás el camino emprendido" ("I'd be lying if I said that death doesn't scare me because at the age of twenty you always value life, but danger never causes me to abandon the path taken") (5). Her eloquent reasoning is met with praise by the men. They are equally impressed when she details her plan for infiltrating the business of the men who have stolen the valuable formula by playing the role of a foreigner named Vasilika Ramosky who is looking for a secretarial position. While the narrative first introduces the secret agent by drawing attention to her beauty, it also allows Diana Fletcher to articulate how she views her responsibilities as a secret agent and to specify how she will retrieve the stolen formula. From the outset, there is more to Mediante's female character than being the object of the male look, evidence of which we find in the conversation that the police officers have once she leaves the room:

> Cuando la puerta se cerró tras ella, dijo Judson:
> – ¡Qué mujer!
> – Es lista como una ardilla – añadió Dorthow.
> – Y valiente y bonita – agregó Mark.
> – Y, sobre todo, consciente de su responsabilidad – terminó Dubois – dando un suspiro. (6)

> When the door closed behind her, Judson said:
> – What a woman!
> – She's as witty as a fox – Dorthow added.
> – And brave and pretty – Mark added.
> – And, above all, aware of her obligation – Dubois finished – with a sigh.

Although her beauty is mentioned, so are her intelligence, bravery, and sense of responsibility. Still, all the male characters who encounter *la señorita detective* underline her attractiveness, with the exception of her boss. Dubois, who exemplifies a proud paternal figure, tells her that she is the only one who can solve this particular case during a later encounter where the secret agent informs him of her progress: "Sólo usted puede llevarla a cabo. Un hombre fracasaría irremisiblemente" ("Only you can carry this out. A man would certainly fail") (11). Dubois guarantees her success early on by confirming his confidence in her sleuthing skills, and perhaps even views her femininity as a manipulative weapon that she can use in her favour, proof of which we find later on in the narrative. An initial sense of female empowerment predominates at the beginning of this first female detective novel because Diana is given a great deal of agency and independence.

Diana's success in solving the case is contingent upon her ability to outsmart the criminals. This requires using her allure with this goal in mind. Once again, the narrative draws attention to her physical appeal when the criminals first meet her: "Vestía de un modo extravagante, pero los dos hombres no se fijaron en el atuendo de aquella mujer, sino en su maravillosa belleza" ("She dressed extravagantly, but the two men didn't notice her attire, but rather her wondrous beauty") (9). Like the policemen from the previous episode, the criminals admire not only her beauty, but also her intelligence, highlighting how lucky they are to be able to hire her (9). Her skill at staging herself appropriately allows her to gain access to the stolen formula, and the capacity to use the voyeuristic male gaze against itself becomes evident during her encounter with Elías Perthes, the guard responsible for protecting the formula. In this episode, Diana realizes that Elías is looking to take advantage of her, so she uses this to her benefit: "Lo que para otro hubiera resultado anormal y hasta escandaloso, a él le hizo gracia, pero no la exteriorizó hasta no ver que ella se llevaba la botella a la boca y la mantenía un rato pegada a los labios. Lo que no se le ocurrió pensar fue que ni una sola gota había pasado por la garganta de la muchacha" ("Another person would have thought it abnormal and even scandalous, but he was amused, though he did not show this until he saw her take the bottle to her mouth and hold it for a while, glued to her lips. It didn't occur to him that not a single drop had passed through her throat") (14). Elías stares at her, believing that she is intoxicated and that he can physically and sexually dominate her, but instead Diana manipulates and outwits him because she deciphers his intentions, and uses these against him. Recognizing that she can easily outsmart him "y como su costumbre era siempre explorar el temperamento de la gente, decidió ensayar con Elías su modalidad" ("and since it was her habit to always explore people's temperament, she decided to use Elías to refine her methods")

(13). Elías underestimates her intellect, and he pays dearly for it when she is able to steal the formula. This episode accentuates a sense of empowerment because the woman sleuth thwarts a potential sexual assault. As previously exemplified in *El clavo* and *La gota de sangre*, the act of misreading the female character can have dire consequences for the male voyeuristic eye/I, and it does so in this instance.

The reversal of the male voyeuristic eye is again employed when Diana meets the reporter, Leslie, on the train as she heads back with the retrieved formula to meet Dubois. In an effort to establish an early amorous connection between the two characters, the novel puts the *señorita detective* on display during this second narrative pause:

> Leslie se fijó en los ojos de aquella mujer. Eran unos ojos lindísimos, negros y rasgados.
>
> Todo su continente era majestuoso y durante un instante el periodista llegó a pensar si no estaría en presencia de alguna augusta princesa.
>
> Su belleza era fascinadora y Leslie ahogó al verla el vocablo poco galante que iba a salir de su boca ...
>
> Era mucho más bonita de lo que había creído observar. Una verdadera preciosidad, un conjunto de perfecciones difíciles de igualar. Sobre todo sus ojos, aquellos ojos orlados de largas pestañas y aquel mirar. (24)

> Leslie noticed the woman's eyes. They were very beautiful, black and narrow eyes.
>
> Everything about her was majestic and for a moment the journalist even wondered if he was in the presence of some high-born princess.
>
> Her beauty was fascinating and when he saw her, Leslie bit his tongue so as to silence the ungallant words that were going to come out of his mouth ...
>
> She was much prettier than she had seemed at first glance. A true beauty, a set of perfections difficult to match. Especially her eyes, those eyes with their long lashes, and that gaze.

Zooming in on the secret agent like a camera lens, the reader is once again in a privileged position to join in on the look, sharing in Leslie's pleasure of gazing at the female agent. Now that the narrative is focalized through Leslie, we not only get a sense of Diana's beauty, but also of her sweet and melodious voice, which is accustomed to being obeyed (24). Like the other men before him, Leslie cannot help but submit to her: "Leslie no creía en el hipnotismo. Tampoco era de los que se dejan dominar muy fácilmente y sin embargo iba comprendiendo que no tendría más remedio que obedecer" ("Leslie didn't believe in hypnotism. Nor was he the kind of person who would let himself be dominated very easily, and yet he understood that he would have no choice but to obey her") (25). Once more, Diana takes advantage of being the object of the male gaze and of being examined by the male voyeuristic eye to obtain what she wants. As female visibility results in male vulnerability, Diana compels Leslie to take the formula to divert the attention of the man following her, and deliver it to her boss, Dubois. Allowing herself to be the object of Leslie's look, Diana seduces him by emphasizing how she would view him if he were to succeed in this endeavour, underscoring how his help would demonstrate his bravery in addition to constituting a service to their country. In this way, the voyeuristic male eye is turned on itself, and plays a part in Leslie's seduction.

Leslie's appearance in the novel, however, weakens the female detective character. The reporter becomes the heroic protagonist, replacing Diana after the aforementioned scene, when she is injected, we later learn, with a paralytic drug by one of the men following her and thrown off the train. This protagonist replacement, and the literal paralysis and weakening of the female character signals that we have reached the limitations of Mediante's innovation in the genre. The story of the female detective can no longer be supported, and the second half of the novel will now follow Leslie's adventures. The plot contains the female character by paralyzing her so that she is unable to move or speak, transforming her into a secondary character who will remain marginalized in a hospital bed until the male hero, Leslie, rescues her. Hence, the shortcomings of this first female detective narrative become evident with Diana's transformation from active subject to passive object/character.

Hospitalized with a mysterious paralysis that baffles her doctors, Diana's allure remains unchanged as her physicians are captivated by the female agent and the eloquence of her gaze (54). The senior doctor, who takes a special interest in her case, tells her, as Dubois has done before, that "admiramos su proceder, su valor y su fe en el desempeño de una misión en la cual hubieran fracasado muchos hombres ... Otro, en su lugar, al sentirse en peligro, hubiera abandonado la empresa o procurado ampararse en alguien" ("we admire your behavior, your courage and your dedication in carrying out a mission where many men would have failed ... Another, in your place, when feeling in danger, would have abandoned the assignment or sought help from someone") (54–5). Once again, an authoritative and paternalistic male figure underscores and reaffirms Diana's value as a representative of the law while emphasizing that she possesses what are traditionally thought of as masculine attributes. Focalized through Diana during her hospitalization and convalescence, during this narrative sequence we also learn how she came to be a secret agent. Thinking that she would become an actress, after trying her hand at the law and at painting, Diana, an orphan at twelve, moved to Geolandia after her aunt's death, where she solves her first case, the case of a stolen pendant: "El detective particular del balneario hizo todas las indagaciones pertinentes, sin conseguir nada ... Ella [Diana] sospechó desde el primer momento en el secretario de la señora robada" ("The private detective, hired by the spa, made all the relevant inquiries, but without success ... She [Diana] suspected it was the lady's secretary from the beginning") (57). Able to prove her suspicion that the lady's secretary, Lewis Maulette, is the robber, Dubois offers her a job in the Secret Service two months later.[9] Mediante, therefore, assigns Diana's character a certain amount of depth, since she is the only one to get a backstory. By providing us with her trajectory, the narrative appears to want to justify Diana's aptitude for this profession, and prepares the reader for the final surprise of the novel – Leslie Bird, now a secret agent like the lady detective, is sent to the hospital to protect her from Lewis Maulette, who has come to kill her since she survived being pushed off the train.

In a matter of a few pages, Leslie kills Lewis Maulette, Leslie and Diana proclaim their love for one another, and Diana is cured of her temporary paralysis. The novel ends with Diana and Leslie being praised by the Minister of Justice, and when asked if there is anything that she desires in return, Diana responds: "'Ya conseguí todo lo que deseaba,' respondió mirando a Leslie cariñosamente con aquellos ojos que tan bien sabían expresar los pensamientos de su dueña" ("'I got everything I wanted,' she replied looking at Leslie affectionately with those eyes that knew so well how to express what their owner was thinking") (64). Married a few days after, Diana has solved the case, and gets her man at the end. What remains a mystery, however, is whether Diana Fletcher will continue her work as a secret agent. Judging from this lighthearted exchange, the reader infers that there will indeed be changes in Diana's professional life:

> – Te olvidas de una cosa –, repuso ella –, y es de que como agente más antiguo, no acepto órdenes de otro moderno.
> – En tal caso sí.
> – ¿Porqué?
> – Porque este agente va a ser tu esposo.
> – Siendo así, ¡me rindo! (63)

– You forget something – , she said – , I'm a veteran agent, and I don't accept orders from a rookie.
– In this case, yes.
– Why?
– Because this agent is going to be your husband.
– Well then, I surrender!

Mediante's *La señorita detective* introduces a new female character type in Spanish crime fiction by distancing itself from Alarcón's hybrid victim/criminal, from Pardo Bazán's femme fatale, and even from Mediante's own female delinquents. Unlike these previous examples, Mediante's Diana Fletcher does not step outside the legal boundaries or trespass the moral codes of her society. Instead, she fights to keep these legal boundaries and moral codes of conduct intact. In fact, she has been accepted into the fold of the patriarchal system, and, using her femininity as a tool of manipulation, she seeks to restore order, and punish those who have disobeyed the law. Although the men who come into contact with her are initially sceptical of her skills, she always passes their inspection, and comes to be accepted and highly regarded by them. Moreover, it is constantly reaffirmed that a man could not have replicated her success in the case, a success that is largely founded upon being able to outsmart her male opponents.

Diana Fletcher's ability to outwit her male counterparts stems from her capacity to cause a series of misreadings that ensure her success. This skill is one she shares with the likes of Gabriela Zahara and Chulita Ferna and with Mediante's Ágata Bellcome and Malva Apiyu. Even if Mediante has repackaged his heroine as a female secret agent, Diana Fletcher is subversive in her use of the voyeuristic male gaze against itself. When Elías, Leslie, and even the policemen look at Diana Fletcher, they become vulnerable, convinced by her performance, and, in effect, she feeds off this vulnerability to obtain what she desires. If we recall, she convinces the policemen that she will be able to solve the case by delivering a brief sermon about how she views her profession whereas with Elías she has him believe that she is intoxicated, leading him to think that he can take advantage of her. Additionally, she persuades Leslie to take the formula, both by employing her allure and by questioning his manhood. Female visibility is directly related to the weakening of the male character, to a heightening of male vulnerability. In different capacities, Diana performs a distinct version of herself for each of these men or groups of men that reverses the violence and power of the male voyeuristic eye against itself.

The first fictional female detective in Spain also anticipates certain characteristics of the modern woman investigator in contemporary crime fiction, such as her quick-wittedness, her bravery, her ability to read her rivals, and her use of her femininity as a tool of manipulation. However, unlike Gabriela Zahara, Chulita Ferna, and more contemporary examples, Diana Fletcher, like Mediante's Ágata Bellcome and Malva Apiyu, is not positioned to denounce a sociopolitical system that is unfair in its reading of and stance towards women. Mediante's female characters do not present a challenge to the patriarchal structure in the same way that Gabriela and Chulita have because they do not stand for a more feminized form of justice. Although it is an advance in terms of having a female detective in the genre, there is a regression because Diana submits to the same order, similar to what occurs both in *Sombras siniestras* and *Fuerzas ocultas*. Her marriage to Leslie reaffirms this, and so at the end of the novel, we are left with the image of the happy couple flying off to their honeymoon. A product of its time period, while *La señorita detective* breaks the mould of the female character by converting her into a sleuth, an innovation considering the regime's censorship, the novel then weakens the character, first by paralyzing her and handing over the heroic protagonist role to Leslie, and then by marrying her off, effectively containing her within a patriarchal system of law and order.

Male Criminalization at the Hands of the Femme Fatale: Manuel de Pedrolo's *Joc brut*

Although many scholars had previously attributed the appearance of the autochthonous detective novel in Spain as a reponse to the social crises during the transition to democracy, Resina has demonstrated that a crime fiction tradition "responsive to local reality" materialized much earlier in Catalonia because of its prior development as a capitalist society compared with the rest of Spain ("Detective Formula" 119). The hard-boiled genre arrived in Catalonia in the 1950s with the return from exile of Rafael Tasis in 1948, whose trilogy of detective novels in Catalan were successful because he created serialized characters in the genre, the journalist Francesc Caldes and police inspector Jaume Vilagut (120). Another Catalan writer who also experimented with crime fiction in those years was Manuel de Pedrolo, who, unlike Tasis, "openly rejected the traditional or formal detective novel" and instead tailored the hard-boiled formula "to Catalan post-war reality," in this way attempting to vindicate the genre in the eyes of the reading public, according to Colmeiro ("Stretching" 62, 63).[10] Both Tasis and Pedrolo employed crime fiction as a forum to underscore Catalonia's problems, but Pedrolo went a step further in attempting to enhance the value of a genre that had been traditionally excluded from the canon of higher literary forms, in addition to being a model for other Catalan writers (61–3). Resina has previously demonstrated that the decade of the sixties is the precursor to the *novela negra* boom, launched by Pedrolo's second detective novel, *L'inspector fa tard* (*The Inspector Is Late*, 1960) (*El cadáver* 49).[11] Pedrolo's crime fiction is considered fundamental for the development of the genre because he introduces elements crucial to the later *novela negra* that merit attention.

Between 1963 and 1970, Pedrolo would also become the director of La Cua de Palla ("The Straw Tail"), a crime fiction series spearheaded by Edicions 62 where he translated and published classic detective and suspense novels into Catalan (Hart, *The Spanish Sleuth* 52).[12] According to Dídac Pujol, "'La Cua de Palla' was the first attempt in the crime fiction genre in Catalan as well as the first literary series published by Edicions 62. Until its appearance in 1963, readers could only enjoy crime fiction in Spanish (or in the original language, usually English or French) due to the lack of such a genre in Catalan" (174). Edicions 62, which continues a strong tradition of publication and dissemination of Catalan literature, began in 1962 when the regime was undergoing a tempering process to better its international image. As a result, it started authorizing Catalan translations of canonic literature, all under the guidance of the Minister of Information and Tourism at the time, Manuel Fraga Iribarne (173–4). During Pedrolo's tenure, explains Pujol, La Cua de Palla would publish seventy-one titles, and thanks to this collection, crime fiction, especially of the hard-boiled variety, gained popularity among Catalan readers, who were now able to purchase it in their native language, and in cheaper paperback form.[13] Unfortunately, the series was unable to survive past 1970 because "the readership was limited and prices could not become cheaper due to larger editions" (178). In his article, "Que falla, 'la cua de palla'?" ("What Isn't Working, La Cua de Palla?"), Pedrolo would later claim that the series did not survive because other Catalan authors were uninterested in publishing crime fiction novels and that the volumes published by Edicions 62 were just as expensive as higher literary forms (45). Additionally, he was the only Catalan author to publish two texts with the series, *Joc brut* (1965) and *Mossegar-se la cua* (*Biting One's Own Tail*) in

1968 (Pujol 177). La Cua de Palla would relaunch in 1981 as "Seleccions de la Cua de Palla" ("Selections of La Cua de Palla"), where it resurrected titles from the former series and launched new titles, starting in 1986 until 1996, when the series came to an end once again (Canal i Artigas and Escribà 71–3; 89–99). The focus of this series, however, would be on publishing hard-boiled American novels in Catalan, while the previous series published a greater variety of both European and North American crime fiction. The reason it did not survive for a second time, according to Pujol, was because readers no longer preferred reading crime fiction as part of a series but rather individual writers instead (180).

Regarded by critics of his works as one of Pedrolo's masterpieces, *Joc brut* centres on the story of Xavier Rius's criminalization. An idealistic young man struggling to survive, Xavier's dull existence is thrown for a loop the day his eyes become glued to an amazing pair of legs at a bus stop. What starts out as a crush and a series of flirtatious yet frustrating encounters with Juna, the owner of these exquisite pair of legs, ends with Xavier's murder of her so-called uncle, Enric Virós, who, according to Juna, is the one obstacle standing in their way to starting a life together since he administers an inheritance that will be hers when he dies. When he is arrested for the crime, Xavier discovers that this has all been part of Juna's elaborate ruse, whose real name is Caterina Freixa, to eliminate her husband so that she can be with her real lover, a young lawyer who she led Xavier to think was her cousin. From the start of the novel, male criminalization is blamed on the female body and its seductive power. The first of four chapters, titled "El projecte" ("The Project"), details the transformation of a law-abiding young man into a killer. I argue that the emphasis on the connection between female visibility and male vulnerability is established from the novel's opening when the first-person narrator and protagonist, Xavier, claims, "Si no hagués estat per les seves cames, no hauria passat res. O potser sí. Però hauria passat a algú altre. Jo ho hauria llegit al diari ... Mai no havia vist unes cames tan meravelloses. Ni uns genolls tan bonics" ("Had it not been for her legs, nothing would have happened. Or maybe it would have. But it would have happened to someone else. I would have read about it in the newspaper ... I'd never seen such marvelous legs, nor such beautiful knees") (43). Since Xavier claims that this pair of legs would have ensnared another man, Juna's power as a femme fatale is reinforced from the outset. What is crucial to Pedrolo's project, according to Colmeiro and Resina, is that the author forces us to see the world through the eyes of the male delinquent and witness the process of his criminalization, drawing us closer to the male protagonist while eliciting feelings of complicity and compassion. While this is true, I propose that it is necessary to analyze the process by which Juna initiates, fuels, and finalizes Xavier's criminalization in addition to his part in this process because this is likewise fundamental to Pedrolo's project. If we are to sympathize with Xavier, as both Colmeiro and Resina suggest, I demonstrate that it is precisely because the femme fatale has succeeded in her endeavour. In the pages that follow, I draw attention to how Juna effects Xavier's criminal transformation by creating a fictional world in which he believes that through murder he will finally emerge a victor.

The first pages of the novel constitute an extended gazing scene, where the first-person narrative paints a detailed physical picture of the woman that Xavier first sees at the bus stop and then again on the bus. Zooming in on her like a camera lens, Xavier's description begins from the bottom up. Starting with her legs, he then examines the rest of her body, resting his gaze on each part of her:

> Duia una faldilla curta, més aviat cenyida, i el cos era digne de les extremitats que mostrava tan generosament. El ventre era llis, d'adolescent, i això posava més en relleu les anques arrodonides que, després de perllongar unes cuixes que s'endevinaven llargues i nervioses, morien en una cintura breu. Més amunt, les sines inflaven la brusa blanca que contrastava amb el seu rostre bru, il·luminat per uns ulls immensos i maliciosos. (43)

> She wore a short skirt, rather tight, and her body was worthy of the limbs that she showed so generously. The belly was smooth, like an adolescent, and it highlighted her rounded buttocks, which continued into her thighs, and which you could tell were long and nervous, and ended at her thin waist. Further up, her breasts pushed up against her white blouse, which contrasted with her tan face, which was illuminated by her immense and malicious eyes.

When she later smiles at him, he notices her meaty lips and deep-set eyes, and the bus ride continues with his gaze falling back down on her legs and then back up to the beginning of her thighs (45). Xavier's gaze continues rising up her body, ending at the opening of her blouse, where the male voyeuristic eye finally comes to rest and lingers on her cleavage. Not only is the female character meticulously examined and picked apart in piecemeal fashion during this first encounter, but she is also portrayed as a different type of woman – a self-assured woman who seductively frightens the male protagonist. Though she intimidates Xavier, this provokes him further, so much so that he decides to follow her: "[N]o tenia aquest aire esfereït de moltes noies que sembla que vulguin arrencar a córrer quan els adreces la paraula, però el to de la seva veu era una mica dur" ("She didn't look like one of those terrified girls who seems to want to run away when you speak to them, but the tone of her voice was a little harsh") (46). It is worth emphasizing that while Xavier will become a victim of this woman, he is the one who initially pursues and even hounds her in this opening scene by following her off the bus. Pestering and begging to let him see her again, Juna's ambition fuels her to use him to her advantage, but only after Xavier has set the stage for her to do so. Accordingly, the conditions for Xavier's criminalization are not as one-sided as the first-person narration would have us believe later on.

What Xavier interprets as self-confidence when comparing her with other young woman during this opening scene is her ability to use his gaze against him. Part of her seductiveness, her charm, and what Xavier finds exciting is that she does not shy away from him or his stare. Instead, she draws him closer with her look and her body, and admits that she finds the way that he has been looking at her amusing when he asks her why she smiled at him on the bus: "Potser m'ha fet gràcia la seva manera de mirar-me" ("Perhaps I thought your way of looking at me was funny") (47). Aware that he cannot take his eyes off her, the femme fatale finds an easy prey in Xavier, and, as in Mediante's crime fiction, the voyeuristic male look is employed against itself. *Joc brut*, a novel interested in exposing the workings of narrative gazing mechanisms, demonstrates how female visibility provokes Xavier to see himself through Juna's eyes. Here, the reversal of the gaze compels Xavier to recognize the misery of his situation and to feel guilty because he continues to live life as a victim. The reversal of the male gaze is employed first to victimize and then to criminalize Xavier.

Although Xavier admits that her beauty is part of what charms him, "[n]o solament eren les cames, era una mena de lluminositat que transcendia l'aparença física, una qualitat misteriosa que, de sobte, emergia en un gest, en una expressió dels ulls" ("it wasn't just the legs. She had a kind of luminosity that transcended physical appearance, a mysterious quality that would emerge suddenly in a gesture, in an expression of the eyes") (46–7). In addition to the way that she is able to hold his stare and look back at him, the enigmatic quality that Xavier describes distinguishes her from other women in a way reminiscent of the femme fatale. We are reminded of Jess Sully's claim that "feminine beauty and masculine power" come together in the figure of the femme fatale (57), and this is what ultimately separates her from everyday, normal women (Allen 3). This mysterious or enigmatic combination of female and male attributes presents a paradox because the femme fatale attracts and seduces with the feminine, but her fatality stems from her appropriation of traditionally masculine characteristics. In *Joc brut*, Juna manipulates the male gaze by reappropriating its power, and so from the beginning of the novel, the narrative evokes the femme fatale's paradox by concentrating the subsequent narrative pauses on her malicious and yet provocative eyes. Perplexed by Juna's contradictory look and the mystery of her gaze, Xavier reflects upon how "[e]ls ulls van desfer camí, però ara eren diferents, irònics, francament irònics. Semblaven contradir les paraules que pronuncià" ("her eyes found their way back to me, but now they were different, ironic, frankly ironic. They seemed to contradict the words that she had said") (49). This is the first of a few instances where her words do not match her body language, and yet while accentuating the contradiction, Xavier cannot help himself and insists on seeing her again, which she consents to by saying that she takes the bus every Saturday at the same time. Enraptured by this woman, Xavier ignores the signs of female deception, and instead, finds himself subjected to, as the title suggests, her games, which in the beginning consist of simultaneously pulling away to then draw him closer.

The mysterious woman, who introduces herself as Juna, disarms him by constantly restaging herself. For this reason, Xavier can never get a clear or lasting read of her, and so he is defenseless against the onslaught of emotions that she activates in him. Like her female criminal predecessors, Juna plays with her own exposure and legibility, but she also authors a fiction that must succeed in criminalizing Xavier by having him obsess over his need to possess her. A consumer market researcher, Xavier's need to consume and penetrate her body is directly related to his job because, like the household products about which he surveys female customers, Juna becomes a product or object that he must possess. Here, Juna's mastery over the erotic is fundamental, since she must be both incredibly seductive and virginal at once, displaying and selling herself as both. More significantly, whereas Xavier fails in his reading of the femme fatale, she succeeds in first reading and then criminalizing him by taking her cues from Xavier himself, from the stories that he shares with her. Consequently, Xavier provides the narrative that she will employ against him, and takes part in his own victimization.

During a second encounter, Juna recounts how she is a village girl living in the city with her uncle and his wife for a month, which leads to Xavier's rendition of his life story:

> Vaig explicar-li la mena de feina que feia, vaig explicar-li tota la meva vida. Que tampoc jo no era de Barcelona, que la mare i jo hi vam venir en acabar-se la guerra que va deixar-la vídua, perquè el meu pare havia mort al front, al costat del vençuts, i mai no havíem rebut cap ajuda. Ella feia feines per les cases, vetllava malalts, jo havia treballat de grum en una oficina, de corredor d'articles electrodomèstics, però no servia per a vendre, potser no servia per a res.
>
> Les paraules se m'anaven fent agres a la boca, revivia en uns moments la meva infància humiliada i famolenca, les aspiracions de la mare que volia per a mi un futur millor i no ho aconseguí, perquè no va poder donar-me estudis, i mai no vam tenir res, ni casa. (58)

> I explained to her the kind of work that I did. I explained my whole life: that I was also not from Barcelona, that my mother and I came here at the end of the war that had made her a widow, because my father had died at the front, on the losing side, and we never received any compensation. She cleaned houses, looked after ill people, I worked as a bellboy in an office, as a home appliance salesman, but I wasn't cut out for sales. Maybe I wasn't cut out for anything.
>
> The words started to become bitter in my mouth. For a moment, I relived my childhood full of hunger and humiliation, my mother's aspirations. She wanted a better future for me and didn't succeed, because she couldn't afford my studies, and we never had anything, not even a house.

Recalling Marianne Hirsch's work on postmemory and trauma, Pedrolo conjures up the memory of the Civil War and depicts post-war Barcelona as a defeated city, a city that housed the war's losers, according to Xavier's rendition of his life story. Through Xavier, Pedrolo creates an instance of postmemory by exposing his protagonist as a victim of the Civil War, but also by allowing him to voice his trauma. If we recall, Hirsch elucidates that "'[p]ostmemory' describes the relationship that the 'generation after' bears to the personal, collective, and cultural trauma of those who came before," which, she affirms, "is thus actually mediated not by recall but by imaginative investment, projection, and creation" (5). Moreover, Hirsch claims that we should understand postmemory "as a *structure* of inter- and transgenerational return of traumatic knowledge and embodied experience" (6; italics in original). Xavier functions as Pedrolo's tool, not only to convey the traumatic aftermath of the Civil War, but also to expose the dangers of forgetting when the crimes continue being disguised under the resulting dictatorship.

What is more, Xavier's longing for Juna mirrors his desire for Barcelona, to succeed in the city and to surpass his father's memory. Both Juna and Barcelona represent Xavier's promise for a better future. Although Barcelona signified a new beginning for Xavier and his mother after the Civil War, now Barcelona is the city that he traverses with a woman who symbolizes his chance to reemerge a winner. From a city that he arrived at as one of the defeated, there is hope, through Juna, that he can finally triumph. And yet, both Juna and Barcelona evoke an element of victimization and trauma. Significantly, Barcelona also represents the traumatic aftermath of the loss of Xavier's father along with hunger, humiliation, and the thwarting of both his and his mother's dreams. In one way or another, Xavier has always been a victim, and Juna employs this knowledge to her advantage by dangling in front of his eyes what he wants, making him hunger for her, and yet humiliating him when he attempts to get closer. Xavier's life story is one of hunger and humiliation, and Juna reproduces these feelings in him by revictimizing him.

Masterfully playing the seduction/victimization game, Juna delays allowing Xavier to kiss or touch her, making him believe that she is a virgin: "Mai no m'ha tocat ningú, Xavier" ("No one has ever touched me, Xavier") (62). To keep him interested, however, she allows for certain affections, but then quickly denies him others, always keeping him starved for more. An avid consumer of a body that he cannot possess, Xavier catches glimpses of a woman who seems to know what she is doing by using her body to provoke him, permitting him to touch her only to increase his desperation. Although she claims to desire him in return, she stops his advances because she wants more than what he can offer monetarily: "Ja saps que sóc exigent. No vull consumir-me tota la joventut ... No sóc egoista, però sóc ambiciosa" ("You know that I'm demanding. I don't want to waste all of my youth ... I'm not selfish, but I am ambitious") (64–5). Even though she does not allow him to touch her, she toys with him seductively:

> Em mirava; tenia el rostre alçat, tot el cos inclinat enrera, la sina oferta, el ventre a tocar del meu. Els llavis li resplendien, humits encara de les nostres besades ...

> Ens havíem enfadat ja una vegada; vam passar-nos tot un capvespre discutint, gairebé insultant-nos, exasperats pel desig, perquè jo tampoc no podia complir allò que li havia promès, no tornar a besar-la, no intentar de tocar-la. Era com un imant. Un imant que cedia un moment i que després es redreçava amb els llavis vermells, cridant:
>
> – No pot ser, Xavier, no pot ser! (67–9)

> She was looking at me; she had her face raised, her whole body leaning backwards, offering her chest, her stomach almost touching mine. Her lips glowed, still wet from our kisses ...
>
> On a certain occasion, we fought, spending a whole evening arguing, almost insulting one another, exasperated by desire, because it was impossible for me to keep my promise to her, to not kiss her, not to try to touch her. She was like a magnet. A magnet that gave in for a moment and then straightened up with red lips, shouting:
>
> – It can't be, Xavier, it can't be!

Fueling his torment, Xavier finds himself in an impossible situation because although he promises to respect her virginal status, she humiliates him to the point of making him beg for her. Exasperated, Xavier finally complains, "No està bé, Juna ... Això és brut" ("This isn't right, Juna ... This is dirty") (70). According to Hart, "With this phrase in which the title resonates, Pedrolo not only foreshadows the novel's tragic conclusion, but also condemns a society in which this kind of sexual game is the norm, and where girls are brought up to use sex as a bargaining tool to get what they want: matrimony, money or favors" (*The Spanish Sleuth* 54). I read this episode differently because I would suggest that the title is invoked to comment on Xavier's victimization. In this instance, he realizes that Juna is indeed playing a game with his emotions and toying with him sexually, but he cannot resist her. Using Xavier's past and his vulnerabilities against him, Juna continues a process of victimization that the war and the dictatorship had already started. The title of the novel is invoked during this scene because Xavier acknowledges that Juna is constantly testing his limits, making him straddle the line between hunger and humiliation.

The real test of Xavier's vulnerable state takes place soon after when she starts planting the seed that her uncle Enric Virós needs to be eliminated. Before telling him that her uncle stands in the way of their happiness, Juna sets the scene by explaining how her aunt left her an inheritance that her uncle administers: "Jo no puc tocar res, res! Quan es morirà tindré les finques, els valors ... tot ... De vegades penso ... Si li passés alguna cosa" ("I can't touch any of it, nothing at all! When he dies I'll have the estates, the investments ... everything ... Sometimes I think ... If something happened to him") (73). Besides detailing the financial situation and voicing her wish for her uncle's disappearance, Juna also underlines that there is a certain urgency to the situation because Virós, who is fifty-six years old, could live another fifteen or twenty years, and she wants to enjoy her inheritance, "ara que sóc jove, ... no quan sigui una pobra dona de quaranta anys" ("now, when I'm young, ... not when I'm a poor forty-year-old woman") (73). Again, Juna underscores the idea that her ambition and her need for her inheritance are also linked to her desire to enjoy her youth. There appears to be a concern with female aging in this narrative, with a female body that loses its allure and potency, which again refers back to Xavier's job as a consumer market researcher. To gain still more traction in getting what she wants, Juna feeds Xavier's desire during this scene by allowing him to kiss her, promising that she could be his forever. Once she has attacked him from all angles,

> Va passar-se la llengua pels llavis i endinsà l'esguard en el meu.
> – Podríem matar-lo ...
> – És un ser inútil, mesquí, egoista, odiós! ...
> Ho escopí apassionadament i els ulls li llampeguejaren amb una ira estranya, gairebé freda a despit d'aquella passió ...
> [L]es seves mans van quedar-se a mig aire, inertes. Després retrocediren cap a la seva espatlla, on s'aturaren, insegures, abans d'esbocar més la brusa i, amb un gest que semblava maquinal, inconscient, desplaçar una mica el tirant dels sostenidors que li havia deixat un séc a la pell. (78)

> She licked her lips and locked eyes with me.
> – We could kill him ...
> – He's a useless, miserable, selfish, hateful person! ...
> She spit this out passionately and her eyes sparkled with a strange anger, almost cold in spite of the passion ...
> [H]er hands remained in midair, lifeless. Then they went back to her shoulder, where they stopped, unsure of themselves, before opening her blouse a little more and, with a gesture that seemed mechanical, unconscious, she moved her bra strap just a little from where it had left a mark on her skin.

Seeing that nothing else seems to work, Juna exploits her body to initiate Xavier's criminalization, proposing that they should murder her uncle so that he can satisfy his craving for her. In response, Xavier runs away, but he later recalls the Juna that has emerged during this conversation: "Algú, una altra persona, havia emergit de les profunditats del seu ésser i em revelava una cara ferotge, sanguinària, una voluntat decidida, capaç" ("Someone, another person, had emerged from the depths of her being and revealed to me a fierce, bloodthirsty face, a determined, capable will") (79–80). Again, Juna's body has apparently betrayed her by making her real self momentarily legible to Xavier. As before, Xavier will ignore this moment of the femme fatale's exposure and rationalizes her behaviour by blaming himself. Refusing to recognize the villainous woman who has revealed herself to him, he paves the way for his own seduction and criminalization by convincing himself that Juna's passion for him has blinded her.

Later, seeing her with another man reignites his hunger for her, and sets the scene for the further humiliation that he is willing to suffer because of her. Clearly, Xavier's jealousy paves the way for his criminalization because he refuses to let another man possess Juna, since she represents his promise for a better life. When Juna and Xavier meet again, and after debating how they can be together, Juna realizes that the only way to convince him to kill her uncle is to offer her body to him, so they arrange a sexual encounter at Xavier's apartment. Given a key, Juna arrives before Xavier, and he finds her sleeping. Studying her during this episode, he acknowledges the contradictions, the different versions of Juna that appear before him:

> El rostre que contemplava, i l'expressió, eren més innocents, amorosits per una mena d'ingenuïtat que desmentia l'actitud vagament voluptuosa del cos ... Vaig mirar-la llargament, seduït per la gràcia animal dels membres immòbils i exposats, pel dibuix dels llavis que havia badat una mica, per la tofa de cabells que li amagaven tot el front i part de la galta. (92)

> The face that I was looking at, and her expression, were more innocent, softened by a kind of ingenuity that revealed the vaguely voluptuous attitude of her body ... I stared at her, seduced by the animal-like grace of her motionless and exposed limbs, by her faded lipstick, by all the hair that covered her forehead and part of her cheek.

Juna quickly reinitiates the game that she has been playing – making her body available to him, then snatching it away. She has staged this scene, and as he tries to make her his, she denies him and even cries, blaming the sordid room that they are in and the misery that surrounds them. She makes him feel guilty about his economic situation, and revictimizes him in this instance by reminding him that he still lives like one of the defeated: "No podria viure en un indret com aquest. No podria" ("I couldn't live in a place like this. I couldn't") (94). Moreover, she reminds him of everything he does not possess, including her. The female body's exposure forces Xavier into a position of vulnerability, and as Juna recognizes this, she whispers the words "L'oncle" ("My uncle") (95).

With the voyeuristic male eye turned on itself, her words have an immediate effect. Insulted and victimized, we witness Xavier experience a combination of trauma combined with an uncontrollable desire for Juna's body. In this moment, the experience of trauma visually manifests itself on the male protagonist's body:

> El cap em donava voltes, em sentia marejat, tancava i obria les mans espasmòdicament, martiritzant-la encara, acariciant-la ... No sabia què em feia ...
>
> La vaig deixar explicar. Ningú no sabia que nosaltres dos ens conseguéssim, per a més seguretat des d'aquell moment deixaríem de veure'ns, escolliríem una nit que ella sortís amb la seva tia i així tindria una coartada. (95–6)

> My head was spinning, I felt dizzy, I closed and opened my hands spasmodically, martyrizing her still, caressing her ... I didn't know what she was doing to me ...
>
> I let her explain. Nobody was aware that we knew each other. To be safe, from that moment on we would have to stop seeing each other. We would choose one night when she would leave the house with her aunt and that way she would have an alibi.

Without intending to do so, Xavier starts planning the murder with Juna, and as they create a blueprint for the crime, her body emerges from the shadows (98). The female body gains exposure because it is linked to crime and takes part in corrupting the law-abiding Xavier. As in Pardo Bazán's *La gota de sangre,* discussed in chapter 1, crime penetrates the male protagonist through the female body. And yet, when Juna realizes that he is staring at her breasts, she conceals them from him (98). By playing with its visibility and invisibility, Juna's body functions to continue victimizing Xavier by simultaneously starving and demeaning him. Indeed, the female body is initially a source of male narrative pleasure in this text, but later functions to alienate Xavier still further (*El cadáver* 50). Knowing that she still has not fully committed him to her murderous plot, she threatens to leave and end their relationship (*Joc brut* 101). In response, Xavier slaps her, but quickly regrets this expression of violence, and soon after, they are once again in each other's arms. Seduction, victimization, and violence are intimately linked in this text via the visibility of the female body. All three come together during this heightened erotic scene, which will ultimately result in Xavier's criminalization.

The episode, however, ends with a final rejection in which Xavier is left famished for her: "El cor em glatia. Però ara ja no ignorava que al final em rebutjaria, com va fer, i que tornaríem a seure al caire del llit amb el bloc obert al nostre davant, repetint apressadament tot allò que havíem dit" ("My heart was beating fast. But now I knew that in the end she would reject me, as she did, and that we would sit down again at the edge of the bed with the notebook open in front of us, hastily repeating all that we had said before") (102). Continuing to torment him, Juna finalizes the murderous plot, and though he protests that they will have no contact in six months, he acknowledges that her plan is perfect (103). More than just making him desire her, she reveals that eliminating her uncle will lead to Xavier's success; a man who she portrays as both worthless and undesirable, but who, unlike Xavier, is thriving. By taking his life, Xavier believes that he will finally emerge triumphant and no longer continue as a victim. Juna simultaneously employs Xavier's narrative and understanding of himself as a victim against him and activates his hunger for her, both of which drive him to commit murder.

In the next two sections of *Joc brut*, "Els fets" ("The Facts") and "La recerca" ("The Investigation"), a transformed Xavier carries out the murder of Virós, and we witness the effects that this has on his life, especially when he realizes that Juna has disappeared. After about nine months, when Xavier suffers the loss of Juna but also of his mother, he starts playing the role of detective to locate the disappeared Juna. Xavier eventually learns that he has been a pawn in her game and that Juna has carried out this plan in order to be with another man. When he finally confronts her months later in her new home, he recognizes the extent of his victimization and how, even then, she continues traumatizing him: "Aquella ràbia freda i sorda que precedeix les explosions frenètiques i el dolor que segueix les grans pèrdues. Un dolor més agut que mai, inimaginable, però cert, operant, el dolor que reviscolava la seva presència. Perquè no podia estar-me de repetir-me: És bella, bella, bella ... Només que ara sense rastre de desig" ("That cold and deaf rage that precedes frenzied explosions and the pain that follows great losses. It was a pain more acute than [I had] ever [experienced], unimaginable, but real, ongoing, a pain that was strengthened by her presence. Because I couldn't stop repeating to myself: she is beautiful, beautiful, beautiful ... Only now without a trace of desire") (187–8). Xavier realizes that his hunger for her wanes because he is now the victimizer whereas Juna was "insegura, sota el meu esguard, sota la meva actitud amenaçadora, ja no era un cos desitjable, potser perquè la tenia al meu poder, sense condicions" ("insecure, held by my gaze, held by my threatening attitude. Hers was no longer a desirable body, perhaps because I held her entirely in my power") (189). And yet, the role-reversal does not last because as his desire for her diminishes, Juna attempts to reestablish the power hierarchy between them by appealing to his former feelings for her, using his pursuit of her against him. Despite what she has driven him to do, she promises that they can still be together, which for Xavier again signifies that he can potentially overcome his victim status.

Although Juna's potential vulnerability transforms her into an undesirable body, once Xavier realizes that she is still within his grasp, he starts believing her lies. Yet again, the femme fatale exerts her enigmatic powers to dominate him:

> Dintre meu una veu, una veu estúpida, no parava de dir: Sí, sí, sí ... I ella se'n va adonar. Però aleshores els ulls la traïren. Fou una cosa breu, com un llampec triomfal que alhora revelava un menyspreu infinit. Tot va capgirar-se, a fora i a dintre ... jo me sentia endut per un menyspreu encara més amarg, més punyent, que el dels seus ulls. Imbècil, imbècil!, em deia. Havia estat a punt de tornar a caure en la trampa. (191–2)

> Inside me a voice, a stupid voice, wouldn't stop saying: Yes, yes, yes ... And she noticed. But then her eyes betrayed her. It was quick, like a triumphant bolt of lightning that at the same time revealed a feeling of infinite contempt. Everything turned around, inside and out ... I felt overpowered by a scorn even more bitter, even sharper, than the one in her eyes. Idiot, idiot! I said to myself. I had almost fallen back into the trap.

As her eyes betray her, Juna's feelings of disdain and contempt towards Xavier become legible. Sharing these feelings, Xavier is victimized once again. Viewing himself through Juna and forced to recognize the truth about their relationship, he is finally able to read her accurately: "M'havia enredat fins al final. Mai no havia dit una veritat" ("She toyed with me until the end. She hadn't told me one true thing") (200). It is worth emphasizing, however, that Juna's body has been transmitting these signals all along. More than once, her look, her eyes, betray her, and yet Xavier fails to read these bodily signals or clues.

Realizing how he has been used and humiliated, he violently undresses her, finally attempting to obtain what he wanted from the beginning: "Mai no havia vist res de tan bell. Però ara era una bellesa muda, enemiga, quelcom que calia destruir ... No va tenir temps de fugir, però. Vaig obrir-li la galta dreta, de dalt a baix. L'altra, no" ("I had never seen anything so beautiful. But now it was a mute beauty, an enemy, something that had to be destroyed ... But she didn't have time to run. I opened her right cheek, from top to bottom. The other cheek, I didn't touch") (192). Instead of satisfying his appetite for her, he marks her for life, and punishes her for his transformation. By defiling the female body, he makes sure that she cannot use it to victimize again. The connection between the visibility of the female body, Xavier's victimization, and his subsequent criminalization is reaffirmed at the end of the story. Although Xavier has been a victim of his society from the beginning, he turns to violence in hopes of possessing the female body, which Juna has him believe will alleviate his condition as a victim. Violence stems from the female body because in Pedrolo's *Joc brut* it is not a source of male pleasure, but instead functions to exploit the vulnerable male body.

Juna, whose real name Xavier will find out is Caterina Freixa, once he is arrested for murder, is able to play this elaborate ruse on the male protagonist in part because, according to Ángel Otero Blanco, "la novela de Pedrolo es la narración de un fracaso, la trágica historia de un individuo que es víctima de las circunstancias en las que le ha tocado vivir. Desde niño, Xavier ha vivido en un continuo e inestable proceso de cambios traumáticos que han provocado en él sentimientos de soledad y alienación social" ("Pedrolo's novel is the narrative of a failure, the tragic story of an individual who is a victim of the circumstances in which he had to live. From the time he was a boy, Xavier has lived through a continuous and unstable series of traumatic changes that have provoked in him feelings of loneliness and social alienation") (57). Upon meeting Juna, however, Xavier is filled with hope because in the beginning she represents his future and his last chance to finally reemerge a winner (59). With/through her, he can ultimately move from those defeated in the Civil War to the side of the victors, overcoming his past victimization and vulnerability by succeeding in the city, Barcelona, that has represented his failure, hunger, and humiliation. Still, we should recall that Xavier also creates the conditions for Juna to manipulate and use him by accosting her in the beginning and again at the end of the novel.

For her part, Juna/Caterina wants to eliminate her husband to inherit his money and legitimize her adulterous affair. She is a woman seeking financial independence, a modern and ambitious woman, but who is also driven, like Xavier, by love. For this reason, she should be read not only as a femme fatale, but also as a *femme moderne*. When Juna realizes that Xavier's victim status can be used against him, she masterfully stages herself to represent the materialization of his dreams while simultaneously revictimizing him and fueling his sexual need for her to the point that he loses himself, trespassing ethical boundaries to become a murderer. Similar to how Gabriela, Chulita, and even Diana Fletcher create and stage misreadings of themselves to manipulate the men around them, Juna/Caterina's staged misreading leads to murder by using Xavier's gaze against him, forcing the male protagonist to see himself through her eyes. Here, the female body, visible enough to make Xavier kill to see what remains covered, is the "object" responsible for his transgression. By erasing the boundaries between victim and criminal, Juna makes a mockery of morality and the law. The femme fatale, in turn, is punished with disfigurement for turning the male voyeuristic eye against itself. Her now marked body will never function like before.

Chapter Three

Parodying the Male Gaze in Lourdes Ortiz's *Picadura mortal*

For as many studies as there are on the *novela negra*, little has been said about the female characters of the hard-boiled genre in Spain until the appearance of the first female detective protagonists. One reason for this is that there are few recurring female characters prior to the boom in female crime fiction. Arguably, some *novela negra* authors employed the female character to at times detract from the serious and violent action at hand and allow its audience to rest pleasurably on the sexualized display of its female characters. For the most part, as John Macklin observes, "the women in the *novela negra* are prostitutes, strippers, barmaids, masseuses, singers, or long-suffering girlfriends, like Pepe Carvalho's Charo. They are almost invariably described by the narrator in terms of their physical attributes, usually breasts, and whether these are small, average, large, or silicone" (59). What Macklin states regarding the women of the *novela negra* is true because the depiction of these female characters frequently concentrates on specific body parts by studying women in piecemeal fashion. The female body remains the site of narrative pleasure, where both the detective and the reader can momentarily escape the cycle of violence and the disillusioning social reality explored in these texts.

Vázquez Montalbán's Pepe Carvalho series, for example, hosts a parade of female characters, whose purpose is to visually and/or sexually entertain the detective and the reader during the moments that they appear in the novel. The most significant recurring female character is Charo, a call girl who also takes on the role of Carvalho's girlfriend.[1] Charo, whose real name is Rosario García López, first appears in *Tatuaje* (*Tattoo*, 1974) along with Carvalho's sidekick, Biscuter, and his friend Bromuro, and remains a constant in the series until *El laberinto griego*

(*An Olympic Death*, 1991), though she will reappear in *El hombre de mi vida* (*The Man of My Life*, 2000) in an attempt to reunite with the detective. Carvalho's inner circle is made up by marginalized characters that he utilizes to satisfy his physical and emotional needs, but that are in need of his help or protection. In Myung N. Choi's opinion, Vázquez Montalbán's inclusion of a prostitute as Pepe Carvalho's sentimental partner demonstrates that "las mujeres representan sólo objeto de satisfacción sexual o que simplemente no vale la pena mantener una relación seria con ellas" ("women represent only an object of sexual satisfaction or simply that it is not worth maintaining a serious relationship with them") (35). I disagree, however, with Choi's analysis of Charo because she is the only woman that Carvalho is able to sustain a sentimental relationship with for years even if it is not exclusive. As their relationship evolves, it becomes less sexual and defined more so by long-term companionship, since the pair grows old together. Furthermore, the connection between the detective and the prostitute could also be considered significant at another level – they both "sell" themselves packaged as a service that only they can offer. The service that Charo provides goes beyond the bedroom because Carvalho's attitudes towards love and relationships change because of her. Becoming more to him than a sexual partner, Charo defies conventional stereotypes regarding women in crime fiction because she does not fit neatly into the traditional roles assigned to females in the genre. Overlapping the line between victim, love interest, and companion, Charo emerges in this series as someone who challenges the detective to realize his emotional potential.

Even though Charo's function in the series should be revisited, as readers who are granted frequent access to Carvalho's bedroom we become quite familiarized with the sleuth's thoughts on heterosexual relationships. Allowed to witness scenes where the woman character is objectified, the reader not only shares in what the sleuth sees, the naked female body, but is also permitted to observe how the detective behaves sexually. According to Susana Bayó Belenguer, "the frequent descriptions of Carvalho's sexual behaviour may therefore reflect the political and sexual liberalization of post-Franco Spain" (*Theory* 230). No longer under the constraints of a dictatorship that repressed "the lower body" to employ Stephanie Sieburth's term, the Carvalho series revels in depicting the detective's sexual prowess in the bedroom, but does so in a critical fashion. The voyeuristic eye in Vázquez Montalbán's detective novels is turned back on itself to question the detective's morality and ethical standards, which is an innovation of the series. Unlike his predecessor Philip Marlowe who exemplifies the chivalric and morality-driven detective, Carvalho's questionable moral compass, especially when it pertains to women and how he objectifies them, comes under some scrutiny.

Although other women in the series are used pretty much exclusively for Carvalho's sexual gratification, Charo maintains a more complicated role in her relationship with the detective. She problematizes his connection to women in the novels by signifying more to the detective than a sexual exploit, but at the same time, he remains unable to commit to her. Interestingly enough, the woman who sells herself in these novels is the one who, in comparison to the other female characters that appear in the series, is the least objectified. Charo never comes into full view for the reader, remaining in the shadows or in the sleuth's recollections. Furthermore, Charo represents Carvalho's fear of aging and death, the fear of being left behind in a rapidly changing society. In *El hombre de mi vida*, for example, Charo no longer reappears as a prostitute, but as a businesswoman who offers to help Carvalho while they embark upon the latter years of their life. From the margins, she makes her way to the centre, becoming an entrepreneur and a potential wife to Carvalho even though he does not accept. The character of Charo perhaps signals a transition period for the female character of Spanish crime fiction, where she moves beyond the object of the male gaze towards a more active, but now conventional role. Charo's new position in the series contains her by having her abide by traditional roles and morality and still maintain her place at the male detective's side.

Female crime fiction writers who burst on the scene in the late 1970s and throughout the 1980s would subvert the conventional portrayal of women and of the female body by employing a woman sleuth's perspective. The female detective introduced during these two decades is a product and a consequence of the feminist movement's rejection and revision of traditional gender roles, which, according to Kathleen Gregory Klein, presented "not only a critique of those earlier stereotypes and a promise for women's roles in a more open future society but also a challenge to the limitations of women's current roles" ("Women" 12). Now that the scrutiny and criticism of society is from a woman's perspective, this required the rewriting of the female character's role in the detective novel. Female characters are no longer secondary or tangential to the plotline, but are now the protagonists who as detectives or pseudo-sleuths solve crimes and deliver justice, and using its first-person narration, the detective's "gender awareness," to use Nancy Vosburg's terminology, becomes one of the critical issues presented that will result in what Vosburg calls "'revisionist' strategies [that] serve as points of departure" ("Genre Bending" 60). This signifies that these women investigators "are conscious of gender as a way in which the social system categorizes, judges, and responds to people," and thus, the female protagonist must find a way to thrive as a detective despite the problem that being a woman in a *machista* society still poses (60).

Kimberly J. Dilley, in her study of female sleuths, proposes that we problematize this literary figure by asking ourselves why such "few women in literature have been called heroic," which is one of the problems that the woman investigator must confront (141). According to Dilley,

> The heroine is most often praised for her dedication to traditional feminine qualities. She is pure, gentle, generous, quiet, stoic in the face of adversity, and responsive to her roles as mother and wife. She epitomizes the feminine. "Hero" is traditionally reserved for masculine behavior: adventure, facing down enemies, taking risk, aggression, independence, and charging in after adversity ... Theoretically, however, women can be heroes; the term is the "universal." For women to do so, however, means struggling against gender stereotypes and risking their femininity. To be "universal" is to be masculine. (141)

The female detective must battle against these particular gender stereotypes that exclude her from what is traditionally considered masculine behaviour and a male-dominated profession. What this implies is that she must adopt masculine characteristics, but this does not necessarily mean risking her femininity because the female sleuth will also employ this to her benefit. Already in the first literary examples of the genre, female investigators experiment with gender fluidity, alternating feminine and masculine attributes to enhance their sleuthing abilities. For this reason, a *bildungsroman* structure forms part of these first modern examples because the woman investigator must combat the undermining of her authority while simultaneously learning how to effectively evolve as an investigator.

In P.D. James's *An Unsuitable Job for a Woman* (1972), Cordelia Gray, considered by some crime fiction scholars to be an innovation in the genre, inherits the practice from her boss/partner, who committed suicide. She must develop as a professional sleuth while solving her first solo case, during which she must confront issues such as her authority as a detective, her memories of the past, her emotional attachment to the victim, and her relationship to Adam Dalgliesh, the policeman she hands the case over to at the end ("Women Detectives" 195–7). Throughout the work Cordelia expresses serious doubts regarding her sleuthing skills, but Maureen Reddy underscores that "[b]y the end of the novel, however, a more mature and confident Cordelia than the one we meet as the novel opens asserts her right to investigate and indeed to choose whatever work she wishes, relying in part on fantasies of her long-dead mother's approval" (196). Other crime fiction scholars, like Birgitta Berglund, do not seem to agree with the idea that Cordelia Gray is such an innovation in the history of the genre. For Berglund, the strategy that P.D. James uses to make Cordelia a protagonist had been employed "sixty years earlier" by Baroness Emma Orczy in *Lady Molly of Scotland Yard* because "[j]ust like Lady Molly, Cordelia thus neither actively applies for nor even chooses her job. Both are pressed into accepting their jobs by men and both fit into the category of women who have to fend for themselves in the absence of male protectors" (149). Still, Cordelia's decision to continue her investigative work is more purposeful than Berglund claims because she is never pressed into accepting the job at the detective agency before the death of her boss/partner, but chooses to do so. Moreover, it is worth taking into account the *bildungsroman* structure of the novel and how Cordelia's identification with the victim propels her to continue working the case despite the resistance that she encounters because of her gender ("Women Detectives" 196). Regardless of its shortcomings, James's novel would provide the subtext not only for the British and American variations of female crime fiction produced during the 1970s and 1980s, but also for women authors working in Spain, such as Lourdes Ortiz, who introduced the first female hard-boiled detective, Bárbara Arenas, in *Picadura mortal*.

Picadura mortal follows the investigation headed by Bárbara Arenas into the disappearance of a wealthy industrialist, Ernesto Granados, in the Canary Islands. Assigned the case by her boss Juan Carlos, Bárbara stays with the Granados family, examining each of them as potential suspects since the Granados children will only receive their inheritance once the body is recovered. In the end, Bárbara discovers that Ernesto Granados was never kidnapped and is alive and that this has all been part of his plan to retain political and economic control in addition to covering up his own crimes following the Spanish Civil War. The novel, which was written in about two weeks, would be Ortiz's only incursion into the crime fiction genre (Pérez and Ihrie, "Detective

Fiction" 168). Part of the post-Franco literary generation, Ortiz, a prolific and genre-versatile author, published *Picadura mortal* to experiment with the genre for the publishing house Sedmay's crime fiction series, Club del Crimen (Crime Club), which was started in 1979 (168). Prior to *Picadura mortal*, Ortiz had already published *Luz de la memoria* (*Light of Memory*) in 1976, a psychological novel that centres on the life trajectory of a man who ends up interned in a psychiatric institution, but her best-known work, however, would come later in the form of the historical novel, *Urraca* (1982), which tells the story of the mostly forgotten Queen Urraca of Spain (Pérez and Ihrie, "Ortiz" 450). Besides her novelistic texts, Ortiz, who has been a professor of art history and communications at the Complutense, has also written plays, short stories, critical essays on literature and communication, newspaper articles, and children's literature.[2]

The year Ortiz published *Picadura mortal*, 1979, has some literary crime fiction significance in Spain, since it coincides with the publication of Vázquez Montalbán's *Los mares del Sur*, Mendoza's *El misterio de la cripta embrujada* (*The Mystery of the Enchanted Crypt*), Jorge Martínez Reverte's *Demasiado para Gálvez* (*Too Much for Gálvez*), and Andreu Martín's *Aprende y calla* (*Learn and Shut Up*) and *El señor Capone no está en casa* (*Mr Capone is Not at Home*).[3] The publication of all these works not only signalled the *novela negra*'s increasing popularity, but also its function as a literary pulpit from which to voice dissatisfaction with the democratic transition. This is particularly meaningful considering that the general elections, the first constitutional general election under the new constitution to take place since 1936, were held on 1 March 1979. That year would also mark the year of the Jornadas Feministas (Feminist Symposia) in Granada that were organized by the Coordinadora Feminista – Federación de Organizaciones Feministas del Estado Español (Feminist Coordinator – Federation of Feminist Organizations of the Spanish State). The Coordinadora Feminista continues to assemble women from different feminist groups to discuss and debate crucial issues pertaining to women, including abortion, sexuality, lesbianism, gender inequality, and gender violence among others and to publicize the feminist agenda.[4] The Jornadas Feministas of 1979 did not focus on one sole matter, but attempted to grapple with the problems affecting women during the Transition, the most central of which was being regarded as second-class citizens. Although positive in their general message, the Jornadas Feministas of 1979, however, also made it clear that there was no one cohesive Spanish feminism, but two primary competing "school[s] of thought" – the equality versus the difference feminists (*Killing Carmens* 15).[5] Mercedes de Grado elucidates that one of the basic goals of the equality feminists was to "erradicar el sistema sexo-género en el que se basa la sociedad patriarcal, el cual establece estereotipos de género que favorecen a los hombres y marginan a las mujeres" ("eradicate the system of sex and gender in which patriarchal society is based, that establishes gender stereotypes that favour men and marginalize women") (37). Meanwhile, what the difference feminists sought to emphasize was sexual difference, seeing their authority as stemming from difference, which is oppressed in a patriarchal system. Underlining power and equality as male-centred values, according to de Grado, the difference feminists in Spain were greatly influenced by French theorists like Luce Irigaray and the Italian concept of *affidamento*, used to describe a specific type of relationship that only occurs between women and that encourages female solidarity (40).

Most feminist scholars agree that the Jornadas Feministas of 1979 represent the beginning of a second stage in the feminist movement in Spain. Following an initial stage of organization and mobilization (1975–9), this second period from 1979 to 1982 was characterized by a split due to the irreconcilable differences within the movement that contributed to a sense of disillusionment (de Grado 29). The third and final stage would take place between 1982 and 1985, which de Grado and others understand as the disintegration of the movement. This disintegration was understood by some as the result of the institutionalization of feminism, which occurred with the government's creation of the Instituto de la Mujer (National Women's Institute) in 1983 and its redeployment of women's programmes that had been initially spearheaded by feminist groups (31). Despite the challenges the movement faced throughout these final two periods, the reforms headed by these feminist groups led to what Anny Brooksbank Jones classifies as "significant changes of consciousness, particularly among women most exposed to the competing demands of public and private spheres" and whose focus now shifted towards their career over the domestic space (387).[6]

Although Lourdes Ortiz's Bárbara Arenas emerges during a crucial moment for the feminist movement in Spain, most crime fiction scholars agree with José Colmeiro's statement regarding *Picadura mortal*: "Estamos evidentemente lejos de una novela policíaca de auténtico planteamiento feminista" ("We are obviously far from a detective novel with an authentic feminist approach") (*La novela policiaca* 227). According to Patricia Hart, Ortiz's sleuth exemplifies "many negative stereotypes about women," and her adoption of positive masculine sleuthing attributes fall short of what is expected from a successful hard-boiled detective (*The Spanish Sleuth* 173). For these critics, it would be up to Maria-Antònia Oliver, who introduced Spain's first female crime fiction series, to develop the 1980s feminized formula of the genre with her private eye, Lònia Guiu. Whereas Oliver's Lònia seems to not care about her appearance and for the most part avoids sentimental attachments, Bárbara is both distracted by men and considerably preoccupied with her looks and clothing to the point of exhibiting jealousy when she encounters other beautiful or better-dressed women. In Hart's estimation, there is a lack of depth to Bárbara's character, and at times the plot reads more like a soap opera than a detective novel (172). Colmeiro characterizes it as such when he calls the novel "un tratamiento suavemente humorístico de las actitudes de una mujer liberada española de los nuevos tiempos con el telón de fondo de una telesaga de magnates repleta de odios, rencillas y pasiones" ("a mildly humorous treatment of the attitudes of a liberated, modern Spanish woman against the backdrop of a magnate's soap opera, full of hatreds, quarrels, and passions") (*La novela policiaca* 227). What both these critics affirm is that though *Picadura mortal*'s subversion of the male canon is bringing a woman sleuth to life, the novel would not set an example for female crime fiction to follow (Hart 172–3). For Robert C. Spires, Ortiz's emplotment of a female detective is not a deviation from the standardized male model, but instead, constitutes an imitation of her male predecessors (204). What these three critics fail to recognize, however, are the parodic elements at work in Ortiz's novel. I demonstrate that parody plays a subversive role, especially when discussing the function of the detective's gaze and the representation and reading of the female body in this text.

As discussed in the introduction, the feminization of crime fiction will partly rely on parody to problematize and invert the male models of the genre, but will also be self-reflective and critical in its imitation of male predecessors. Once again, I am invoking Linda Hutcheon's definition of parody as "a form of imitation, but imitation characterized by ironic inversion" (6). I argue that Ortiz, in her imitation of the male-centred genre, employs parody to recreate the gazing scenes of the *novela negra*, but does so to reverse the gaze – thus, feminizing the "eye." While the inversion and replacement of the male "eye" by a female "eye" is one feature of Ortiz's strategy, I suggest that another tactic consists of mocking the male-dominated *novela negra*'s sexist scenes by objectifying the male characters during the lovemaking episodes, but also by producing a new look directed at the female body. The performance of the "eye" that informs the politics of female visibility in male crime fiction comes under scrutiny in Ortiz's novel.

Picadura mortal's mechanism of subversion relies on a reformulation of the politics of visibility in the genre that I describe as a twofold approach. First, the narrative refocalizes the attention away from the female body as an object and problematizes these moments of objectification, and second, the novel recreates these scenes with male characters in a parodic form. Sally Munt has previously pointed out "the common convention that satire, as protest art, suits feminism's desire to parody patriarchal norms and forms" (*Murder* 197). This transgression of the male-gendered form occurs, according to Munt's study of early female crime fiction authors, "through parody. Texts by these women tended to disrupt male authority myths and deployed stereotyped female characters satirically, against themselves" (204). This, I would argue, is the formula that Ortiz employs in *Picadura mortal* against the male hard-boiled genre because she uses parodic inversion to destabilize the male gaze and its authority. Through humour, Ortiz's novel unveils the myths surrounding the male detective and performs certain female stereotypes to satirize and undermine them. Recalling Munt's characterization of parody as a disruptive force against authority, I am claiming that seen through the lens of parody *Picadura mortal* can be read as an investigation of female gender roles. Put succinctly, parody is the main textual strategy utilized by Ortiz to redefine the politics of female visibility in the genre.

Furthermore, there are various instances in *Picadura mortal* where the novel reflects upon its generic condition and the myths surrounding the detective's portrayal to render them false. Lynn McGovern has previously demonstrated that "through the subtle use of parody it humorously challenges such issues as greed, status, bourgeois standards, and gender roles in modern society" (260), employing a female sleuth to act out "hyper-masculine postures and attitudes in a way which throws a parodic light on the genre's conventional 'tough guy' protagonist" (262). From the beginning of the work, Bárbara makes the following connection between the Granados case and the genre, "allí todo parecía montado para una representación, una representación de una mala novela policiaca" ("everything there seemed to be ready for some sort of performance, a performance of a bad crime novel") (22). Another instance of this generic self-consciousness occurs when Carlos, Ernesto Granados's youngest son, appears towards the end of the novel after Rosario has been murdered, and says the following to Bárbara: "A ustedes les encantan las hipótesis románticas del tipo: 'el asesino sólo aparece al final.' Yo no estaba aquí hasta ahora, luego yo debo ser el asesino ... Siempre me han apasionado las novelas policiacas" ("You love romantic theories like 'the killer only appears at the end.' I wasn't here until just now, so I must be the murderer ... I've always been passionate about detective novels") (145). Moreover, Bárbara is critical of her role as a detective because she lets passions and impulses drive her instead of reason. When she feels that she is not following the sleuth stereotype, she calls herself "una detective de fin de semana" ("a weekend detective") (60). Other characters will also point out Bárbara's investigative flaws when she does not meet the standards of the stereotype. For example, when Rosario, Ernesto's daughter-in-law, mentions that unlike others in her profession, she is not a master of subtlety (29), or when Nora, one of Ernesto's granddaughters, points out that private detectives should be audacious people, without fussiness (37). Using this form of self-conscious reflection and satire, both the generic and the detective stereotypes come under comical scrutiny and function as a targeted critique of the genre.

Scholars, such as Choi, McGovern, and Alison Maginn, have also proposed that *Picadura mortal*'s imitative qualities along with its humorous and self-critical elements constitute a subversive reading. In contrast to Hart, Colmeiro, and Spires, McGovern argues that Ortiz employs both male and female stereotypes of the hard-boiled novel to demonstrate their absurdity, but more importantly "for the purpose of consciousness-raising" (259). Whereas McGovern focuses on the consciousness-raising aspect of the novel, Maginn adds that despite being modelled after the male detective, Barbara defies "sexual schemas" by "exploding the mythical male figure of the hard-boiled detective," reversing certain elements of the male-centred, *machista* genre (55). More recently, Choi has expounded upon both of these claims by establishing how Ortiz uses parody and imitation to ridicule not only the male detective, but also the genre by placing her female protagonist in ridiculous situations where she appears inept and clumsy (96). Although I agree that parody is employed to critique the patriarchal values associated with the male sleuth and raise awareness of the prevailing stereotypes, I am arguing that parody in Ortiz's novel functions both to reflect upon, problematize, and subvert the male perspective of the *novela negra* by creating a series of inversions with respect to the ways that the gaze operates in the genre.

The opening scene of the novel already emphasizes the destabilizing role that parody will play. During this episode, Bárbara Arenas awakens beside a young blonde man, and regretting her one-night stand with this unfulfilling lover, she describes the situation as follows:

> Mientras contemplaba a mi lado el cuerpo dormido de aquel muchacho rubio, tan tiernecito por otra parte, me preguntaba cómo puedo ser tan tonta para a mis veinticinco años no tener todavía claro aquello de que "quien con niños se acuesta ..." Por eso, mientras bostezaba y empezaba a imaginar los modos y maneras que me permitirían salir de aquella cama, sin tener que volver a repetir el largo y lamentable *toma y daca* de aquella noche, añoraba que la cosa se pusiera movidita, y lo de movidita no iba en el sentido que el lector puede estar presintiendo. (9; italics in original)

> While I looked at the sleeping body of that blonde boy next to me, who looked so tender after all, I wondered how I could be so foolish, for I was twenty-five and I still haven't learned that "if you sleep with boys ..." That's why, while I yawned and began to imagine what I'd have to do to get out of that bed, without having to repeat the long and regretful *give-and-take* of last night, I longed for things to get moving, but moving in a different way from what the reader might sense.

Reading it only as an imitation of male models, Spires incorrectly suggests that this beginning sequence "could be taken out of a Vázquez Montalbán or any other macho detective novel" (204). This passage, according to Spires, sets the stage for a female sleuth who will play at being a male detective, even by engaging in "casual sexual encounters" (204). Patricia Hart and James Mandrell also misread this scene by highlighting that it repeats misogynistic patterns instead of showcasing a truly liberated woman (Hart 173; Mandrell 67–8). Again, these are oversimplifications of Bárbara's characterization that do not take into account the parodic inversions of the male forms of the genre. The reader is supposed to be reminded of the *machismo* in the male detective novels, and juxtapose it to this sex scene where the man's sexual performance is lackluster at best.

Diverging from critics' traditional reading of the opening scene as a mere copy of male detective fiction, I agree with Maggin's interpretation of the episode as "an interesting reversal of macho *donjuanismo*" that functions like a critique of Iberian *machismo* and highlights "a profound sexual frustration on the part of Spanish women" (47, 48; italics in original). Compared with the erotic scenes that we find in the Carvalho series where the detective flaunts his sexual prowess, Ortiz creates a reversal of this by having *Picadura mortal* open with the comical aftermath of a disappointing passionate encounter. Although at first glance this scene might imitate one found in a male detective novel, instead we wake up with our detective the morning after her unsatisfactory one-night stand contemplating her young blonde lover, and witness how she tries to avoid an encore of the night before. Additionally, in her first-person narration Bárbara plays with the reader's expectations of this scene by informing her audience that though she wants things to get moving, it is not in the way that the reader suspects. The narrative not only pokes fun at the sex scenes that we would traditionally find in the hard-boiled male detective novel, but also at the reader's voyeuristic expectations of the genre to watch this unfold.

Instead Bárbara searches for a way to put an end to the young blonde's continued advances when the phone call that she receives from her boss, Juan Carlos, provides the perfect excuse to put an end to the amorous encounter that he wants to reinitiate:

> [L]a mano buscadora del niñito prometía juegos y lindezas, que llevaban a un punto al que no me apetecía volver, así que con muestras de fastidio infinito por llamada que iba a cortar "el más excelso momento de amor jamás vivido" – nunca hay que ser demasiado dura para no desalentar al partenaire, que en otros casos y quizá con otra puede llegar a mejores resultados – , me levanté de la cama, me disculpé y con tono de lástima dije aquello de que una "desgraciadamente siempre está en acto de servicio." (10)

> The young man's seeking hand promised me games and niceties that led down a familiar path I had no desire to revisit, so showing signs of infinite annoyance for a call that was going to cut short "the most sublime moment of love ever experienced" – you should never be too hard on your partner so as to not discourage him, who in other situations and perhaps with someone else might achieve better results – , I got out of bed, apologized, and with a pitiful tone I said that "one unfortunately is always on call."

Bárbara accepts the case that Juan Carlos assigns her not only so she can put an end to the encounter with the young blonde, but also to not hurt his fragile ego too severely. The disappointing love scene ends with Bárbara giving him a kiss and sending him out the door (11). Moreover, the "rubito," the blonde she has been describing, holds one final disappointment when we learn that he is so concerned with his image that his hairstyle takes hours to perfect (11). Ortiz reverses and thwarts our expectations of this sexual encounter by taking an episode meant to produce narrative pleasure to one that is frustrating for the female detective, but comical for the reader.

What critics like Maginn, McGovern, Hart, and Spires fail to pinpoint is that the opening scene of the novel demonstrates that the dynamics of the gaze in crime fiction have changed. Using the first person, the narrative immediately hands over the "right to look" to the female protagonist, who inverts the male gaze that we traditionally encounter in the genre. According to Priscilla Walton and Manina Jones, detective novels with women protagonists, "by self-consciously reversing the male gaze of character, author, and reader, stage alternative practices of spectatorship, and significantly, produce corresponding theories of agency. Because of the conventional gendered power dynamic of the gaze, the appropriation of the narrative 'I' of the private eye novel by women is always an ideologically loaded move" (159). This is underscored in *Picadura mortal*'s introductory scene. Commanding the gaze, Bárbara asserts her control first by examining her lover's body, describing him as "tiernecito" and referring to him as a "niñito," and then by rejecting his foreplay that morning, effectively emasculating the young man. Yet, even after denying him, Bárbara feels pleasure in gazing at his body while he prepares to leave: "[C]ontemplaba con una cierta nostalgia el donaire del joven que, en calzoncillos, volvía a recuperar su apostura y su prometedor talante" ("With a certain nostalgia, I stared at the grace of the young man who, in his underwear, regained his good looks and his promising disposition") (10). The female detective, now the primary spectator, controls the viewing and the reading of the body, the narrative power once held by the male sleuth. What this allows for is to "place the power dynamics of the gaze itself under surveillance" and to "use the reflexive possibilities of the 'I' narration either explicitly or implicitly to subject the gaze to investigation and reformulation" (Walton and Jones 159). Parodying the male variation of the genre during this opening scene and throughout the various gazing episodes that occur in *Picadura mortal*, Ortiz places the look under surveillance, and problematizes the performance of these gazing scenes.

Picadura mortal is a novel preoccupied with sight, with the power of the look, and thus, this poses an additional challenge for Bárbara, who must defy the male gaze that seeks to convert her into its object from the moment that she sets foot on the Canary Islands. When she first arrives at the Las Palmas airport, she is greeted by Ernesto Granados's eldest son, Adolfo, who, while surprised she is a woman, rewards her with a smile because he finds her attractive: "Me tasó con los ojos, demorándose quizá excesivamente en mis caderas – una sabe cuál es su punto fuerte" ("He sized me up with his eyes, maybe lingering excessively on my hips – a woman knows what her best physical assets are") (13). Taking the objectifying look a step further, his brother, Roberto, endeavours to visually undress her when he meets her at the Granados mansion, and so the narrative pauses to underline how he stares at her: "[T]enía unos ojillos húmedos y lacrimosos, ojillos brillantes de esos que la desnudan a una" ("He had small, moist, tearful eyes, bright little eyes of the type that can strip a girl naked") (14). From this initial meeting, she gathers that "aquel gordito podía saltarme encima en cualquier momento; en muy pocas palabras me transmitió su nada grata opinión acerca de las mujeres" ("that chubby man could jump on me at any moment; in short he conveyed to me his not-at-all positive opinion about women") (15). Bárbara's assumption proves correct because Roberto later attempts to fondle her, and since she denies his advances, he then tries to pay her for sex (71). Insulted that he would treat her like a low-class prostitute, she hits him in the back of the neck, and kicks him once he is on the ground, explaining that although the detective profession may have its setbacks, misogynistic comments and behaviour should not be tolerated (71). For this reason, she resorts to violence to thwart Roberto's unwelcomed advances and insulting proposition.

In later episodes, however, Bárbara will confront the male gaze more directly from the beginning, and her defiance signifies returning and undoing the male look like in her exchange with Guillermo, Roberto's son-in law and a major heroin supplier in the Canary Islands: "Tardó en contestarme y se dedicó a observarme con detenimiento. Yo le correspondía de la misma manera: era un joven larguirucho y desproporcionado con la nariz ligeramente torcida y una prominente mandíbula cuadrada" ("It took him a while to answer me and he was focused on watching me closely. I corresponded in the same way: he was a lanky and oddly proportioned young man with a slightly crooked nose and a prominent square jaw") (75). By reversing Guillermo's stare in this instance, Bárbara repossesses the agency of the gaze, and in doing so, she solidifies her authoritative position while converting him into the object of her eye. During her narrative of investigation, Bárbara becomes more adept at overturning the objectifying male gaze and using it against itself, a technique employed by Federico Mediante's female detective and women delinquents and Manuel de Pedrolo's femme fatale.

For example, held captive by one of Guillermo's henchmen later in the text, she uses her attractiveness to seduce him so that she can get a hold of his gun. In her rendition of the scene, Bárbara emphasizes the exchange of looks that takes place between them, and how she lures him into her trap:

> Me miró con cara de vacile y luego se acercó despacio como si intentara calcular qué trampa le estaba tendiendo.
>
> Le miré con esa coquetería que quiere decir: "Me muero por tus huesos." Es inverosímil, pero los hombres en general están siempre dispuestos a creerse cosas de ese tipo ... en cuanto estuvo con las manos en el cierre intentó acercarse más; una todavía confía en sus encantos. Creo que intentaba besarme en el cuello cuando me eché hacia atrás con fuerza dándole una terrible culada; no había calculado mal e inmediatamente se dobló hacia delante. (89)

> He looked at me with a hesitant face and then approached me slowly as if he were trying to figure out what kind of trap I was setting for him.
>
> I looked at him suggestively, insinuating: "I want your body." It's unbelievable, but men in general are always willing to believe things like that ... as soon as he had his hands on my zipper he tried to get closer; I still trust in my ability to seduce. I think he was trying to kiss me on the neck when I pushed back hard, aiming right for the groin; I hadn't miscalculated and immediately he doubled over in pain.

Using his gaze against him, she ensnares him with her suggestive glance, and in this way, is able to get away from her captor. Walton and Jones claim that for the readers of female crime fiction it is empowering to witness a woman defeat those that threaten her because it represents women being able to overcome the patriarchal forces that endanger them (176–7). What is more, a woman who employs her physicality to defend herself against her attackers subverts the notion of the hero and the heroic in the genre because according to Dilley, "[p]art of what appears to be an unwritten rule for traditional women characters is that while they can be abducted and locked up by criminals, they are safe from 'vulgar' physical assaults such as kicks, punches, and blows to the head. They are allowed the role of the nurturing heroine, but the role of hero is usually reserved for men and their adventures" (142). This, however, is not the case in *Picadura mortal*. Barbara enacts her revenge, and symbolically regains control over her body while breaking with the role of the nurturing heroine and becoming heroic by subduing the same man that had previously threatened her with a knife to her back. Bárbara's gaze and body are her weapons in this instance, weapons that are activated when she finds herself vulnerable.

Alicia Giralt establishes that Bárbara breaks with the traditional female stereotypes of the time because she also enjoys a sexual freedom that is traditionally associated with men and male detectives in the genre (96). The aforementioned introductory scene is one of two amorous encounters that take place in the novel, neither of which the reader is privy to unlike the sex scenes in the Carvalho series and other male crime fiction that are more graphically detailed for the reader. In this second episode, her sexual encounter is with Chema, a friend of the teenager María Granados, who provides her with some information regarding the case. Bárbara describes the episode using the following tone and language:

> La hierba me pone romántica, aquel muchacho tenía un no sé qué y, de vez en cuando, se puede echar una canita al aire: ... Fuimos hacia la playa y cuando todo acabó me sentí bien. Realmente Chema era un buen chico y su aire de experto no era una fachada; se había portado y esas cosas siempre le dejan a una en plan dulce. Creo que a él tampoco le pareció del todo mal. (129)

> Weed makes me romantic. There was something about that boy and, from time to time, you can have a little fling: ... We went to the beach and when everything was over, I felt good. Chema was really a good guy, and the impression of experience he gave off was not a façade: he went above and beyond and when that happens it always makes me all sentimental. I think he thought it wasn't too bad either.

What is noteworthy about this episode is Bárbara's use of a masculine vocabulary to depict the encounter by employing phrases such as "canitas al aire," according to Giralt (96). In this instance, Bárbara not only imitates the masculine detective language, but "imita también el contenido semántico. Esto es especialmente obvio cuando se trata de discutir sobre otras mujeres" ("also imitates the semantic content. This is especially obvious when it comes to discussing other women") (97). The example Giralt utilizes to illustrate this point is Bárbara's portrayal of Adela, Ernesto Granados's daughter-in-law, where the narrative highlights the following: "Era mayor, pero todavía era hermosa, aunque vestía un camisero sencillo y estaba sin pintar. Podría tener cuarenta y cinco años; era una mujer delgada, señora de su casa y madre de familia, pero de esas madres de familia que reconfortan al que llegan" ("She was older, but still beautiful, although she was wearing a simple, long shirt and didn't have makeup on. She could have been around forty-five years old; she was a thin woman, the lady of her house and a mother, but one of those mothers who comfort whomever comes in") (63). Giralt interprets this portrayal as one that demonstrates how the female sleuth has adopted phallocentric prejudices because "[t]eniendo en consideración que Adela tiene unos treinta años, es difícil creer que una mujer emancipada del patriarcado la calificaría de 'mayor.' La palabra 'todavía' es aún más relevante, ya que es el patriarcado el que yuxtapone belleza a juventud" ("considering that Adela is about thirty years old, it is difficult to believe that a woman emancipated from the patriarchy would qualify her as 'old.' The word 'still' is even more relevant, since it is the patriarchy that links beauty and youth") (97). Although there might be some truth to this argument, despite the fact that Giralt miscalculates Adela's age, I consider that Giralt's reading of this scene is not particularly convincing. Bárbara's limited encounters with Adela suggest that she reads her as another woman in the Granados household who is taking on a role. Whereas her sisters-in-law, Margarita and Rosario, employ their seductiveness to enhance their performances, Adela embraces a more maternal role in the house, and draws attention to herself as the suffering mother and wife because everyone suspects that her husband Roberto is having an affair with Rosario. A better illustration for Giralt's argument would have been the encounter between Bárbara and Rosario, where Bárbara even reimagines Rosario in pornographic attire as discussed later on. Regardless of the example used to prove her argument, Giralt overlooks that Bárbara's adoption of the male perspective on the female body is a parody of the gazing scene in male detective novels. The novel's opening sequence accentuates that with its inversion of the look readers are supposed to recognize these male models and see through the imitation to detect the performance of the gaze that is taking place.

Prior to her meeting with Rosario, Bárbara will first encounter Margarita, Ernesto Granados's much younger wife, who according to our sleuth conserves her seductive yet innocent schoolgirl aspect in spite of her husband's disappearance: "La dolorida esposa resultó ser una rubia con aires de colegiala, pasada por revista francesa de modas, ... Un bombón, que sabía llevar su posible viudez con serenidad casi olímpica" ("The suffering wife turned out to be a blonde with the appearance of a schoolgirl, like the ones in French fashion magazines, ... She was a hot little number who knew how to bear her possible widowhood with almost striking serenity") (14). Seeming angelical in front of the rest of the Granados family, once the two of them are left alone, Bárbara also describes her as "dicharachera y atrevida" ("chatty and daring") (15). In fact, she holds a great surprise for Bárbara and the rest of the family, since we come to find out that she marries Ernesto Granados as part of Carlos Granados's plan to take over the estate. Carlos Granados, Ernesto's youngest son who was banished by his father for using the family business to traffic drugs, seduces and employs Margarita to gain reentry into the family fortune. This initial characterization of Margarita – a woman who plays the part of the angelical stepmother by dressing like a young girl – continues throughout the novel until the death of her counterpart, the more seductive and womanly Rosario. Once the narrative eliminates Rosario due to her apparent heroin overdose, Bárbara notes a change in Margarita because she dresses in more grownup attire and applies makeup: "Se había cambiado de vestido ... y el cansancio la favorecía. Se había dado un rouge muy suave que acentuaba las ojeras y había pintado con kool los párpados, resaltando el azul lánguido de sus ojos semibrillantes. Hermosísima y muy creíble" ("She had changed her dress ... and fatigue favoured her. She had applied a very soft rouge that emphasized the dark circles under her eyes and wore eyeshadow, highlighting the languid blue of her half-bright eyes. She was beautiful and very believable"); however, we later learn that those bags under her eyes are due to having spent the night with her lover Carlos (152). Margarita's initial depiction as an angelic beauty sets the stage for the narrative's sketch of Rosario, the more womanly and mischievous-looking *comehombres* (*"man-eater"*).

Before her encounter with Rosario, Bárbara is told by Margarita that she is a sickly woman, though we later learn she is more of a hypochondriac, with a heroin addiction. The relationship between Margarita and Rosario is complicated by the fact that Rosario's husband, Adolfo, is attracted to and has formed some sort of alliance with Margarita whereas Rosario appears to be having an affair with Roberto, Adolfo's brother and Adela's husband. From the start of her stay at the Granados's house, Bárbara understands that the women of the family are clearly at odds with one another, but with an even greater amount of vitriol directed at Rosario in particular. Still, Bárbara acknowledges the control that this woman has over the rest of the household because "la presencia de Rosario llenaba la casa como ausencia que tenía un peso" ("Rosario's presence filled the house like a heavy absence") (25). Passing by her room during her first day at the Granados's mansion, Bárbara hears Rosario's whimpers and sighs, and already, there is an attraction to the mysterious woman behind those doors. Filmic in nature, the moment that the two women meet provides us with this narrative picture:

> Estaba de pie, en medio del cuarto y, evidentemente, se había preparado para recibirme. Nuevo choque. La imagen física de la Rosario que tenía delante no era la de la debilidad. Era una mujer de unos treinta y tantos años, bastante hermosa. Llevaba el pelo recogido en un moño tirante, moño dificilísimo, a lo Cleo de Merode o a lo Romero de Torres. Era alta, y el quimono con que se cubría, un estrambótico quimono de seda verde, se plegaba dejando entrever un cuerpo joven. Si se colocara junto a Margarita uno, sin vacilar, hubiera situado a Rosario en el lugar de la mala perversa, la come-hombres de la literatura y el cine ... Parecía un gato dispuesto a saltar y la boquilla que sostenía entre los dedos, así como la decoración de su cuarto, revelaba un gusto decadente que hacía pensar en las *garçonnières* de principios de siglo. Una especie de Mata-Hari de las islas. (25–6; italics in original)

> She was standing in the middle of the room and, evidently, she was ready for my visit. A new shock. The physical image of Rosario that I had before me was not that of a weak person. She was a woman in her mid-thirties, quite beautiful. Her hair was tied in a tight bun, a very complicated bun, similar to the ones of Cleo de Merode or Romero de Torres. She was tall, and the kimono that covered her, an eccentric green silk kimono, worn open, revealing a young body. If she were positioned next to Margarita, anyone, without hesitation, would have placed Rosario in the role of the perverse, bad woman, the man-eater of literature and cinema ... She looked like a cat ready to pounce and the cigarette that she held between her fingers, as well as the decoration of the room, revealed a decadent taste that led me to think of the *garçonnières* of the beginning of the century. A kind of Mata-Hari of the islands.

Using Rosario's hairdo as the point of comparison, the narrative invokes the French dancer of the Belle Époque, Cleo de Merode, and the female portraits of the Spanish painter Julio Romero de Torres to accentuate her dark seductiveness. This scene allows for a textual pause to eroticize Rosario and to seduce the spectator both within (Bárbara) and outside the text (the reader) by adding details like the opening in her kimono that highlights her young body and by comparing her to a cat ready to attack. Unlike the depiction of Margarita, here the narrative sexualizes the character of Rosario in a *crescendo* movement, enticing the reader first with intertextual references, then reminding us of the *comehombres* character in film and literature, and ending with the reference to the erotic dancer and courtesan, Mata Hari, the epitome of what it means to be a femme fatale. In this homoerotic seduction scene, Bárbara slowly falls under Rosario's spell, and the reframing allows for an exploration of non-heteronormative gazing pleasures.

By comparing Rosario to Mata Hari, we are reminded of the performer-turned-courtesan, who was accused, tried, and executed for treason. Arriving in Paris after divorcing the father of her two children in 1904, Mata Hari, the stage name for the Dutch-born Margaretha Geertruida Zelle, "began her dancing career ... already a *femme fatale,* as a woman whose sexuality was not confined to marriage and as a divorcee who did not fulfill the maternal ideal," according to Rosie White (75; italics in original). Employing her knowledge of the East Indies that she acquired during her stays in Sumatra and Java to enhance her performative persona, Mata Hari drew on the public's enthrallment with the orient and fascination with figures like Salomé, who would also inspire dancers like Maud Allan, who were quite popular at the time (Sully 51–3). Jess Sully has previously suggested that orientalized dancers like Mata Hari and Maud Allan become a sort of bridge between the femme fatale that appeared in late nineteenth-century artwork and the femme fatale of early 1920s films before she was reborn in the film noir of the 1940s and 1950s (52–3). Once past her prime as a dancer but still using the political contacts that she had obtained, Mata Hari would transform herself first into a courtesan and later, due to economic necessity, into what many consider an unsuccessful "spy," since she sold information to her military and diplomatic contacts (White 78). Charged with treason by the French authorities, she was executed "not for her great success as a master spy but because she was a symbol of the contagion of decadence and treason that seemed to be undermining France, especially in 1917" (Proctor 126).

White clarifies that Mata Hari should be thought of as a representative of "the changing roles of women in modern Europe" (72) because she "had come to represent the most feared and desired aspects of modernity in the person of the modern woman, and for this reason she was executed" (74). What is emphasized here is Mata Hari's subversive relationship to space, her ability to infiltrate different social and public spheres that were normally out of reach for ordinary women. For this reason, "[h]er trial was an attempt to fix that mobility within the regime of French sexual and imperial relations. It was thus not important what Mata Hari had actually done, but rather what she *represented*," according to White (74; italics in original). In addition to underlining Mata Hari's mobility, Pat Shipman characterizes her as "a shape-shifter" because she was also able to shift her image, to switch to a different persona when needed (142). Her image, first as an exotic dancer and later as a courtesan, a persona that she was able to control at first, works against her when she is accused of disclosing information. Put differently, her leaked image, a leaking that she was responsible for, explains her execution by the French government. White's study of Mata Hari further emphasizes how her performances and persona promoted a dangerous femininity that could not be relegated to the private sphere:

> Her final audience, the prosecution at her trial in Paris in July 1917, imagined her as the threat of unconfined femininity – worse, a woman who allegedly engaged in the masculine sphere of international intelligence. In these terms Mata Hari offers a transgender, transracial account of modernity, slipping between masculine and feminine, public and private, self and other, Occident and Orient. (75)

In thinking about Mata Hari's "otherness," we are also reminded of Helen Hanson and Catherine O'Rawe's suggestion that the problem with the femme fatale is that there is a "slippage" in how she is understood, which is made clear when we think of how Mata Hari has been traditionally represented (4). This slippage, according to Hanson and O'Rawe, has to do with women's connection to the public space, and hence, the boundaries that come to be blurred between the categories of *flâneuse* or street walker, actress, courtesan, and prostitute in traditional interpretations of femmes fatales (4; Doane 263). What makes her threatening and even deadly, I would underscore, is directly linked to her claims to space. If we recall, the image of the femme fatale (re)emerges or is revamped when "woman's revised relation to space" occurs in the nineteenth century, as Mary Ann Doane has signalled (263). Since female power and influence extend beyond the domestic sphere, this dangerous and mobile woman must be punished for her spatial transgressions that likewise rely on her employment of her sexuality.

Ortiz's use of Mata Hari in the formulation of her femme fatale, Rosario, plays with the slippage or the leaks of this figure, and serves to caricature the femme fatale in this episode with Bárbara. And yet there is also an indication that the novel is conscious of its investigation of gender roles and women's relation to space, which is made evident with the matriarchy that now predominates after Ernesto Granados's disappearance. The wealthy industrialist's disappearance opens a space for someone in the family to reclaim political and financial control, not only over the household, but also, the narrative implies, over the Granados's financial empire in the Canary Islands. This vacuum of power causes the three women – Margarita, Adela, and Rosario – to be at odds with one another, made evident during their exchanges with Bárbara. Indeed, all three women try to form an alliance with Bárbara to shift the power struggle in their favour. The scene between Rosario and Bárbara, however, complicates this because the female detective seemingly falls into the trap that the femme fatale has prepared for her in an attempt to seduce her:

> Relamía el vaso y me miraba con aquellos ojos de gata alerta. Sonrió y su sonrisa era como todo el marco: de *bibelot* de vitrina erotica ...
>
> Fue como un relámpago, pero de pronto pude imaginarla de pie con grandes botas negras y el látigo en la mano: foto o cromo de revista porno, lleno de sugerencias; a sus pies podía ver al gordinflón, resoplando. Idílica imagen. (28–9; italics in original)

> She licked the glass and looked at me with those watchful cat eyes. She smiled and her smile just about filled the room: she was a *trinket* in an erotic display ...
>
> It was like a bolt of lightning. Suddenly I could imagine her standing, wearing high-heeled black boots and holding a whip in her hand: like a very suggestive photo or illustration from a porno mag; at her feet I could see the chubby man, panting. A delightful image.

The passage refers to its own staging of the female character, admitting how Rosario is displayed to be gazed at. Indeed, Rosario's eroticization reaches its highest point when Bárbara pictures her as a dominatrix with her brother-in-law, Roberto Granados, at her feet. Ortiz has taken the narrative pause that we find in male-centred crime fiction when a female character appears on the scene and exaggerates it to the point of making it pornographic, drawing attention to the text's amplified parody of this episode. For Maginn, *Picadura mortal*'s use of "textual self-referentiality ... shows that both Ortiz and her character Bárbara Arenas are conscious of being in a deformed or parodied detective novel" (53). It should be noted that textual self-referentiality is present in most works of the genre since its origins. In the first novel featuring Sherlock Holmes, *A Study in Scarlet*, for instance, Holmes favourably compares himself to Edgar Allen Poe's C. Auguste Dupin. Ortiz, however, employs self-referentiality differently in *Picadura mortal* because she effectively demystifies a scene that we find in traditional crime fiction by vulgarizing it, deforming it to the extent that it becomes a caricature of the semi-pornographic encounters in Manuel Vázquez Montalbán's Pepe Carvalho series and other male-dominated *novelas negras*.

To emphasize this point, the same pornographic image of Rosario is repeated later on in the text: "Por un momento volví a imaginarme a Rosario con látigo y botas altas y a Roberto jugando a perrito faldero, perrito indómito" ("For a moment I again imagined Rosario with a whip and high-heeled boots and Roberto playing the lapdog, an untrained little dog") (98). Again, Rosario appears as the dominatrix with a subdued and animalized Roberto, visualized as a small lapdog at her side. Clearly, this image emphasizes the sort of control that Bárbara imagines that this woman possesses not only over Roberto, but also over the Granados estate. Rosario is seductive because she is beautiful and appealing, but more significantly, due to her domination over men, which Bárbara interprets by picturing Rosario with a whip in her hand. Although Maginn's claims of textual self-consciousness refer to the novel in its entirety, her statement that "it is, rather, a perverse copy, which deforms and ridicules the more staid conventions of that genre" (54) holds true in this gazing and staging scene of the female body. Ortiz's imitation of male models in the way that she describes female characters is meant both to parody, and as Patricia Johnson asserts more broadly about female crime fiction, to "decenter some of the archetypes, male and female, that the form has constantly structured itself around" (98). James Mandrell's reading of *Picadura mortal*, on the other hand, suggests that scenes like this are dangerous in that they can be interpreted "as evidence of an internalized performance of that misogyny which ends up recapitulating and actually confirming many of the negative gendered aspects of the genre of detective fiction" (67). While it is true that these performances underscore the misogynistic character of traditional male crime fiction, a simultaneous inversion also occurs, beginning with the fact that the looks exchanged are between two women. This scene does two things – it inverts the traditional episode, but also plays with different spectatorship scenarios because Rosario then takes over and controls the stare directed at Bárbara's body. By decentring these archetypes through parodic inversion, the heteronormative gazing episode in traditional male crime fiction is rejected, and replaced with an alternative exchange of looks between the two women.

The gazing scene is further complicated because the once-spectator, Bárbara, now becomes the object of Rosario's gaze:

> Me miró de arriba a abajo y automáticamente mi lado competitivo femenino se sintió defraudado por no haberme preparado suficientemente para la primera entrevista. Mis tejanos y mi blusita blanca, con el pañuelo de batista en torno al cuello, resultaban provincianos frente a aquel despliegue de *fumoir* y aquel olor a sándalo en la alcoba. (26; italics in original)

> She looked me up and down and automatically my competitive feminine side kicked in, and I felt disappointed that I hadn't prepared enough for the first interview. My jeans and my little white blouse, with that cambric handkerchief around my neck, were provincial when confronted with that display of *fumoir* and the smell of sandalwood in the bedroom.

This episode acts out different scenarios of looking – inverting the subject and object roles to further disrupt the traditional gazing scene in crime fiction, which is usually one-sided, with the male detective eyeing the female body. By reversing the gaze, Rosario takes control of the encounter, which Bárbara quickly recognizes: "Estaba aceptando su reto y de algún modo estaba perdiendo la calma. Tenía que reconocer que hasta entonces ella conservaba el control" ("I had accepted her challenge and somehow I was losing my cool. I had to admit that she was still the one in control") (29–30). In a second instance of studying Bárbara, Rosario vocalizes her thoughts on the female sleuth to her: "Tiene gracia: ancha de caderas, pechos pequeños pero bien colocados, desenvoltura de lengua y encima regeneracionista. ¿Qué otros papeles juega?" ("You have such grace: wide hips, small but well-placed breasts, a smooth talker, and a regenerationist besides. What other roles do you play?") (29). As Adolfo and Roberto have done before her, Rosario objectifies Bárbara during this episode, describing her in piecemeal fashion by homing in on her breasts and hips, similar to what the female detective has done to her. What this accomplishes is that Rosario momentarily strips the detective of her authority. While the men of the novel attempt to usurp Bárbara's authority with their misogynistic comments, Rosario uses seduction and a reversal of the investigator's gaze to overpower her.

The seduction scene, however, also serves to demystify the image of the hard-boiled detective as an unfazed, confident sleuth by identifying her insecurities. Both Hart and Maginn have previously demonstrated that Bárbara's insecurities have less to do with her profession and are almost always based on feeling inadequately dressed or sensing that she is not the centre of male attention, according to her confession in a later episode: "[E]n este asunto había demasiadas mujeres y el papel de primera fila que siempre me gustaba jugar estaba muy disputado. Tenía que prescindir de rabietas y competitividades para empezar a ver claro" ("In this matter there were too many women and the role of leading lady that I always liked to play was very much up for grabs. I had to forget about tantrums and competitiveness and begin seeing things clearly") (57). Bárbara's complaint about feeling inferior to Rosario, especially in the way that she is dressed, is one that is repeated throughout the novel, highlighting this particular concern. Upon entering Rosario's room, she feels her control dissipating almost immediately, and she is forced to reestablish her authority to counteract the insecurities that the femme fatale produces in her (26–7). Bárbara even compares herself to a troubadour who is there to entertain the mysterious woman who now reigns over her: "La princesa raptada llamaba al trovador para que la pusiera al corriente de aconteceres mundanos, mientras ella languidecía en el sofá. Magnífico, pero mi espíritu trovadoresco estaba de capa caída y tenía muchas cosas que hacer" ("The kidnapped princess summoned the troubadour to bring her up to speed on worldly events, while she languished on the sofa. Magnificent, but my troubadour spirit was crestfallen and I had many things to do") (28). Therein lies the threat of the femme fatale because she rules by combining masculine domination with feminine attractiveness and seduction, manipulating "the element of gender ambiguity" (Sully 57). Power and beauty come together in the figure of the femme fatale, which like her mobility endangers and threatens because she is fluid and not fixed, meaning that she also transits between the masculine and the feminine. The brief exchanges between Rosario and Bárbara accentuate this aspect of the archetype because Rosario is able to level the playing field between the two women, even criticizing the sleuth by saying that she is not a master of subtlety. The first-person narrative concedes a temporary victory to Rosario in this scene because Bárbara recognizes that the one in control is the temptress while she remains in an inferior position and must find a way to reassert herself.

More significantly, the encounter between the two women lays bare the formula employed by the hard-boiled male detective novels for these gazing and seduction episodes. As Walton and Jones have previously proposed, "The hard-boiled convention that allows descriptions of sexual encounters is adapted to accommodate the representation of lesbian eroticism. It is also used to provoke a self-consciousness about the power dynamics of the heterosexual erotic look" (163). In the scene between Rosario and Bárbara, the power dynamics of the look itself come under examination because each woman takes control of the encounter when she is the one studying the other. Although the episode replicates the tension and the seduction game of the male form of the genre, it subtracts the sexual component that traditionally follows, thus toying with the reader's possible expectations and highlighting the sexism of the male gazing scene, one in which we have come to expect seeing the naked female body come into view for our narrative pleasure.

Lastly, the seduction scene finally juxtaposes the two women, the two sides of the female archetype that the narrative has come to caricature – the angel of the house, Margarita, versus the temptress, Rosario – by exaggerating their portrayals. In thinking about Adolfo's relationship with the two women, Bárbara reveals that "[p]ensé que Adolfo debía vivir aquel aire mundano como cárcel y suspiraba por la refrescante Margarita, como contraste con la 'Mujer' que guardaba en aquel santuario" ("I thought that Adolfo must have experienced that worldly air like a prison and that he must have longed for the revivifying Margarita, instead of the 'Woman' he kept in that sanctuary") (26). Not only does the good girl versus the female seductress come under scrutiny, but also the spaces that these two women inhabit and what they represent – one is refreshing and lively while the other is stifling and decadent. This decadence, mixed with a certain erotic spiritualism, is part of Rosario's enigma as a type of femme fatale. Put differently, there is already a certain fatality that characterizes Rosario, and the space that she inhabits, the smells that emanate from her room, suggest this from the beginning. This woman with a capital W is relegated to a certain space within the house, confined to control and limit her, and yet, her rule over the household is undeniable.

Recalling Munt's idea on how female stereotypes can be used satirically against themselves in women's crime fiction, when the narrative brings Bárbara, Margarita, and Rosario together in a dinner scene, the exaggeration of their roles caricatures them. In its ridiculing of Margarita and Rosario, the narrative pokes holes in its own depiction of the two women, as McGovern has previously underlined. The following contrasts are drawn out during the dinner scene:

> Rosario había descendido y se había vestido para la comida como si de princesa oriental en gira por el mundo se tratara ... No entendía por qué, pero el despliegue ornamental de Rosario conseguía ponerme nerviosa y en condiciones de inferioridad; lo último que estaba necesitando.
>
> Margarita tampoco estaba mal: su estilo de niñita grande, resaltaba ante la nuera. Sus volantes y puntillas, sacadas del *Marie Claire* de turno, volvían ridículo el traje rojo, hindú de la hijastra crecidita. (58; italics in original)

> Rosario had gone downstairs and had dressed for the meal as if she were an oriental princess on a tour of the world ... I didn't understand why, but Rosario's ornamental display made me feel nervous and inferior; the last thing I needed.
>
> Margarita wasn't bad either: her teenage style made her stand out from her daughter-in-law. Her ruffles and lace trims, taken from the latest issue of *Marie Claire*, made the stepdaughter's red, Indian dress seem ridiculous.

Although the two Granados women represent the more traditional female roles that we are used to encountering in crime fiction whereas Adela will later represent the faithful wife and mother, Bárbara fails to fit either stereotype even though she employs her physical attractiveness and her powers of seduction to obtain information pertinent to the case and to get out of potentially dangerous situations. In her study of crime fiction's female characters, Dilley suggests that "[t]he woman investigator does not succeed because she looks and acts like a man. She neither scorns masculine society – becoming 'ultra-feminine' – nor adopts it as her own – becoming an 'honorary male'" (138). Instead, female detectives reveal "the struggles of many women in trying to make a place in a society predicated on a particular set of gender assumptions. They do not preach feminism; they just try to live it" (138–9). Dilley's characterization of the female sleuth corresponds with how Bárbara conducts herself throughout the novel because she disrupts the traditional good/bad woman binary by not fitting into either category. Still, Bárbara finds herself competing against both Margarita and Rosario, who make her feel not only inadequate but like an outsider.

Using Dilley's analysis of the female hero of women's detective novels, I propose that *Picadura mortal* exposes gender stereotypes while trying out new narrative functions for women in the genre. For this reason, Bárbara remains on the side of the spectator. She is on the outside looking in at the two stereotypes that by the end of the novel will come undone when she realizes that Margarita has been manipulating the family all along to gain control of their fortune and that Rosario's bad girl image is a façade that she employs to conceal her heroin addiction. Ortiz inverts the conventions of the male form of the genre not only by parodying women's traditional roles in hard-boiled novels, but also by having her female sleuth transit between masculine and feminine attributes. Bárbara's fluidity between male and female characteristics represents a new type of detective hero, one who utilizes her physicality and aggressiveness in addition to her sexuality, signalling in this way a reevaluation of gender stereotypes for the detective hero in Spanish crime fiction. Consequently, *Picadura mortal* can be read as a detective novel that is interested in investigating gender roles during a time period when women's private and public lives were undergoing a major transition. What is more, the investigation and the resolution of the case are secondary to the subversion of the male models of the genre, and Bárbara's spectator position, the inversion of the male sleuth's gaze, forms part of the female investigator's trajectory to becoming the detective protagonist.

In their analysis of Sharon Short's Patricia Delaney series, Walton and Jones draw attention to how "[t]he trajectory of her [Patricia's] career is an obvious version of the shift (or flip) from object of the male gaze to active subject" (171). What makes Patricia Delaney particularly interesting is that before becoming a detective she worked as a stripper, making the inversion from object of the gaze to subject even more pronounced. Although not to this extreme, the trajectory from object to subject is also stressed in *Picadura mortal*, and proves useful when analyzing the birth and boom of the modern hard-boiled female detective. Because she occupies both positions at different moments, Ortiz's Bárbara demonstrates the oscillation from passive object to active subject that occurs throughout the text as she seeks to solidify her sleuthing authority. With Rosario, for example, she takes on both subject and object roles until the final gazing scene when the sleuth encounters Rosario's dead body:

> Sin demasiadas ceremonias abrí la puerta. Había una atmósfera pesada, casi irreal, y me resultó repelente volver a entrar en aquel santuario. Rosario estaba tendida sobre la cama y su postura me pareció todo menos

> natural. Estaba retorcida en un curioso serpenteo y su cabeza colgaba de uno de los lados de la cama; llevaba el camisón revuelto y uno de los brazos caía junto a la cabeza siguiendo la diagonal que formaba con el resto del cuerpo ...
>
> Me acerqué a ella: todavía estaba caliente; mientras nosotros comíamos abajo, Rosario había muerto en su habitación, sin que nadie, como de costumbre, hubiera reparado en sus grititos. En el suelo estaba la jeringuilla y casi al mismo tiempo pude ver las picaduras que salpicaban su brazo. (116)

> Unceremoniously, I opened the door. The atmosphere was heavy, almost unreal, and the thought of entering the sanctuary again disgusted me. Rosario was lying on the bed and her pose seemed to me anything but natural. She was twisted into a curious shape and her head hung from one side of the bed; her nightgown was dishevelled and one of her arms lay next to her head, following the diagonal line of the rest of her body ...
>
> I approached her: she was still warm; while we ate downstairs, Rosario had died in her room, without anyone paying attention to her muffled cries, as was often the case. The syringe was on the floor and almost at the same time I could see the stings [track marks] that dotted her arm.

The title of the novel is taken from this episode, for the "picaduras" refer to the track marks on Rosario's arms that are evidence of her addiction. This particular dose of heroin, this "picadura mortal," has killed the seductive Rosario, and we are left with the visual aftermath of her overdose, which Bárbara will later confirm as murder. Bárbara discovers that González, Ernesto Granados's right-hand man and administrator, learned about Rosario's affair with Roberto and tried to blackmail her until she decided that she would no longer pay and that she would inform others about his attempts to bribe her. González becomes her heroin supplier to keep her quiet and to continue obtaining money from her (168). Ultimately, the one who decides that she must be killed is Ernesto Granados himself though we never ascertain why. Apparently, Rosario was privy to knowledge about their involvement with Guillermo's heroin trafficking business in the Canary Islands, which could expose both men. This idea that the femme fatale possesses damning information that threatens the patriarchal system reminds us of the reasoning behind Mata Hari's execution. According to White, Mata Hari's threat was connected to the idea that "the female spy as *femme fatale* employs private means to influence public life, thus mobilizing fears about women's domestic power across the board. Mata Hari fitted the stereotype and filled a convenient role as scapegoat" (78; italics in original). Reminiscent of this interpretation of Mata Hari, Rosario is killed because Ernesto Granados suspected that she would betray him and jeopardize the family's socioeconomic influence over the island. Put simply, Rosario was the one woman in the Granados household who was feared.

Following Bárbara's gaze, the narrative first depicts the surreal and repellent atmosphere of Rosario's sanctuary, and, after Bárbara sees Rosario's dead body, then illustrates how she is positioned on the bed in a curious serpent-like position, recalling the femme fatale's association with Eve, temptation, and sin. Different from what Glen Close finds in his study of the eroticization of the female cadaver in the male hard-boiled novel, Rosario's body is not put on display during this episode. And yet, while the dead body is not objectified in this way, Bárbara is finally able to read Rosario. She becomes legible for the female detective because the "picaduras" on her arm are now made visible, but, more crucially, because she can no longer confront and return the detective's stare. Rosario's death contributes to solidifying the subject position for the female detective as the threat of the femme fatale type becomes undone. Similar to the male detective model, the femme fatale must be eliminated to reinforce the sleuth's authority. Ultimately, the power struggle between Bárbara and Rosario ends because the female private eye has the final look.

It is only at the end that Bárbara comes to understand that the whimpers and the seductive aroma surrounding Rosario are all part of her addiction, an addiction that has been used to eliminate her. Part of Rosario's enigma, which contributes to her stereotyping as a femme fatale, is directly linked to her drug use. The aroma of fatality that envelops her from the moment that Bárbara enters her room is eventually associated with the effects of her heroin use. Moreover, this scene recalls what author Sarah Dunant has argued regarding the use of female victims in crime fiction, explaining that "within crime fiction women have been particularly targeted for mutilation and depersonalization" (17). Indeed, Dunant claims that "[t]he corpse itself has a brutal lack of identity. You will notice that very often such corpses have no face. Who they are is not important. It is their body and what has been sexually done to it that is the point" (17). Interestingly enough, the Sedmay edition of the book's cover illustrates this scene – a black and white photograph of a woman representing the dead Rosario.[7] Similar to the type of cover page that one is likely to find on the classic North American hard-boiled novel, the photograph recreates Rosario's dead body, placed precisely on the edge of the bed with her head and left arm dangling towards the floor according to the narrative's description. In the picture, her left hand still holds the syringe, and there is a glass of alcohol and a pack of cigarettes with an ashtray next to it. If you look closely at the left arm, you can even see the track marks, the "picaduras." With no knowledge about the book's plot, a first-time reader could suppose that the main crime has something to do with the overdosed woman on the cover, when the crime that Bárbara is asked to solve involves the disappearance of a man. Although there is nothing particularly erotic or sadistic about the photograph, even before the reader enters into a relationship with the text she is confronted with the image of a female corpse. Ortiz's Bárbara Arenas represents an innovation in the genre and subverts certain masculine norms, and yet, it is the passive image of a female corpse on the cover page that provides the initial frame for reading the first hard-boiled female detective in Spain.

What is also striking about the use of this cover photograph is that Bárbara addresses a female reader at certain points in her narrative, particularly when she is faced with misogynistic situations. Giralt has previously highlighted that Bárbara, as an autodiegetic narrator, is complicit with an implied and ideal female reader who has also been the victim of *machismo* (94). Indeed, the narrative includes the female reader in the misogynistic situations that Bárbara suffers like the one with the Granados's administrator, González. In this moment, the female sleuth explains, "Era de esos que nos odian visceralmente: tipo reprimido, que supura mala leche" ("He was one of those people who hate us viscerally: a repressed guy, someone oozing bad blood") (44). According to Giralt, by using the pronoun "nos" ("us") Bárbara attempts to establish an alliance with her female readers by creating a sense of solidarity when faced with male misogyny (94). Thus, it is this female reader, a potential ally, who is introduced to the novel with the cover picture of a dead woman, which undoes any sense of female solidarity or empowerment. From the start, she is placed in what would appear to be a male-spectator position.

If we recall, the spectator position in cinema is traditionally regarded as masculine because it is active whereas the image understood as body in its passivity is feminine. Addressing the problem that this causes for the female spectator in her addendum to "Visual Pleasure and Narrative Cinema," Laura Mulvey would later suggest in "Afterthoughts" that the female spectator finds herself shifting between a masculine and a feminine position (29). Mulvey compares this female viewer with a woman protagonist in certain melodramatic films that are "shown to be unable to achieve a stable sexual identity, torn between the deep blue sea of passive femininity and the devil of regressive masculinity" ("Afterthoughts" 30). Both accept a temporary masculinization of their position and fluctuate between adopting a male versus a female gaze. And yet, like the female protagonist whose masculine identification is not fully accepted, "[s]o, too, is the female spectator's fantasy of masculinisation at cross-purposes with itself, restless in its transvestite clothes" (37). The problem is spatial, one of proximity, because, as Doane argues, "For the female spectator there is a certain overpresence of the image – she *is* the image" (22; italics in original), and this results in "a tendency to view the female spectator as the site of an oscillation" (24). For this reason, the female spectator's identification with a masculine viewpoint invokes the transvestite metaphor because a masculinization of her position occurs to distance herself from the image (25).

A possible alternative to the female spectator's transvestism would be the masquerade, which in Doane's words, "in flaunting femininity, holds it at a distance" (25). Here, an excess of femininity will produce the distance necessary from the image, and what this accomplishes is that the image can perhaps become legible for the woman viewer. The masquerade "involves a realignment of femininity" because "[t]o masquerade is to manufacture a lack in the form of a certain distance between oneself and one's image" (26). It is a spatial solution to the female spectatorship problem by overfeminizing. The masquerade, consequently, in "destabilizing the image ... confounds this masculine structure of the look" by "disarticulating male systems of viewing" (26). In effect, the masquerade creates a defamiliarization of the image, and it in this space of defamiliarization that the woman spectator can perhaps produce a reading (31–2).

Employing this theoretical framework to analyze *Picadura mortal*, perhaps we can read the mutual gazing and seduction scene between Bárbara and Rosario as one in which a masquerading effect takes place to destabilize the spectator position. Here, the masquerading effect distances Bárbara from Rosario by invoking images of courtesans and *comehombres* figures in addition to picturing Rosario in erotic dominatrix attire. The narrative oversexualizes, perhaps even overfeminizes Rosario, the object of the detective's eye. By oversexualizing the character of Rosario and creating this distance, Bárbara, as the spectator and active looker, feels no sort of identification with the feminine, with the woman she is gazing at. This overtly sexual objectification makes Rosario legible to the female spectator, but the result is that Bárbara is seduced by the erotic images that she projects unto Rosario.

Unmasking its own performativity, the narrative reveals the workings of the gazing performance in the male forms of the genre. *Picadura mortal* draws our attention to how male crime fiction's politics of female visibility, its portrayal of the female body, is complicit in reproducing the sexist patriarchal ideology that Bárbara Arenas and the female detectives born after her must confront and battle against. For this reason, the novel constantly plays with the reader's assumptions and expectations to reveal and revoke them. As Dilley suggests more generally about women's detective novels,

> Murder is a device for focusing attention, but it also signals the breakdown of order in the community. Order must be created out of the chaos. The women are not necessarily looking to restore order in the sense of that which was before. It was because of that "order" that there was a breakdown. The community of the individual mystery novels gives the detective permission to dig into lives and their secrets and to critique what caused the murder in the first place. In the details of the everyday, the detective finds the clues to society's secrets and oppressions (139–40).

Dilley's analysis is relevant here because there is no restoration of the patriarchal order in Ortiz's *Picadura mortal*. Instead, the novel puts forth a commentary that serves as a rejection of an established system that continues to subjugate women. According to Talbot, *Picadura mortal* forces us to problematize what the true crime is because the novel "condemns an entire historical period. The search becomes, at last, a revelation about a regime" (164). Bárbara's discovery of an old photograph leads her down an investigative path that ends up having far greater political implications because it unearths the original crime, since it appears that Ernesto Granados murdered a Republican soldier during the Spanish Civil War to pose as him and in exchange, inherit his land and wealth. In the epilogue, we discover that Bárbara will revisit the Canary Islands to expose Ernesto Granados for the serial murderer that he is, but as Talbot emphasizes, "by not including the final outcome of Bárbara's investigation, Ortiz rejects the patriarchal sense of closure as she rejects the patriarchal regime of Franco" (167). Munt has previously asserted that "[l]esbian and feminist writers interfacing with masculine genres tend to estrange through using parody, which accentuates the reader's sense of superior distance. Parody addresses a highly knowing audience, through the use of style; it is closely connected to pastiche, its sceptical, deflationary intention highlighting the presence of ambiguity in its target" (*Murder* 77). With the female sleuth's eventual return to the Canary Islands, we realize that the parodic inversion that characterizes the novel also has a liberating function in Ortiz's *Picadura mortal* because Bárbara will continue to bring chaos to the Granados's order and consequently will disrupt the family's power over the island.

By reversing the male eye and reappropriating it into what Maginn terms a "deformed parody," Ortiz paves the way for a new politics of visibility in the female crime fiction that will follow because one of the ways that the gendering of crime fiction destabilizes the genre is by exposing its gazing and policing function of the female body. Put differently, parody is the textual practice that reveals in order to transform the function of female visibility in the genre. Again, this reminds us of Dunant's words on the subject when she explains that "the body – especially the female body – has become a cultural battlefield over which men and women are, albeit obliquely, facing and confronting each other in print" (14). By revisiting the role of the femme fatale to create a series of homoerotic seduction scenes, Ortiz challenges the legibility of the female body in traditional male-centred crime literature. The femme fatale type, Rosario, only becomes legible to Bárbara when she is a dead body because Ortiz employs the female corpse to signal the tendency in male crime fiction to overexpose and even erotize women-as-victims. Instead, in *Picadura mortal*, Rosario's dead body becomes evidence of the Granados family's involvement in the heroin trafficking business. The femme fatale, as a marked body, signals the wrongdoing and corruption of the upper echelons of society and testifies to crimes that would otherwise remain invisible. Similarly, in Maria-Antònia Oliver's Lònia Guiu series, discussed in chapter 4, the female body gains visibility when it is mistreated and abused, and becomes the site through which gender violence comes under examination and deliberation. Whereas in male crime fiction it is the fetishizing of the female body that is responsible for its silencing, the containment and silencing of the female body occurs via rape and other forms of sexual assault in the female crime fiction that will follow Ortiz's *Picadura mortal*.[8]

Chapter Four

A New Politics of Visibility in the Lònia Guiu Series

In 1970s Barcelona, a group of writers who collectively called themselves Ofèlia Dracs came together in an effort to experiment with different genres to attract a new generation of readers in Catalan.[1] This group of Catalan writers expressed similar concerns about the social and cultural status of the Catalan language and its literature, but also held a new vision for Catalan popular literature that would prompt its revival ("Catalan Culture" 302). As a result, each short story collection that was published by the group examined a different genre, such as erotica, horror, detective tales, science fiction, and even a cookbook (Cònsul 32).[2] A member of Ofèlia Dracs, Maria-Antònia Oliver experimented for the first time with crime fiction in the 1983 collection titled *Negra i consentida* (*Hardboiled and Spoiled*) with her short story, "On ets, Mònica?" ("Where Are You, Mònica?").

Oliver arrived in Barcelona from her native Majorca in 1969, and formed part of Ofèlia Dracs, alongside her husband Jaume Fuster, also a Catalan author and writer of detective novels.[3] While she is now best known among crime fiction scholars for her Lònia Guiu trilogy, during her forty years as a writer and translator Oliver has published everything from television scripts to children's literature. A recurring theme in her creative endeavours, however, has been women's issues and the socio-ecological upheavals experienced in Majorca during and after the dictatorship, both of which have acquired a special protagonism since she began her literary career in 1968 with the publication of two short stories, "El meló" ("The Melon") and "La drecera" ("The Shortcut"), and in her first novel, *Cròniques d'un mig estiu* (*Chronicles of a Half Summer*), which was published two years later in Barcelona by Club Editor (Cortés and Escandell 11–13).[4] Like others of the literary generation of the 1970s in Barcelona, Oliver's avant-garde and experimental phase came about when she published a series of short stories in the 1980s in conjunction with the other Ofèlia Dracs authors (25–6).

Negra i consentida brought together the different Ofèlia Dracs members' interpretation of the crime genre. While some of the authors had already experimented with the detective genre, others, like Oliver and fellow Majorcan Antoni Serra, wrote their first detective story for this particular collection ("Catalan Culture" 306–7). Oliver's "On ets, Mònica?" features Lònia Guiu, the female sleuth protagonist that reappears in Oliver's detective novel trilogy and that has garnered both domestic and international acclaim. Even though Lourdes Ortiz introduced the first female detective protagonist in Spain with Bárbara Arenas in *Picadura mortal,* Oliver is the first author in Spain to create a crime fiction series whose main character, the private eye, is female. With her Lònia Guiu trilogy, Oliver defies the notion of the male-dominated crime genre at various levels: by replacing the male detective hero with a female detective whose sidekick is male (as well as gay) and by shifting the focus of the main crime to gender violence, making all other crimes secondary to this one. Using "On ets, Mònica?" to introduce her female hard-boiled detective, Oliver turned her attention to the detective novel and tackled a legal system that, despite its democratization, was still considered hostile to female victims of sexual violence.[5] Hence, Lònia's clients and/or the victims she encounters are always female, often Majorcan women like herself, and children who have been exploited, and the crimes that Lònia investigates are always of a sexual nature, though these will often be intertwined with ecological crimes as well.

The focus of most of the scholarship on Oliver's crime fiction has been on Lònia's self-transformations and how these have been intimately tied to her feminist convictions and the evolution of these beliefs. Scholars such as Shelley Godsland and Nancy Vosburg have done extensive work on the connection between Lònia's self-transformations and her feminist awakenings, which lead her to identify with the victims of her cases, women who have been subjected to gender violence. For his part, José Colmeiro's "The Spanish Detective" emphasizes how Lònia's identification with the victims of her cases leads to identity crises in each of the novels, which then result in feminist realizations that promote solidarity and strengthened female networks. In my study of the Lònia Guiu series, however, I want to draw attention to another crucial aspect of the trilogy – the link between narrative hybridization and the representation and spectatorship of the female body. I emphasize how the female body and perspective are represented within the framework of female victimization to arrive at an understanding as to how Oliver is redefining both the victim and the politics of visibility in crime fiction. By writing a hybrid narrative that is both a detective story and an examination of the self, Oliver has led the reader into an examination of crime fiction's treatment of gender violence and of the female body. This has the disconcerting effect of bringing both the detective protagonist and the reader into the very sphere of violence, and it is here that the female body becomes visible. Unlike the representations of women's bodies in traditional male crime fiction that are displayed to be attractive and pleasurable to the reader, in Oliver's trilogy, the female body gains visibility when it is mistreated and viciously abused.

"On ets, Mònica?" already brings together many of the themes that are underscored in the trilogy such as: Lònia's self-transformations and the reaffirmation of her authority as a female detective, the sexual victimization of women in the form of rape and Lònia's emotional attachment to these victims due to her feminist awakenings, her network of female friends who aid her during her investigations, her rage against the raping of the land that results from its overdevelopment, her relationship with her partner-sidekick Quim, and her travels outside of Spain. Along with the themes first presented in the short story, we also get a preview of Lònia's personality and what traits will characterize her, such as her vegetarianism, her lipstick fetish, her bluntness, and her witty sense of humour. From the beginning of "On ets, Mònica?" and throughout the trilogy, there is an inversion in the gender roles that we traditionally encounter in classic detective fiction because it is now the female detective's gaze, her perspective and voice that dominates the first-person narrative with the objectification of Víctor, the male client who hires Lònia to find his missing wife, Mònica. Víctor, who has come to the detective agency expecting to find a male detective, contracts Lònia, thinking he will be able to deceive her into believing that his wife escaped with her friend Patrícia, whom Víctor has hired to role play both his wife and herself so that he can gain ownership of Mònica's land by the seashore. In her role as Mònica, Patrícia temporarily convinces Lònia that Mònica's disappearance is the result of their lesbian love affair, and this facilitates a permit for Víctor to build on Mònica's land. At the end of the story, Lònia discovers that Mònica is dead and that Víctor is somehow responsible for her death and disappearance. Though we never learn how Mònica was killed, the motive becomes clear to Lònia when she makes the connection that Mònica would not allow Víctor to develop her land because she was keeping it from being violated. Mònica did not want her land to endure the rape that she was suffering at the hands of her husband, and because she would not consent, he killed her. Oliver's first experiment with crime fiction combines two themes that will reappear intertwined in the trilogy – the raping of a woman's land and the victimization of the female body.

Like the short story, *Estudi en lila* (1985) reintroduces us to a quick-witted and sassy female detective in her mid-thirties with an extensive lipstick collection, who, after learning her lesson with Víctor, no longer takes cases from male clients. In this first installment of the series, Lònia, with the help of her partner, Quim, investigates two cases simultaneously – that of a Majorcan teenager, Sebastiana, who has disappeared in Barcelona, and another, brought to her by the elegant antiquarian, Elena Gaudí, who has hired her to find three men. The cases involve two women of different social classes, but we learn that the crime that binds them is rape – both Sebastiana and Gaudí have been raped on Barcelona's city streets. Whereas Sebastiana commits suicide in Lònia's bathtub as a form of revenge against her parents, who accuse her of provoking her own rape and resulting pregnancy, Gaudí's goal is to find her rapists, so that she can castrate them as her form of vengeance. Lònia, who catches up to Gaudí when she is about castrate her final assailant, allows Gaudí to get away with her crime, for in the process of locating her rapists, the female detective is groped, beaten, and almost raped, thus experiencing sexual victimization first-hand. As a result, she feels a sense of solidarity towards both victims. Although we never get a description of Lònia in the crime fiction series, the female body appears when violence is enacted upon it, when it becomes a victimized body. When the sleuth is a woman, the politics of vulnerability in crime fiction are reformulated because the detective's body is now always in danger of being violated and penetrated by the masculine.

After discovering that Gaudí's rapists are also part of a seedy underworld involving arms trafficking and an international prostitution scheme, *Estudi en lila* ends with Lònia selling the case to a fellow detective, Lluís Arquer, in return for a flight to Melbourne to escape the effects that the rape of both women have had on her life.[6] Lònia's guilt over Sebastiana's suicide, however, results in another search for a teenage Majorcan girl in the second novel of the trilogy, *Antípodes* (1987) (*Antipodes*, 1989). On her flight to Melbourne, Lònia meets Cristina, a teenage socialite whose disappearance ends up forming part of a web of lies that involve her uncle's desire to inherit and develop her land by the Majorcan seashore. The topic of the raping of the land is once again revisited in this novel and linked to the prostitution and victimization of the female body. To acquire her land, Cristina has been sold off to an international ring of sex traffickers, and Lònia, who is unable to penetrate Melbourne's underground world of sex slaves, is forced to hire Henry Dhul, an Australian detective, who becomes her lover. Lònia, who is ready to give up her profession for love, is ultimately deported and forced to return to Barcelona after being deceived by Henry and Cristina into believing that Cristina is dead. Guilt compels Lònia to continue with the investigation, which will lead her back to her homeland, Majorca, and it is here where she infiltrates the brothel. In an effort to uncover who is behind the sex trafficking scheme and to protect Cristina's land from being developed, she goes undercover and is forced into prostitution.

Once again, the female body attains visibility when Lònia becomes a victim of male aggression, but unlike *Estudi en lila,* here the detective body is penetrated by the masculine. Forced to prostitute her body, Lònia experiences a new sense of solidarity – this time towards female victims of prostitution. In *Antípodes,* vulnerability and female victimization are redefined by problematizing what constitutes a victim because Lònia realizes that all women are forced to prostitute a part of themselves. This topic is taken up once again in the final novel of the trilogy, *El sol que fa l'ànec* (1994) (*Blue Roses for a Dead ... Lady?,* 1998), which opens with Lònia beating up the pimp of a group of prostitutes in the city streets of a downtrodden neighbourhood of Barcelona. While the prostitutes celebrate her victory by screaming her name, Lònia admits feeling embarrassed despite acknowledging that she enjoys the publicity that she gets as the main character in two novels by her friend, the author Maria-Antònia Oliver. With this metatextual mention, the exposure of the female body and its mobilization is now linked self-reflexively to crime fiction, specifically to the first two novels of the series where the detective body only becomes visible when it is vulnerable and penetrated.

In *El sol que fa l'ànec,* Lònia is hired to find Júlia, a young woman whose disappearance will have Lònia uncovering a child prostitution ring that extends from Germany to Majorca. Throughout the novel, Lònia draws attention to her own fictionality, highlighting the tensions that exist between the author and the detective, and yet Oliver assists in providing the clue that will aid her in solving the case – the meaning of the song, alluded to in the title of the novel, that will help her expose the reason for Júlia's disappearance. Lònia discovers that both Júlia and her employer Catalina have been accomplices, aiding Tomeu and his men in charge of the sex trafficking of children. Once again, the higher class in conjunction with a corrupt Majorcan police force is responsible for the horrendous victimization of these children, with the exception of sub-commissioner Maiol, a friend of Lònia's deceased father. As in *Antípodes*, the violence stems from the Majorcan elite, whose aim is the appropriation of land belonging to a woman, in this case Catalina's land, Son Pont. What is more, and similar to the novels that precede it, *El sol que fa l'ànec* portrays a police force that conceals the horrific and depraved crimes committed by the upper echelons of society. Maiol, however, proves to be the counterpart to these corrupt policemen by helping Lònia bring Tomeu (the administrator of Catalina's land), his men, and the police involved to justice. Lònia's victimization is once again made visible because she is threatened with rape, but unlike *Estudi en lila* and *Antípodes*, she is not the only victim whose assault is made available to the reader, for the novel presents a series of vignettes depicting the rape of children by both men and women. Yet again, the sleuth experiences the cycle of violence, but this time is forced to witness it as an outsider without being able to defend those that are being victimized. The emotional attachment that she develops towards these children surpasses what she has felt in her previous cases, so much so that she breaks down in tears at the end of this sequence, and decides to take justice into her own hands by assaulting the man responsible for spearheading these crimes. Since the legal system rarely protects or sides with the female victims in Oliver's trilogy, Lònia's private system of justice and not a male form of justice prevails in these narratives because rape has marked both female and children's bodies. These sexual crimes are now viewed from and resolved via a female point of view, or more precisely, from the point of view of a woman who has been a victim herself. Because the detective is also a victim, Lònia bypasses a legal system that is inefficient in punishing rapists.

Throughout the series, Lònia's first-person narration details an individual identity crisis that mirrors a generalized female collective identity crisis that appears to have been rooted in the changing of women's roles upon their entrance into the workforce in the early 1960s and during the transition to democracy in the 1970s and 1980s, as discussed by Godsland in *Killing Carmens*. Oliver demonstrates how the changes in consciousness during the feminist mobilizations in Spain manifest themselves in the character of the career-minded Lònia and her friends, in particular the gynecologist Mercè, who is responsible for the detective's feminist awakenings in *Estudi en lila*. Lònia and her friends not only reject traditional domestic roles and redefine what constitutes a family, but also become advocates for victims of male aggression.[7] Despite the sociopolitical changes that Spain has undergone and the rights women have attained in this post-dictatorship society, Lònia realizes that all women, regardless of status and social class, continue to be the victims of men. The series emphasizes how powerful men, because of their social status and a complicit and at times corrupt police force, get away with their crimes. Nina Molinaro has previously clarified in her study of Oliver's *Estudi en lila* and Alicia Giménez Bartlett's *Ritos de muerte* (*Death Rites*) that "[r]ape happens because the societies reflected in the novels are organized to facilitate it happening" ("Writing" 110). This, I believe, is the disillusioning realization that Lònia reaches at the end of the first novel of the trilogy – her society has also become a victimizer of women, an aid to rapists, by allowing them to remain in the shadows. Lònia recognizes that justice is not possible, for there is no way within the legal system to avenge the crime of rape.

As we accompany Lònia in her cases, we are also privy to her flashbacks and her internal world. We witness how she must rediscover and redefine herself as a *detectiva*, a woman detective, as she refers to herself, in a post-dictatorship society because her sleuthing function and identity have also changed in accordance with this political and societal transformation.[8] Lònia's redefinition is clearly linked to the new types of cases that she is asked to solve that involve the more widespread and indiscriminate social problem of sexual violence against women (see Vosburg's "Genre Bending" and Godsland's *Killing Carmens*). Oliver's Lònia, however, seems to be unaware of her own potential role as a victim in a social system that devalues women and the female body. What is more, she underestimates her own vulnerability in a system that is dangerous to women, a system that mistreats and abuses the female body. She becomes a victim of the same crime that she investigates, and finds that there is no solution, no guarantee that a stop can be put to this cycle of sexual violence.[9]

In light of her victimization, the female detective's body becomes the site for a discussion of gender violence and for redefining victimhood in the genre. While most scholars mention the victimization that Lònia suffers at the hands of her assailants, critics have not examined how Lònia's body (as a victimized body) is put on display in Oliver's crime fiction. Using this new representation of the female body, Oliver problematizes the reader's role in the reproduction of the patriarchal ideology that motivates gender violence. Oliver, as Maureen Reddy has previously claimed about female crime fiction, educates us on how "to read as feminists," or, better said, "how to read as women" ("Feminist Counter-Tradition" 176). Though I agree with Reddy that female crime fiction authors feminize their readers, I would specify that Oliver succeeds in feminizing the gaze that falls upon the female body in her detective novels, thus challenging and redefining its function in crime fiction. Oliver draws our attention to how male crime fiction, in its portrayal of the female body, has been complicit in reproducing the sexist patriarchal ideology that Lònia must confront and battle against in the series.

The Birth of Lònia Guiu in "On ets, Mònica?"

With "On ets, Mònica?," Oliver follows the mould that Lourdes Ortiz had broken four years earlier in *Picadura mortal* by positioning a female character at the centre of the narrative, but this time with a male sidekick. Though we learn very little about Quim from the short story, what we do gather is that Quim, whom Lònia refers to as her business partner, turns out to be more of a secretary and less of a partner. From the beginning of "On ets, Mònica?" and throughout the trilogy, Lònia continually reasserts her authority as a detective by exerting her control over men and reminding them of her power. In the short story, it begins with her objectification of Víctor, resulting from her need to have the upper hand in the relationship with her male client. She cannot help but focus on each of his features and gestures, and surveys his every movement while fantasizing about him.

Despite finding him physically appealing, Lònia is also immediately suspicious when Víctor explains that his wife, Mònica, has been missing for three days now, and he has not contacted the police. He assures her that this is not a case of infidelity and that the reason he has not contacted the police is that Mònica's parents do not want anyone knowing because they are high-society people who require discretion. For the most part, the cases that Lònia investigates in the trilogy involve the wealthier social classes and are usually a critique of their moral debasement and corruption. Víctor, who will be no exception, asks Lònia to solve the case because as a woman, perhaps she can ascertain where Mònica has gone: "M'ha sorprès trobar una dona en aquest ofici, però per a la feina que jo li encomano, crec que és millor una dona que un home ... perquè li serà més fàcil posar-se dins la mentalitat d'una altra dona i, en conseqüència, de seguir-li la pista" (121–2) ("I was surprised to find a woman doing this kind of work, but for the job I want you to do, I think it's better to have a woman than a man ... because it'll be easier for you to get inside the mentality of another woman, and that way you'll do better at tracking her down") ("Where Are You, Mònica?" 373).[10] Since it involves the disappearance of a woman, a potential female victim, Víctor admits that in this case a female detective is preferable, so it is a suitable job for a woman. And yet Víctor, we come to find out, hires her because he thinks that he will be able to mislead her by employing Patrícia to play the role of Mònica.

Indeed, Lònia is so deceived by Patrícia's role-playing that while she feels some sort of complicity with Mònica (played by Patrícia), she does not feel the same way towards the femme fatale Patrícia. Although she never meets the real victim, Lònia feels an affinity towards her, first when she meets Mònica's dog (which takes an immediate liking towards her), later when she rifles through Mònica's makeup, specifically her lipsticks (one of which she takes with her because she cannot help herself due to her lipstick fetish), but eventually, and most significantly, because Mònica refused to develop her land. Justice prevails at the end because Lònia is finally able to tell the two women apart when she sees pictures of the real Mònica, who wears less makeup and does not wear the high-heeled shoes that Patrícia (as Mònica) had on when they met. The picture positions the cosmetically enhanced high-heeled femme fatale sidekick against the victim, who does not wear makeup and has opted for more comfortable shoes to walk the land near the seashore that she has kept Víctor from destroying. Oliver contrasts two types of female characters that we find in traditional crime fiction, but she also revisits the role of the female victim, making her the figure that the female private eye identifies with because she has been strong-willed and has protected her land from being violated. Because this is a cause that Lònia shares with the victim and due to the affinity that she feels towards the victimized woman, Lònia realizes that Mònica viewed the construction on her land as rape, comparing it to the abuse that she suffered at the hands of her husband. Once she deciphers the truth, Lònia hands Víctor over to the authorities, but we never learn what happens to Patrícia, the female criminal/femme fatale, who is also Víctor's lover. Apparently, the female criminal has eluded punishment and no one seems to care, whereas her male counterpart must face justice. At the end, Lònia decides that she can no longer trust or for that matter take on male clients and that female solidarity and helping women clients will take precedence.

To make all of these connections, Lònia relies on her network of female friends, asking her friend and colleague Adela, a psychiatrist, for help after learning that Mònica had been seeing a psychiatrist herself. The theme of female friendship and the use of women's professional networks is first presented in the short story and continues to be developed throughout the trilogy. More than just friendship, Oliver's crime fiction demonstrates the power of female solidarity at work. The help that her friends offer allow her to bring her cases to a close with greater ease, but this is not the only role female solidarity plays in Oliver's crime fiction. More significantly, female solidarity results in Lònia's identification with the female victims of sexual abuse, which compels her to advocate and act on their behalf. Lònia recognizes that even Mònica, a woman of a high social class, is not immune from sexual victimization.

Thanks to Adela's inquiries about Mònica's psychotherapy sessions, Lònia ascertains that Mònica went to a psychiatrist not because she was a lesbian (which Víctor and Patrícia had led her to believe) but because Víctor raped her repeatedly. Lònia summarizes the case to Víctor with the following information:

> Anava al psiquiatre no pas perquè fos lesbiana, sinò perquè l'obligaves tant si ella en tenia ganes com si no. I si no en tenia ganes era perquè li feies fàstic. I inconscientment se sentia violada. Per això no volia que fessis la urbanització al lloc que ella més estimava. Era com si volgués preservar la terra de la teva violació, ja que no se sabia preservar ella mateixa. (145)

> She didn't go to a psychiatrist because she was a lesbian, she went because you forced her to make love with you whether she wanted to or not. Naturally, she felt raped. So she didn't want you to develop the place she loved most. It's as if she wanted to save the land from being raped, since she wasn't able to save herself from it. (396–7)

Her summary of the case shatters the silence that Víctor imposed on his wife, and brings to light the rape of two bodies – Mònica's rape and that of her land. In some of Oliver's detective and non-detective fiction, the brutality of female victimization goes hand in hand with the desire to savagely overdevelop, to build indiscriminately on undeveloped beautiful land, a phenomenon known as balearization.[11] According to Biel Horrach Estarellas, Majorca has become a prime example of the effects of balearization because of the overwhelming amount of construction that took place on the seashore during the late 1960s and early 1970s to boost the tourism industry, without taking into account the destruction of the beaches and ecosystem.[12] Oliver condemns balearization as a form of savage capitalism both in this short story and in the trilogy by linking this crime against nature to sexual crimes committed against women. Lònia's identification with the victims (Mònica and her land), which is not typical of the classic detective formula or of most hard-boiled fiction, does form part of the characterization of this particular female sleuth. This differentiates Oliver's contribution to the genre from that of her male predecessors in Spain.

From the short story onwards, we gather that Oliver's Lònia adopts certain masculine traits that distinguish her from the more traditional female characters in crime fiction. For example, she is able to engage successfully in a car chase and uses martial arts to defend herself. Despite refusing to carry a gun for fear that she might end up using it, Lònia is not afraid to inflict violence when necessary, and, like her masculine counterparts, she receives her fair share of beatings too. While an emphasis is placed on Lònia's more "masculine" traits, the female sleuth's fetish – buying and collecting lipsticks – is particularly feminine. These sorts of fetishes are common in detective fiction, but the fact that she never uses the lipsticks and that the fetish is more about collecting them suggests the contradictory nature of this symbol. Her lipstick fetish is not only "a gratifying act of self-affirmation," as Colmeiro has noted, but also another way of being a part of a female community ("Spanish Detective" 190).[13] Put differently, the gap between women of differing social classes can be bridged by having this cosmetic product function like a common denominator between women. Her clients, who know about her fetish, give her lipsticks to thank her – for example, Gaudí and Sebastiana in *Estudi en lila* and the prostitutes in *El sol que fa l'ànec* – which again reaffirms how, in the act of giving this particular gift, there is something all women can potentially share. While it is true that there are differences between the lipsticks that Lònia receives as gifts, it still reminds us that Lònia can perform the function of a bridge or mediator between women and the social classes that they belong to, since she is an advocate for all of them. Men, like her friend Jem in *Antípodes*, will also present her with lipsticks to make her feel better, but they also employ her lipsticks against her, as they do in *Estudi en lila*.

The men who ransack her office use her lipsticks to smear her walls and destroy her papers, making her feel powerless (93–4). Whereas men can potentially use her fetish against her, women celebrate and thank the female detective with lipsticks. Seen in this way, lipstick becomes a symbol of female solidarity, solidarity among all classes of women against gender violence.

Then again, Lònia normally buys lipsticks for herself during moments of crisis or confusion, or of feeling powerless when she feels her investigation is stalled, though she will also buy them to celebrate a break in a case. Symbolically, Lònia mostly purchases lipsticks in her moments of vulnerability because it seemingly buys her a sense of power or authority. The same occurs with Elena Gaudí. After Gaudí escapes at the end of the novel, Lònia discovers that Gaudí has used red lipstick on her bathroom mirror to write the date she was raped – 15 May – and finds that Gaudí's calendar had stopped on 15 May with that date circled in red. Even on the package that she has left Lònia, Gaudí dates it 15 May. For Gaudí, lipstick serves as a reminder of her rape, but a reminder that will lead her to avenge her assault by castrating each of the men who gang-raped her that night, signifying the power to move beyond victimization. Lipstick, therefore, signifies not only revenge, but also power, for both Lònia and Gaudí.

Additionally, Lònia, a shortened form of her name, Apollònia, has been named after Saint Apolònia, the saint who protects dentists. This particular saint was a virgin martyr whose torture consisted of the violent extraction and/or shattering of her teeth during the emperor Phillip's reign in Alexandria. This connection between her name, her teeth, and the phallic connotations of a cosmetic product that adds colour to the lips is worth pinpointing, considering that Lònia has opted to rename herself once she arrives in Barcelona to break with a very conservative name from Catholic tradition. Colmeiro has previously argued that Lònia's act of renaming has more to do with a reaffirmation of the feminine: "She is a woman-identified woman, who has renamed herself (her given name was 'Apollònia') to erase the trace of the masculine inscription (Apollo), the symbolic patriarchal marker present in every woman, thus figuratively mutilating the male" ("Spanish Detective" 185). While I would suggest that the act of renaming herself has more to do with breaking free from her past than with a break with the masculine, as Colmeiro postulates, I propose that the female detective's lipstick fetish symbolizes a struggle between the feminine and the masculine – between vulnerability versus power and authority. The ambiguity of this contradictory fetish/symbol represents Lònia's tendency to be feminine, but also her attempts to break with the feminine and with her femininity.

The Detective Turned Victim: The Victimization and the Visibility of the Female Body

Despite all that we know about Lònia, from her insecurities to her lipstick fetish, we never get a physical depiction of the private eye. Though Lònia claims that she has not read Oliver's novels (which angers her author-friend), Lònia confirms the lack of her physical description in Oliver's works when the receptionist at the German consulate, who has read both *Estudi en lila* and *Antípodes*, compliments her by saying that she is pretty: "És molt més guapa que així com la descriu ella" (*El sol* 66) ("You're a lot prettier than she describes you") (*Blue Roses* 33).[14] Lònia responds to her compliment by pointing out that "l'Oliver no m'ha descrita mai! Només en una ocasió va posar que tenia els cabells foscos i que era bastant alta" (66) ("Oliver has never described me. Just one time she said I had dark hair and I was pretty tall") (33). Knowing how she has been described in Oliver's novels would suggest that she has either read them or has attained this knowledge in some other fashion. Either way, this lack of a physical description provides a stark contrast with the detailed descriptions of the female characters in male detective fiction, in particular when we encounter the femme fatale or the male detective's sexy sidekick, whose physical attributes are indeed highlighted. Kathleen Thompson-Casado has previously underscored that in female crime fiction the woman detective is not described to avoid her objectification, giving her professional skills greater distinction by contrast (140). In both the short detective story and in the trilogy, the absence of Lònia's physical description serves to highlight Oliver's rewriting of how the female body is now staged in crime fiction.

We do, however, witness how Lònia's body is victimized throughout the series, since the first-person narration details the extreme violence and pain she endures. Oliver uses these episodes not only to criticize how violence is employed in male crime fiction, as has already been suggested by Godsland and White, but also to make the victimized female body available by creating a binary or a doubling, where the protagonist is both a detective and a victim of sexual assault.[15] In male-centred crime fiction, the detective will be subject to the occasional beating, but will not be sexually assaulted, as Lònia is in the trilogy. Oliver employs these episodes of violent confrontations between the detective and their criminal counterparts to further shift the generic form.

This recasting of the detective as a victim of sexual assault is clearly problematic because, as Kathleen Klein accentuates, "Rape transforms the detective into a victim, moves him from the dominant position to the subordinate one in the power struggle and the linguistic configuration (criminal/victim)" ("*Habeas Corpus*" 180). This is true for Lònia, who narrowly escapes being raped in all three texts, and in *Antípodes* is forced to prostitute herself, which makes her feel as if she has been raped. The sexual nature of the assaults that she endures transforms her into a victim of gender violence. According to Klein, "the victim ... is, despite biology, always female ... the Woman is the body in the library on whom the criminal writes his narrative of murder. On top of that narrative, the detective inscribes his narrative of investigation" (173). What changes, then, when the detective is also the victim?

By having her female detective experience sexual victimization first-hand and by putting her assaulted body on display, Oliver creates the new binary of detective/victim and deconstructs the sexualization of the female body in traditional crime fiction. In *Estudi en lila*, Lònia first doubles as a victim when she goes to the house of one of Gaudí's rapists, Gòmara, and is greeted by his henchmen. She describes how she fights off Gòmara's men, who are not only physically assaulting her, but are also attempting to rape her:

> Jo vaig aguantar mentre em tocaven com si fos un home. Però quan les mans del grassonet s'entretengueren més del compte per segons quines parts del meu cos li vaig esvergar una galtada que el va deixar perplex ...
>
> – Agafa-li els braços! Agafa-li els braços – cridava enfollit al filipí, mentre jo li feia caure una pluja de cops de puny a la cara – . Ja veuràs aquesta melindrosa com espernegarà de gust d'aquí a una estona.
>
> Quan em va esqueixar la brusa i els sostenidors vaig seguir el consell del Quim ...
>
> Tenia les mans del català damunt cada mamella. I els seus baixos se m'oferien indefensos. Repenjant-me a l'esquena del filipí, li vaig encastar els dos genolls a les parts sense os i immediatament els meus pits foren lliures. L'home es cargolava a dues passes, gronyint com un porcellí. (81)
>
> I put up with it with it while they searched me as if I were a man. But when the fat guy's hands started playing freely with certain parts of my body, I let loose with a slap that caught him off guard, ...

> "Grab her arms! Grab her arms!" he screamed at the Filipino, enraged, while I kept showering his face with punches. "We'll see how this prude's going to squirm with pleasure in a little while."
>
> When he ripped my blouse and bra off, I took Quim's advice ...
>
> The guy had a hand on each tit, and that left him defenseless below. Leaning against the Filipino, I penetrated his boneless parts with both knees, and my boobs were set free inmediately. He curled up a couple of paces away, groaning like a stuck pig. (*Study in Lilac* 66)

Unlike the attacks the male detectives face, in the case of the female private eye she is at risk of also being sexually assaulted. This transforms the episodes of violence that we are used to finding in traditional crime fiction into terrifying assaults that replicate the violence against women, which Lònia combats in this novel. In this instance, the female body appears only to be undressed and assaulted, and her vulnerability is emphasized because the detective has lost control, albeit for a moment, over her body. Lònia, however, is able to regain power over her body, taking advantage of Gòmara's men fondling her to disable her attackers. These instances of victimization also serve to empower Lònia, to embolden her to fight.

Moreover, violence in the Lònia Guiu trilogy is linked to rememorations and flashbacks, for a causal relationship exists between these violent episodes and the memories that are triggered by these assaults. Following the aforementioned attack, she is able to get away, but later wakes up after being knocked unconscious and locked up in a room at Gòmara's house. Wondering if Gòmara's men have sexually assaulted her, she describes looking down at her clothes, but quickly realizes that she has not been raped. It is then that she feels the lump on her head, which triggers the following childhood memory:

> I els ulls em començaren a plorar de dolor mentre amb la mà em palpava un bony descomunal, com el que m'havia fet quan tenia set anys, un dia abans de la primera comunió, quan em vaig barallar a pedrades amb na Joana perquè deia que mumare havia pagat a les monges perquè jo anàs la primera de la fila a combregar ...
>
> Em vaig veure reflectida al mirall del tocador amb cara de bleda assolellada pel record melangiós. Però ja no era una nina de primera comunió. (85–6)

> My eyes started watering with pain as my hand palpated an enormous lump, like the one I'd gotten when I was seven, the day before first

> communion. I'd had a rock fight with Joana because she said that my mother had bribed the nuns so I could be in the first row for communion ...
>
> I saw myself in the mirror, like a dummy struck by the nostalgic memory. But it wasn't a first communion any more. (69)

Throughout the trilogy, the violence inflicted upon the female body conjures up these childhood memories for Lònia, reinforcing the vulnerability that doubling the detective as victim entails. In both *Estudi en lila* and in *Antípodes*, the victimization of Lònia's body will result in her recollection or flashbacks of childhood memories. Though her appearance is not described, Oliver makes her detective turned victim available for the reader during this scene. What becomes available, however, is not a description of Lònia as we would expect when she stands before the mirror, but instead a childlike vulnerability. Facing her vulnerability, however, empowers her to fight back, and so she is able to disarm the criminals by rendering them unconscious to make her escape.

Although the beating that she receives in *Estudi en lila* leaves Lònia with some temporary bruises, others, especially those inflicted in the Majorcan brothel in *Antípodes* are permanent – for example, the blow to her right ear, which leaves her practically deaf and will require surgery, and the knife scar on one of her cheeks. This particular assault occurs immediately after spending an afternoon with one of her ecologist friends, Queta, at the Cala Mura beach in Na Morgana, which is in danger of being overdeveloped, of being savagely victimized by Cristina's uncle. This episode, which begins with Lònia's astonishment at Cala Mura's beauty, ends with her musings that the purity of the land is no longer possible because, while swimming, a plastic bag covers her breasts and when she gets out of the water, she realizes that tar coats one of her feet (*Antípodes* 166). Cala Mura has already been touched, prostituted, and as these reflections end, an episode of horrifying violence, during which the detective protagonist is savagely assaulted, is intertwined with flashbacks of childhood abuse and memories of the beating done to her friend Joana, one of her roommates when she was a university student in Barcelona, for political reasons (170–1). By linking these three beatings, an association between child abuse, rape, and political violence is established.

Lònia, who has discovered how the sex trafficking ring in Majorca works – under the guise of a marriage and a tourist agency – has been able to infiltrate the brothel by playing the role of a prostitute, Perla. In trying to gather evidence, she is caught in the act. As one of the men at the brothel beats and slaps her, the face that she sees is that of her teacher Sister Magdalena: "i després una altra galtada, i una altra, i una altra, prou!, basta!, no me pegui més!, no me pegui més, sor Magdalena! ... La suor freda em feia enganxar la pols de guix que saltava de la pissarra, tot mesclat, baves, suor, mosques" (168) ("and then another slap, and another, enough! stop! don't beat me any more, stop beating me Sister Magdalena! ... The cold sweat made the chalk that fell from the blackboard stick to me, mixed with spit, sweat, flies") (146). As in *Estudi en lila*, the violence inflicted upon Lònia conjures up her body's memory of physical suffering, but this time in the form of a vivid flashback that intertwines the current beating with one from her childhood past, where Sister Magdalena beat her for not knowing how to solve the problems on the board. The past and present converge in the pain that her body is being made to experience, the bruises and marks on her chest and thighs. Moreover, it is significant that once again Lònia's childhood body, the body in its most vulnerable state, is reimagined in this scene.

From the description of the state of her body – blood and snot trickling down her nose, tears coming out of her eyes, and bruises on her chest and thighs – another picture of the female detective/victim, though vague, emerges. Doubling as a female victim, the scene continues *in crescendo* until the men have left her completely naked and are about to rape her: "M'havia obert les cames. I jo em sentia lassa, com una pepa de pedaç sense mobilitat pròpia, vexada però incapaç de fer cap esforç per tornar a ajuntar les cames; però l'altre home va dir: 'I ara boixaries amb aquest pelleringo? Encara li donaries gust, betzol.' I em varen tirar la roba damunt" (172) ("He had spread my legs. I felt helplessly exhausted, like a rag doll without its own mobility, furious but unable to make any effort to bring my legs back together; but the other man said, 'And now you want to fuck this trash? You'd still give her pleasure, you ass!' And they threw my clothes on top of me") (149–50). Once again, a description of Lònia, even in this rudimentary form, becomes available because she is assaulted and threatened with rape. The assaulted body attains visibility in this scene because her transformation into a victim has taken place.

When one of the men grabs Lònia and pulls her by the hair, she has yet another flashback of her childhood self, during which a neighbour pulled her hair so that she would not leave:

> Però aquell home m'havia agafat pels cabells i me'ls volia arrabassar. Quins cabells tan fins que tens, guapa ... I quan ho vaig contar a mumare,

> ella es va posar a cridar, porc, me sentirà aquest porc, gorà, poca-vergonya! I va armar una escandalera a tot el carrer, i la veïnada plorava i plorava, i s'enrabiava amb mi, ets una mentidera, Polita, es meu homo no t'ha estirat els cabells. Sí, que els m'ha estirats, primer no, però quan jo me'n volia anar perquè no volia que els m'embrutàs, perquè sempre duu ses mans molt brutes, llavors sí que els m'ha estirat. (172)

> But the man had grabbed my hair and was trying to pull it all out. What nice hair you have, cutie-pie ... When I told Mom about the man, she started yelling, pig, animal, that pig'll hear from me, he has no shame! She raised a stink in the whole neighborhood, the neighbor was crying, she was furious at me, you're a liar Polita, my husband didn't pull your hair. Yes, he did, not at first, but when I wanted to leave so he wouldn't get it dirty, because his hands were always dirty, he pulled it, all right. (150)

This second flashback of her childhood body, this time a body threatened by a pedophilic neighbour, serves to continue emphasizing Lònia's loss of control over her body, her mounting vulnerability, and the female detective's return to a childhood state of feeling unprotected, exposed, and threatened. In effect, she has previously described the same glee experienced by both the nun and this man upon savagely beating her when she says, "però mai no havia notat el rabejament que notava en la monja. Fins ara, que l'havia tornat a notar en aquell home que coneixia però no recordava" (171) ("but I'd never noticed such glee as the nun had when she did it. Until now, when I saw it again in that man I knew but didn't remember") (149). Unlike in *Estudi en lila,* where the criticisms against the Catholic Church remain somewhat veiled, here the critique is quite explicit, and a link between the institution of the Catholic Church and the present victimization of the female body is clearly established.

In Oliver's short story, we have already seen the link between sexual violence (against women) and economic violence (capitalism against nature) established, but this section in *Antípodes* adds a third interesting element – political violence against people who protest. Lònia's present and past beatings converge with the torture suffered by her activist friend Joana, who was held and beaten for seventy-two hours, the maximum time (three days) that the police could keep a person in custody in Spain before being required to present him/her before a judge: "Era com un record llunyà que no em pertanyia, com si algú m'ho hagués contat. Dos homes que apallissaven una dona perquè la volien fer parlar i ella tenia la memòria emblanquinada pel pànic" (170) ("It was like a faraway memory that wasn't really mine, as if someone had told me about it ... Two men had beaten up a woman because they wanted to make her talk and her memory was blanked out by panic") (148). In *Estudi en lila*, we learn that Lònia's roommates are politically active, especially at the University of Barcelona during the Transition period in Spain, and she describes the bruise that another one of her roommates, Margalida, has suffered after the police storm the university during a student gathering. Lònia views Joana's actions as heroic regardless of whether her memory went blank from panic or not. Joana represents the brutality carried out against those who oppose the political establishment during the end of the Franco regime and during the beginning of the Transition. Apart from the potential political implications, the fact that at that moment of victimization Lònia associates in her memory the beatings that she received from Sister Magdalena and the beatings that her friend Joana received (from the police) may point to how the female body still suffers from similar forms of mental and physical torture even after the transition to democracy.

As in the short story, the land and the female body mirror one another in this scene – for balearization, this form of savage capitalism, is the equivalent of being prostituted and savagely raped, and in Lònia's case, the same assailants who intend to violate Na Morgana's Cala Mura beach are the same men who try to beat her into submission. By having the hard-boiled detective turn into the sexually assaulted victim, Oliver uses Lònia to exemplify the condition of the female victim of gender violence in this instance, and experience the powerlessness of victimization. Moreover, as we will see in her scene with Inspector Vargas (which takes place in the brothel), the author also has her female detective experience what it feels like to be forced to prostitute herself to maintain her cover as a sex worker. Lònia even compares herself to Maria Goretti, saying that she did not resist as the Catholic martyr had done, who preferred to be killed instead of being raped. While Lònia admits that Inspector Vargas did not force her and that she did not resist, she still feels it was an assault on her body.[16] She reveals that:

> Només una cosa bona hi va haver: vaig menysprear aquell home com supòs que menyspreen els clients totes les putes del món, fins i tot les que no en són conscients. Fins i tot les que no fan l'ofici obligades com les del xalet del Terreno. I aquell sentiment de superioritat enfront del mascle que

> tenia damunt em va fer sentir solidària amb totes les dones que no tenien l'oportunitat d'experimentar-lo. (194)

> There was only one good thing: I felt such scorn for that man, just like all the whores in the world must feel about their customers, I guess, even the ones who aren't conscious of it. Even the ones who aren't forced to work like the girls in the chalet at Terreno. That feeling of superiority over the male who was on top of me made me feel solidarity with all the women who hadn't had a chance to experience it themselves. (171)

Although her friend Lida has emphasized that no prostitute has sex for pleasure, Lònia comes to truly grasp this during the aformentioned narrative sequence. The feeling of solidarity towards other prostitutes that she describes during this episode results in her later realization in *El sol que fa l'ànec* that all women prostitute themselves in one way or another, regardless of whether it is the prostitution of the body or of the mind. The feelings of scorn drive Lònia to feel superior to the man that lies on top of her, and though vulnerable in this scene, this shared vulnerability emboldens Lònia to free all the women at the brothel who have been forced into prostitution and that she now feels connected to because she has prostituted herself. This vulnerability, as previously discussed, is another source of empowerment. What is more, the fact that the victimization of the female body is narrated by a female voice adds an emotional and subjective component, which distinguishes it from the more rational and objective traditional male description of victimhood. This is particularly true in Oliver's crime fiction where the victim recounts her own sexual assaults, and the reader experiences these assaults as they happen. Like Lònia, the reader cannot escape the cycle of sexual violence.

While in *Estudi en lila* and in *Antípodes* Lònia does not blame herself for her attacks, in *El sol que fa l'ànec* she does feel responsible because she allowed herself to be followed and finds herself at the mercy of two men who beat and undress her:

> El que tenia darrere em va estirar els braços cap amunt i em va fer veure la padrina, el malparit. I el que tenia davant va estrènyer les cames i em va ficar mà a l'entrecuix, tot alhora, que els genolls em varen fer cre-crec i la cotorra em va cantar de dolor ...
>
> I a l'entretant m'havia obert el zig-zag dels pantalons i me'ls baixava. Però només podia fer-ho fins a mitja cuixa. Llavors em va esqueixar les bragues. I se'm va quedar mirant el parrús, sense saber què fer. (142)

> The one behind me pulled upwards on my arms and it wracked me with pain, the sonofabitch. The one in front of me tightened up on my legs and stuck his hand in my crotch at the same time. My knees went creak-creak and I was singing the blues ...
>
> Meantime he'd undone my zipper and was pulling down my pants. But he could only get them down to mid-thigh. Then he ripped off my undies. And there he was staring at it, without knowing what to do. (74–5)

Similar to the other scenes where she is attacked, the female sleuth is threatened with the act of rape, but her assailants are unable to follow through because while they try to capitalize on her momentary state of vulnerability, Lònia is able to use their perception of her vulnerability against them, taking advantage of any opportunity to fight back and prevail over her attackers. *El sol que fa l'ànec* adds an additional element by narrating a second attack, where for the first time one of her victimizers is a woman. Although this attack is not sexual in nature, the woman participates in breaking Lònia's finger. In this way, the scene anticipates the appearance of female aggressors later in this novel who participate in acts of sexual violence against children

Sally Munt has previously characterized the female detective as "a moral watchdog from the Other who paces the streets in order to expose sex/gender oppression" (*Murder* 197). This is the case in each of Oliver's novels that form part of the trilogy. Oliver's female detective protagonist, Lònia Guiu, is this watchdog, this advocate for female and child victims of sexual assault and exploitation. In women's crime fiction, "[t]he constituent parts of Woman-as-victim are being dissected and investigated by Woman-as-hero" (202–3) because only the female detective can uncover "the artifice of gender via an investigation into patriarchal effects" (207). Throughout Oliver's crime fiction, however, women-as-victim are investigated by the detective-as-victim. As readers of Oliver's trilogy, we are always threatened with the possibility of witnessing the rape of the detective, something unheard of in male crime fiction. Oliver forces her readers to remain alert, on edge, because the consequences of these violent episodes for Lònia, being raped, are far more sinister than what we traditionally expect from the detective genre. We can rejoice, however, because Lònia is always able to defeat her attackers. Vulnerability becomes yet another weapon in her arsenal, which she uses to outsmart her criminal counterparts. Lònia is successful because she can see through the eyes of the victim and take on the perspective of those who have been sexually assaulted, a new perspective in the genre that compels a reconsideration of victimization.

Recasting the Victim: (Re)defining Detection, Victimhood, and the Prostitution of the Female Body

What would seem like a contradiction to readers of the genre, a detective/victim, becomes commonplace throughout the Lònia Guiu trilogy. This doubling of the protagonist is not something new in crime fiction. For example, in *The Murder of Roger Ackroyd* by Agatha Christie, the narrator also doubles as the criminal. The doubling of the detective/victim, however, is novel in Oliver's series because the texts experiment with this hybridity, a technique that is now being employed by contemporary female crime fiction writers. The doubling of Oliver's protagonist represents a transformation of the genre, thus subverting its conventions. Consequently, what it means to be a victim, to be associated with victimhood, is likewise redefined in the Lònia Guiu series. In *Estudi en lila*, for example, Oliver not only transforms the female detective into a victim, but the female victim, Elena Gaudí, also doubles as a criminal. We come to learn at the end of the novel that Gaudí is looking to avenge her rape, committed by three men from a high social class who can avoid being punished by a patriarchal legal system. After locating the first two men, Gòmara and Antal, that Gaudí has asked her to find, Lònia discovers that both have died under mysterious circumstances and that they were both castrated. Once she sees through Gaudí's web of lies, she reaches Pierre Jovel's home in time to see her client enacting the final stage of her revenge – the castration of the third man who gang-raped her.

In this moment, Gaudí paints a picture of her rape by the three men and confesses that her intention was to castrate, but not kill, her rapists since she wanted each of them to remember what they had done. She recounts her rape and her castrating revenge to Lònia: "El dia quinze de maig aquests tres homes em varen fer entrar a un portal i em varen violar. Un darrera l'altre ... I jo he decidit capar-los, un darrera l'altre" (180) ("The fifteenth of May, those three men forced me into an entryway and they raped me. One after the other ... And I decided to castrate them, one after the other") (149). Lònia is struck by Gaudí's cold and monotonal voice during her rape narrative, but her thoughts turn to Sebastiana, the pregnant Majorcan teenager who has committed suicide in her bathtub. Lònia allows Gaudí to castrate Jovel because all three women – Sebastiana, Gaudí, and herself – have been victims of sexual assault: "Na Sebastiana dormia en un llit de llençols vermells estampats amb roses de vòmits. A mi m'havien intentat violar dues vegades a can Gòmara. A la Gaudí li ho havien fet tres vegades seguides" (182) ("Sebastiana had slept on sheets stained with vomit. They'd tried to rape me twice at Gòmara's. They'd gang-banged Gaudí") (150). Gaudí, in essence, castrates her rapists on behalf of all three women. For her part, Lònia becomes an accomplice to the female criminal by allowing her to elude the justice system because she identifies with Gaudí's need for vengeance. In *Estudi en lila*, the female victim doubles as a criminal because justice would not have been served otherwise, which compels the detective to accept the role of her accomplice.

Whereas Gaudí moves forward after eliminating those who have victimized her, Sebastiana has not been so lucky. She commits suicide in Lònia's bathtub because, according to the suicide note that she leaves Lònia, her death is her revenge and a way of punishing her parents. After learning that she had been raped and was now pregnant, they called her a pig, and blamed her for being raped and for humiliating them. Upon finding her in the bathtub full of blood and vomit-stained water, a traumatized Lònia remarks how "[u]na ganyota d'oi li enlletgia la boca. I un solc profund entre les celles era el rastre que havia deixat el dolor físic. Però ara ja no hi havia dolor. De cap classe" (146) ("[a] grimace of disgust twisted her mouth, and a deep wrinkle between her brows were evidence of the physical pain. No pain now, of any kind") (120). Beyond her initial comment upon meeting Sebastiana that she looked like a pale and needy teenager, we get no further physical depiction of the teenager until now, when her description is provided to give evidence of the pain that she has endured. What is put on display here is the female body in pain, the pain of victimization.

The impact that Sebastiana's rape and suicide have on Lònia reiterates how this detective begins her journey of self-exploration. Lònia first demonstrates indifference towards Sebastiana's situation by handing over her case to Quim, but after learning that Sebastiana has been tricked by a landlady to overpay for an apartment, and upon confirming that the girl is pregnant, Lònia assures her that she will not tell her family if she agrees to stay with her. Despite these initial maternal inklings, we are reminded that for the most part she feels no real empathy towards Sebastiana until she is almost raped herself. Initially, Sebastiana represents the typical girl looking to escape Majorca to find a better life for herself in Barcelona, but she becomes a victim of the city, a fate that Lònia suggests is far too common. Although Colmeiro suggests that "the process of Lònia's identification" does involve both women, Lònia's process of resolving Gaudí's case draws her closer not to Gaudí, but to Sebastiana ("Spanish Detective" 185). To emphasize her identification with Sebastiana, the first image that is conjured up when she permits Gaudí to complete Jovel's castration is of Sebastiana sleeping on vomit-stained sheets. Lònia recognizes herself, her past, and her victimization in Sebastiana, who is, according to Colmeiro, in large part responsible for her identity crisis in *Antípodes* (186).

The attachment that she comes to feel towards Sebastiana is founded upon their shared conservative and religious upbringing in Majorca, and the key moment occurs when Lònia stresses to Sebastiana in front of her Majorcan friend and social worker Jerònia, who still subscribes to these traditional values and morality, that she understands her situation: "'Ja veig que [els teus pares] són dels que creuen que una dona només és violada si es deixa ...' Jo també havia estat d'aquesta classe de gent. Fins que un dia ho vaig dir davant la Mercè i la Mercè em va deixar l'opinió feta una coca" (97) ("'I see. They're [your parents] the kind that believe if a woman is raped, it's because she went along with it.' I believed that once myself. Until one day I said it in front of Mercè, and she tore my opinion into shreds") (79). Lònia feels a newfound connection with Sebastiana because she has almost been raped herself, and though she does not tell Sebastiana that she has been assaulted, Lònia recalls the story of Maria Goretti, an Italian virgin-martyr and canonized saint. Two different understandings of rape victims' roles in their own attacks are underlined in this episode. Jerònia proudly explains how Maria Goretti was an adolescent girl who was almost raped, but knowing that this would be a mortal sin, allowed herself to be killed instead. Whereas Jerònia highlights Maria Goretti's bravery, Lònia counters this admiration by emphasizing that even at a young age she believed that Maria Goretti's actions were irrational and senseless and that rape victims are never to be blamed for their rape. Lònia uses her past, her Catholic upbringing in Majorca, and her rebellion against it, to persuade Sebastiana to not blame herself, but to rightfully place the blame on her victimizer instead.

Reappropriating the Maria Goretti story, Lònia dispels the notion that rape victims who do not fight off their attackers consent to their attacks, and she counsels Sebastiana to stay in Barcelona and have an abortion, which in her case would be legal.[17] Lònia, who has not taken a stand on the issue before, decides that she must now confront Jerònia, who wants to return with Sebastiana to Majorca, and argue for what she believes is best for the teenage victim. Significantly, Lònia has become a true advocate for Sebastiana, and in so doing, she advocates for herself as a victim as well. Her identification with Sebastiana puts into perspective her own victimization as she is finally able to admit that she too has been a victim of gender violence.

In *Antípodes*, however, the victim, Cristina Segura, does not elicit the same type of identification and empathy that Lònia feels towards Gaudí and Sebastiana. On the contrary, Lònia takes a dislike to the Majorcan teenager almost immediately:

> Era una mossa de casa bona, és a dir, mitja melena rossa – tenyida – , cara de pa, els ulls pintats subreptíciament de manera que semblava que els tenia blaus encara que els tingués marrons, vestida amb roba cara i discreta, accessoris destrament combinants, manicura impecable amb ungles rosades d'una llargada perfectament justa. Allò que sa tia Antònia en deia una al·lota fina. La vaig fer d'uns divuit anys ...
>
> Em va caure com una pedregada seca, pobre al·lota. Era el prototipus de nena filla de papà, beneitona i creguda, estufada i satisfeta d'ella mateixa, del seu estatus social, a qui tot li havia sortit bé fins ara i creia que aquest privilegi era degut, no a la casualitat, sinó als seus propis mèrits. (29)

> She was a girl from a well-off family, longish blonde hair – dyed – and a pasty face, eye makeup applied discreetly so the eyes seemed blue even though they were brown, expensively dressed, with well-chosen accessories, impeccable manicure with pink fingernails of exactly the right length. What Aunt Antònia would call a fine young lady. I guessed she was about eighteen ...
>
> She came on like a ton of bricks, poor kid. She was the prototypical spoiled brat, simple-minded and pretentious, vain and satisfied with herself and with her social status, someone for whom things had gone well so far, and she thought it was due to her own merits rather than to chance. (13)

This description of Cristina, which draws attention to her accessories and social status rather than her physical or sexual attributes, underscores the difference between Oliver's emplotment of the female body and the descriptions of women's bodies in traditional crime fiction.[18] From the outset, Lònia underscores that Cristina with her dyed blonde hair, her expensive dress and accessories forms part of the Majorcan elite, the same upper class that will be responsible for the crimes committed in *Antípodes* and in *El sol que fa l'ànec*. Unlike what she experiences with Sebastiana, Lònia does not identify with or feel empathy towards Cristina, and, as Colmeiro signals, the reason that Lònia feels compelled to investigate her disappearance is to help assuage her guilt over Sebastiana's suicide ("Spanish Detective" 186). Lònia's drive to solve Cristina's case is never really about Cristina.

When Lònia realizes that she has been deceived by Cristina to protect land that she is now thinking of developing, she disregards the fact that Cristina has been a victim of sex trafficking and slaps her three times for each of the victims of the case – the Australian grandmother, the cleaning lady, and herself. Even though Lònia recognizes that Henry has betrayed her both personally and professionally by deceiving her into believing that the teenager is dead after falling in love with her, she only seeks revenge against Cristina: "M'havien estafada. Tots dos. Però només tenia necessitat de venjar-me de na Cristina" (234) ("They'd really stuck it to me. Both of them. But I only wanted vengeance on Cristina") (210). Despite sharing the experience of being forced into prostitution, Lònia does not view Cristina as a victim because she learns that the teenager will build on the land that Lònia believes she is saving from being violated. We are reminded that Lònia has sworn to protect the land and admits to feeling maternal towards it, emphasizing Oliver's concern with the phenomenon of balearization in Majorca. Instead, Cristina will continue the raping of Na Morgana that her uncle had commenced.

Other than the aforementioned women and Na Morgana, the other victims in *Antípodes* are the prostitutes that Lònia encounters in the Majorcan brothel. Yet even before her encounter with these prostitutes, Lònia has begun questioning what constitutes the prostitution of the female body when she reencounters Cristina on Lida and Jem's boat. Her conversations with Lida prompt her to realize that all women face having to rent some part of their body to a man. As she interviews the girls working at the Segura family's hotel in Majorca, she compares their situation with the one faced by prostitutes, recalling what Lida has previously argued:

> Creus que hi ha cap puta que ho sigui per gust?, m'havia dit na Lida. Bé, el que és jo, abans m'estimaria més llogar el cony com les putes que no les mans com aquestes noies. En definitiva, per què el cony ha de ser més sagrat que qualsevol altra part del cos? Si una dona volia llogar el seu cos

> a un home per boixar, no hi tenia el mateix dret que si el volia llogar per escriure-li les cartes i els informes a màquina? O per rentar-li els plats i els calçotets i, en aquest cas, ni tan sols cobrar? El mal era que sempre fossin les dones que haguessin de llogar qualque cosa, la cotorra, les mans, l'esquena o el cap. (137)

> Do you think there are whores who do it for pleasure? Lida had said to me. I myself would prefer to rent my cunt like the whores than my hands like these girls. In the end, how come the cunt is always considered more sacred than any other part of the body? If a woman wanted to rent her body to a man for fucking, didn't she have as much right to do that as she had to rent herself to him to write his letters or do his typing? Or for washing his dishes and underwear and not even get paid for it? The problem is that it's always women who have to rent something, her box, her hands, her back or her head. (116)

By asking whether it makes a difference how the female body is sold to men, Lònia appears to equate these as equal forms of prostitution and suggests that one is no better than the other. Moreover, Lònia claims that all women should have the right to choose how and why they want to rent their bodies. Still, it is not until she witnesses one of the prostitutes, who she nicknames Babyface in the Majorcan brothel, take her place with a client that she comes to understand what the prostitution of the body entails: "[O]bria les cames en un gest habitual. Vaig veure que tancava els ulls i premia la boca. Vaig veure com aquell bèstia se la tirava, gairebé amb la mateixa indiferència que ella havia obert les cames" (191) ("[S]he spread her legs with a habitual gesture. I looked on as she closed her eyes and held her lips tightly together. I saw how that pig took her, almost with the same indifference she had") (168). Lònia is struck by the "poca il·lusió, tan poc desig, tanta indiferència, en aquell acoplament, era un acte tan mecànic, que se'm va encongir el cor" (191) ("little illusion or desire, so much indifference in that copulation, it was such a mechanical act it made my heart cringe") (168). When Lònia finds herself in a similar position with Inspector Vargas, we are reminded of this scene with Babyface. Forced to experience the same indifference that she saw on Babyface's countenance, Lònia reflects upon the following thought: "Però vaig pensar que m'haurien fugit per sempre més les ganes de boixar. I mira que m'agrada!" (193–4) ("I thought I'd lose the desire to fuck forever. And I really like it!") (170). Lònia equates this feeling to one of victimization. In her view, all the prostitutes who experience this indifference and loss of sexual desire are victims.

After beating up a pimp on behalf of a group of prostitutes in *El sol que fa l'ànec*, Lònia arrives at a similar conclusion that resonates with her realizations in *Antipodes*: "[H]i ha dones que venen el cos i el cap i són considerades esposes i mares de família. Què té més, vendre el cony d'una manera o d'una altra?" (22) ("[T]here are women who sell their bodies and their brains too, and they're considered wives and mothers. What difference does it make which way you sell your cunt?") (7). Lònia likens being a wife and a mother to a woman selling her sex because for her, they are merely different ways of prostituting yourself. Emphasizing this point, she argues that wives and mothers sell not only their bodies, but their minds as well, making their form of prostitution perhaps worse still. It would appear that Lònia represents a form of feminism that is in favour of prostitution like any other line of work, giving women the right to choose how to employ their bodies. Taken together, these scenes seem to suggest that the character has come to the realization that a great majority of women rent or sell some part of themselves to men in some form or another because they are forced to do so. By redefining the prostitution of the female body, Oliver again projects an incriminating perspective on gender roles and positions.

While the investigation in *El sol que fa l'ànec* centres on finding a missing girl named Júlia in Majorca, Júlia's disappearance forces Lònia to examine a new type of crime – the sexual exploitation of children. Apart from the distinctive nature of the crime in this novel, another departure from the two novels that precede it is that we find the most graphic examples of victimization in this work, in a series of vignettes that portray the rape of little boys and girls by both men and women: "Infants acaronats, infants atupats, infants pessigats, infants besats, infants mossegats, infants penetrats per tots els forats del cos, infants emporuguits, terroritzats. I homes i dones – més homes que dones, però en aquest cas era el mateix – despullats, en una orgia desenfrenada i malèfica" (208) ("Kids being hugged, beaten, pinched, kissed, bitten, penetrated through all their orifices, scared kids, terrified kids. Men and women – more men than women, but in this case it was all the same – all naked, having an unending and evil orgy") (113). Apart from the scenes where Lònia is assaulted, this is the only other episode in which the crime is narrated and visualized as it happens. She feels utterly helpless since she cannot defend this group of victims. Instead, Lònia becomes a witness to the children's assault and trauma, in this way transforming the reader from a mere spectator to a witness of child abuse.

Using a first-person narrative, Oliver depicts the process of Lònia's traumatization upon witnessing the violation of these vulnerable bodies. The rapists' power during this sequence becomes clear to Lònia because she is present as they defile the children. Despite the fact that Júlia and her employer Catalina are both victims of Tomeu and those who help him in the sex trafficking of children, they are also accomplices, since they both knew why these children were being brought over to Majorca. For this reason, Lònia remarks that she feels no pity towards Catalina: "No me feia gens de pena ... I d'això sí que ella n'era tan culpable com els altres, encara que no s'hi sentís, encara que se'n cregués víctima" (183) ("I didn't feel one bit sorry for her ... And she was just as guilty as the others, even though she might not think so, even though she might think she was a victim, too") (98). However, Lònia still feels some sort of obligation to defend both Catalina and Júlia at the end of the novel, but it stems from the guilt that she feels because she was unable to protect the children from being raped. When she finally catches up to Tomeu, "li vaig clavar una puntada de peus als collons per la mort de na Catalina i un cop de conill a la nuca per la mort de na Júlia. No era que em sabés greu que fossin mortes, perquè també elles eren culpables. Però, culpables o no, eren dones – i prou greu que em sabia, mecagondena – i ja no es podrien defensar com els que eren vius" (209) ("the kick to his balls was for Catalina's death and the rabbit punch to his neck was for Júlia's death. Not that I was so grieved for them, because they were guilty too. But guilty or not, they were women – and I was grieved about that, damn it all to hell – and they couldn't defend themselves like the live ones back there") (113–14). What Oliver uncovers in this final installment of the Lònia Guiu trilogy is that no woman or child is immune from gender or sexual violence and that this violence is a systemic problem nestled in the governing patriarchal institutions. Recognizing the vulnerability both of the children and of Júlia and Catalina, the female sleuth "supports a personal justice," as Vosburg has previously demonstrated, which is emphasized in this novel when she retaliates against Tomeu on behalf of all his victims ("Genre Bending" 67).

This belief in a personal form of justice is best exemplified in *Estudi en lila*, where Lònia enables Gaudí to avenge her rape by castrating her rapists. In *Estudi en lila*, Lònia "refuses to reestablish the status quo," leaving open for debate the question of whether there is "a proper response to rape" ("Genre Bending" 67). What Gaudí's rape in the Plaça de Sant Jaume, the heart and institutional centre of Barcelona and of Catalonia, reinforces is the notion that women continue to be victims of the patriarchy and that rape is both "ritualized and repeated," as Molinaro asserts, which is precisely the "social disorder" that Lònia confronts and takes action against ("Writing" 104). Gaudí, henceforth, has punished her rapists and gotten away with it because she appeals to Lònia's personal sense of justice, even though Gaudí practices a more extreme form of female justice, like the one conveyed by the lilac-coloured graffiti slogan on Barcelona's city buildings saying, "contra violació, castració" (191) ("Against rape, castration") (155).

Oliver's answer to sexual violence in her Lònia Guiu series is to allow the female victims to tell their story of victimization and violation, to retake control over their narrative, and to break with the narrative that rape and gender violence has imposed upon them. In addition, Oliver is continually defining what it means to be a female victim under this system by including prostitution as another form of gender victimization. While the private eye's particular sense of justice and evasion of the legal system are not exclusive to Oliver's detective fiction, the fact that Lònia's sense of justice is intimately tied to crimes relating to violence against women is both novel and pivotal to understanding Oliver's work (see *Killing Carmens* 32–3). Thompson-Casado has previously argued that because in Oliver's crime fiction any woman can be "the target of sexual violence, Oliver carefully avoids the imputation of guilt to the victim," demonstrating that a woman cannot be accused of provoking her own rape (145). What this realization does is create a community of women inside the text, who collaborate with one another to assure their well-being and rebel against a legal system that does not advocate for them and that conceals the truth. Oliver's readers are compelled to look for what becomes visible in the series because it is through visibility that we arrive at Oliver's form of truth – a truth that becomes apparent when the pain of sexual violence is exposed in the narratives. By following the moments where the assaulted body appears, we also arrive at Oliver's redefinition of victimization and justice in the trilogy.

Like Lònia, we are forced to ask ourselves if the legal and social responses to rape and other forms of gender and sexual violence are adequate and fair to victims, or if the extremes that these characters have gone to are in some measure justified because there is no suitable punishment for these crimes. According to Godsland, Oliver "deploys the genre to assess social responses to rape," to present the lack of legal action with respect to gender violence (*Killing Carmens* 29). With her crime fiction series, Oliver places us in the uncomfortable position of problematizing our reactions to sexual and physical violence in addition to having us identify with the victims of these assaults, whereby we must question what kind of justice we wish to see upheld. In an era of protests against femicide and gender violence, such as the global feminist movement of *Ni una menos* (*Not One Less*), we must ask if we are mere spectators to this sort of victimization or if we will rebel against a system that continues to be complicit with victimizers instead of aligning itself with victims.

From Intertextuality to Metatextuality: Supplanting the Male Crime Fiction Model

By using intertextual references to invoke detectives from other works or the detective stories themselves, Oliver adopts a traditional trait of the genre and has her female detective stand alongside classic male detectives from both Spain and the anglophone world, not only as a ploy to give her protagonist authority as a detective, but also to underscore the particular nature of the crimes that Lònia fights against. In *Estudi en lila*, for example, the intertextual references are used to contrast Oliver's detective fiction model with classic male crime fiction. The title *Estudi en lila* is a play on *A Study in Scarlet* by Arthur Conan Doyle, in which we are first introduced to Sherlock Holmes. Holmes, in a reference to the title, compares his investigation of the murder to "a study in scarlet" to his sidekick, Doctor Watson, explaining that "[t]here's the scarlet thread of murder running through the colourless skein of life, and our duty is to unravel it, and isolate it, and expose every inch of it" (28). In the epilogue to *Estudi en lila*, the explanation that Lònia gives to her colleague, the detective Lluís Arquer, a detective from Jaume Fuster's series of detective novels and thus another intertextual reference, about her case has a similar tone except a study in lilac is a study not of murder, but of rape.[19]

Lònia meets with Arquer to sell him the portion of the case, the international arms and sex trafficking, that does not deal with Gaudí's rape. As Lònia points out to Arquer, "No has vist mai cap pintada color lila d'aquelles que diuen contra violació castració?" (191) ("Haven't you ever noticed the graffiti done in lilac saying 'Against rape, castration?'") (155). Here, Oliver invokes the feminist campaigns against gender violence that took place in Barcelona during 1977 and 1978, along with other parts of Catalonia and Spain, when this lilac-painted slogan could be found on the walls of city buildings (*Killing Carmens* 28; *Una inmensa minoria* 181).[20] Godsland has already noted that these manifestations were planned "to highlight their situation as victims of male violence and to petition for changes to legislation in a bid for heightened protection" (28). In Conan Doyle's novel, there is a clear and direct association between scarlet and blood (or murder), but in Oliver's novel "lila" could be understood in two ways: the colour of rape or the colour of the feminist discourse about sexual violence, since the colour lilac (or purple) has traditionally been associated with the feminist movement. When Lònia refers to the colour of the painted slogan, the implication is that the people who wrote those words are feminists, who would perhaps argue in favour of the kind of justice that Elena Gaudí has tried to obtain (*contra violació, castració*). Thus, the title of the novel can suggest both a study on sexual violence and a study on feminism.

Furthermore, this conversation with Arquer also suggests that Lònia's awakening as a feminist in the novel has been complete. After this allusion to the title of work, Lònia hands Arquer photocopies of rape reports of men who, despite being well-off and without any type of problems, had gone on to rape women. In this way, Lònia prepares for what Arquer will say regarding her decision to allow Gaudí to evade punishment for her castrating revenge (195). Oliver's *Estudi en lila* challenges misconceptions of rape by positing that rapists and their victims can be any age, race, or social class. Lònia, who will not reveal the identity of Elena Gaudí, the rape victim/female criminal-castrator, to Arquer, not only demonstrates her complicity with Gaudí, but, more significantly, she defends the motives that led the victim to commit the crime to avenge her rape.

This encounter with Arquer, which we will return to, is not the first. During Felip Antal's funeral (one of Gaudí's rapists), Lònia sees Arquer and wonders if he is also investigating Antal, stirring up a sense of competition and a flashback of what appears to be a private detectives' association meeting, where both Vázquez Montalbán's Pepe Carvalho and Fuster's Lluís Arquer, are present. Lònia describes the scene and their attitude during the following episode:

> Ell i el Carvallo estaven a un racó, mirant-s'ho tot i tothom amb ulls de perdonavides ... Què s'havien cregut? I si no els agradaven els seus col·legues, per què venien a l'Agrupació?

La veritat és que jo tampoc no m'hi trobava gaire a plaer, allí. Però no em considerava superior als altres, i em va molestar que em mirassin per damunt l'espatlla i amb les celles alçades. (69)

He and Carvalho had been in a corner, looking at everything and everyone with menacing eyes ... Who did they think were? If they didn't like their colleagues, why did they come to the meetings?

As a matter of fact, I wasn't enjoying myself at all either. But I didn't consider myself superior to the others, and it bothered me that they looked at me with arched brows. (55–6; italics in original)

The sense of superiority that both men exhibit towards their colleagues angers Lònia, and yet, the fact that she is there, beside two well-known private detectives that form part of the canon, signifies that she has inserted herself into their world despite their attempt to shun her. Whereas Carvalho ignores her, Arquer cannot help but invite her out to a vegetarian dinner. This encounter with both Carvalho and Arquer is significant because three traditions come together here – the male detective novel written in Castilian, the male detective novel written in Catalan, and now the female detective novel written in Catalan.

In *Estudi en lila*'s epilogue, Lònia and Arquer meet in the same restaurant that they had dined at three years ago. After a flirtatious exchange, Lònia explains that her investigation has concluded because she located Gaudí's three rapists, and Gaudí, in turn, has obtained the revenge and satisfaction that she desired, the castration of her rapists. Lònia informs Arquer that she will sell him the arms trafficking and prostitution case because she too has been tempted to commit the same crime as Gaudí: "Perquè jo hauria fet el mateix, si a mi m'haguessin fet el que li varen fer a ella. I me'n vull anar per no tenir la temptació de fer-ho" (191) ("Because if they'd done to me what they did to her I would have done exactly the same thing. And I want to leave so I won't be tempted to do it") (155). The case that she hands to Arquer does not involve female victims, and thus, Lònia is no longer interested in pursuing it. Once the victim's truth has been told and the perpetrators of gender violence have been punished by Gaudí, Lònia's job has concluded.

In *Antípodes*, Lònia briefly encounters, without knowing who he is, Antoni Serra's Celso Mosqueiro. Serra, a Majorcan-born writer and also part of the Ofèlia Dracs group, developed a crime fiction series featuring a Portuguese ex-policeman turned detective, Celso Mosqueiro, modelled after the hard-boiled tradition.[21] Like Oliver, Serra, a Catalan nationalist and defender of the Catalan language, is also a political, environmental, and cultural activist in both Majorca and mainland Catalonia. Hart differentiates Serra from his predecessors, in particular Tasis, Pedrolo, and Fuster, in that, though they all write their detective novels in Catalan, "Toni Serra goes one step further, showing an endearing relationship to his native Mallorcan that is distinct from the others" ("Catalan Culture" 310). Serra's Mosqueiro, though Portuguese, speaks in Majorcan and not the standardized Catalan of the *Principat*, and from the second novel onwards, Mosqueiro's cases all take place in Majorca (311).[22] Mosqueiro appears in Oliver's *Antípodes* at Na Morgana, where Lònia spends an afternoon at the Cala Mura beach with Queta, a lesbian ecologist who aids her during her investigation of Cristina's disappearance, which is the episode precisely before Lònia suffers the worst beating that she will receive in the trilogy. Lònia asks Queta who the strange man swimming in the pristine water is, to which Queta responds, "Un portuguès ... Crec que era policia, abans ... Li diuen Mosqueiro. Ara viu dins aquest llaüt, ve molt per aquí. És una mica estrany" (166) ("A Portuguese guy ... I think he used to be a policeman. They call him Mosqueiro. Now he lives on the boat, and he comes here a lot. He's a little strange") (144). The appearance of Mosqueiro in *Antípodes* is one more intertextual reference Oliver employs to draw attention to another male detective fiction writer, but this time a fellow Majorcan author. Critics have not emphasized the importance of these intertextual references found in Oliver's crime fiction series, even less so when it pertains to Serra's appearance in *Antípodes*. In fact, Serra and Oliver share a number of themes pertaining to Majorca; for example, the savage capitalism provoked by the tourism industry, which led to the overdevelopment of the Majorcan seashore. At the end of *Antípodes*, we are reminded by the female detective that the Cala Mura beach at Na Morgana, precisely where she has seen Mosqueiro, will continue to lose its purity by being prostituted and victimized by the Majorcan elite.

Contrary to the first two installments of the trilogy, Oliver's intertextual references in *El sol que fa l'ànec* are now to her own work, her previous detective novels – *Estudi en lila* and *Antípodes*. What this suggests is that Oliver has worked through her male canon of detective fiction, referencing male sleuths such as Holmes, Carvalho, Arquer, and Mosqueiro to then add her own Lònia Guiu to this group. Interestingly enough, Oliver positions her protagonist at a distance from herself, for Lònia, the character, dissociates herself from the Lònia that forms part of Oliver's fiction. By creating these various levels, a conflation of diegetic levels occurs. Although Oliver does not make an appearance in the novel, she is a being that inhabits Lònia's world in *El sol que fa l'ànec*, since Lònia mentions the author on various occasions, but mostly to suggest that Oliver is critical of how Lònia handles her job: "[V]aig recordar el que m'havia dit un dia na Maria-Antònia: que sempre em ficava en camisa de set canes, que no pensava les coses abans de fer-les i per això em sortien malament, o no tan bé com jo esperava" (73) ("I remembered something Maria-Antònia had said to me: that I always bit off more than I could chew, that I didn't think things through before jumping in and that's why things didn't turn out right, or at least not the way I wanted them to turn out") (36). Lònia also reflects upon how Maria-Antònia defines their relationship and contrasts that with her view of it: "L'Oliver i jo ens entenem molt bé, a ella li agrada dir que som molt amigues, però jo m'estim més no deure-li favors. Perquè després se'ls fa pagar" (147) ("I got along fine with her, she likes to say that we're great friends, but I prefer not to owe her favors. She wants you to pay them back") (78). What is more, character and author are at odds not only with respect to Lònia's detective skills, but also with regard to how close they truly are. Any time that Oliver is mentioned, the narrative hints at a tension between the author and the character.

Oliver is first introduced as a character in the opening scene of the novel when a group of prostitutes scream out Lònia's name in celebration because the sleuth has defended them against their pimp. Lònia, in turn, feels embarrassed that people might think she is a prostitute: "[P]er què no m'havia agradat sentir el meu nom en aquell carrer. I no era perquè jo sigui modesta, que no en som gens, que prou que m'agrada quan l'Oliver escriu les històries que jo li cont i les publica, i com més èxit té, millor" (21) ("[W]hy I hadn't liked hearing my name being cheered on that street. It wasn't because I was modest, I'm not at all, I love it when Oliver writes the stories I tell her and then she publishes them, the more they sell the better") (7). Lònia admits to enjoying the attention that Oliver's novels have garnered her in the beginning of *El sol que fa l'ànec* when she compares her embarrassment at having prostitutes shout her name to her lack of modesty when it comes to her appearance in Oliver's novels. Lònia is aware of the fiction that she forms a part of though she also seems to struggle with losing her self to Oliver's crime literature.

Lònia will later reiterate to the receptionist at the German embassy that she provides Oliver with the stories she includes in her novels, authorizing her or Oliver to publish her endeavours as a private detective. Still, she reaffirms that she is not Oliver's character: "'Doncs sí, som la Lònia detectiva, però no som de l'Oliver,' vaig voler deixar clar. 'Som de mi mateixa. L'Oliver només explica el que jo li cont'" (66) ("'Well, yes, I'm the detective, but I'm not Oliver's,' I wanted to set the record straight. 'I'm strictly my own. Oliver just explains what I tell her'") (33). Surprised, the receptionist, who is also a reader of Oliver's novels, asks her to clarify whether "vostè és la d'*Estudi en lila* i la d'*Antípodes*? Així, allò que diu a les novel·les és veritat?" (66) ("you're the one in *Study in Lilac* and *Antípodes*? And all that stuff in the novels is true?") (33). By including the title of both of her novels, Oliver then allows her character to engage this fictional reader and place some doubt on the authenticity of what the author has transcribed, though Lònia affirms that most of it has happened to her (66). By having the receptionist acknowledge that she exists beyond or outside of Oliver's two novels, the girl has confirmed the existence of Lònia the detective as distinct from Oliver's detective. Consequently, the female sleuth reclaims her name, and emphasizes that "sempre estaria agraïda a aquella noieta, que m'admirava i em trobava guapa i, sobretot, que m'havia donat carta de naturalesa. Era com si m'hagués fet una cèdula d'identificació per mi mateixa. Jo era jo. I n'estava contenta" (67) ("I would be forever grateful to that girl, who admired me and thought I was pretty, and especially since she'd given me a sort of reality license. It was as if she'd given me an identification card. I was myself, I really existed. I was glad" (34).[23] Despite maintaining that she is not a reader of Oliver's crime fiction, this interaction with the receptionist points out that Lònia is acutely aware of how she has been portrayed in Oliver's novels, and, for the most part, appears to agree with her depiction. She uses the encounter with the receptionist, however, to reaffirm that she "owns" her self and her story, whereas Oliver just recounts the material offered to her. By publishing Lònia's adventures, Oliver has made her invisible except as a character, and Lònia combats this invisibility outside of Oliver's novels during this narrative sequence where she confirms that she is not a product of Oliver's imagination.

Like Lònia's network of female friends, Oliver aids Lònia during her investigation of Júlia's disappearance by telling her to contact Montserrat Planes (a translator) and Josep Maria Pujol (a professor of medieval literature at the University of Tarragona) to help her decipher the meaning of "El sol que fa l'ànec," which happens to be a verse of a popular song titled *Va anar a fer cuieres* and is where the title of the book comes from.[24] The verse is repeated over and over again by Catalina's mother, Catalina being Júlia's former employer, and upon hearing it, Lònia recalls reading the song's verses in a postcard that Júlia sent her mother. To uncover the mystery of this song that keeps reappearing in the novel, Quim recounts how Oliver has introduced him to Pujol, who in the novel provides Quim with the meaning and significance of the song because he claims to have heard it near Ripoll, the capital of Ripollès, in the provice of Girona, Catalonia: it is a song that was adapted orally (phonetically) from the song the townspeople heard in Castilian, and though it makes no sense in Catalan, it became popular. Hence, Pujol and the song itself exist outside of the text and draw attention to Oliver's interest in Majorcan and Catalan culture, folklore, and traditions.[25] Despite acknowledging that Oliver has helped her solve the case, Lònia remains critical of Oliver's profession: "[J]o vaig pensar que les escriptores – i els escriptors – són unes mentideres, que treballen amb mentides i que potser arriba un dia que no saben distingir una veritat" (73) ("[I]t occurred to me that writers, both female and male, are liars; they work with lies all the time and maybe the day comes when they can't tell the difference any more") (36). By making this statement, Lònia not only problematizes what we have read thus far, but also pits us against Oliver, encouraging us to uncover the truth in her crime fiction. We are reminded, however, that the truth in the Lònia Guiu trilogy is directly linked to Oliver's reworking of the politics of visibility in the genre. As readers, we are encouraged to track these moments where violence against the most vulnerable are staged and recognize the law's indifference or impotence in its handling these cases. It is in these instances of visibility that the "truth" of the series is revealed.

As previously underscored, Oliver invokes the origins of the genre with her reference to Conan Doyle's *Study in Scarlet*, in addition to having three traditions of the male detective novel in Spain meet within her narrative. In so doing, she opens up a textual space for her female detective alongside Vázquez Montalbán's Carvalho, Fuster's Arquer, and Serra's Mosqueiro. According to Klein, in the pairing of detective/criminal, "it is apparent that the detective is always male, always in the dominant position in the pairing. Consequently, we see the dilemma writers have faced in using a biological female in a definitionally male space" ("*Habeas Corpus*" 173–4). The problem consists of the male space that defines crime fiction, and "[t]he result has been to call into question at least one side of the phrase 'woman detective,' rendering it an oxymoron. If female, then not detective; if detective, then not really female" (174). In order to resolve the "[i]f female, then not detective" dilemma in female crime fiction, "women detectives emphasize their deviancy, their distance from the proper role of Woman" (174; 177). We see this distancing and deviancy effect in Oliver's trilogy: Lònia can move through the world, role-playing, chameleon-like, switching between social and linguistic registers because she rejects the traditional roles afforded to women and intentionally positions herself as an outsider. Lònia, along with her sidekick Quim, is always on the margins, but moving back and forth between the margins and the centre. For this reason, she has the capacity to infiltrate both the underbelly of the urban areas, and also the upper echelons of society.

More significantly, the character of Lònia is deviant, in terms of the tradition of the genre, because she doubles as a victim, because she experiences gender violence first-hand. Oliver confronts the traditionally masculine space of crime fiction by using the scenes where the female private eye is assaulted to guide her reader's gaze to the new representation of the female body in the genre – the victimized body. There is no pleasure in the viewing of the female body, for when Lònia's body finally becomes visible it is always in danger of being raped. As both the detective and the reader find themselves encircled by gender violence, we realize that the female detective turned victim poses a problem for the genre because the narrative of investigation now goes hand-in-hand with a narrative of sexual victimization. Lònia, however, does not remain a victim. She fights back and is able to reestablish the power and hierarchy configuration of the detective/criminal. Though she temporarily doubles as a victim, in the end she ends up having the upper hand in these power struggles.

Priscilla Walton and Manina Jones have previously suggested that the female detective occupies an "outsider" position (173–4). She is always on the border between spaces, legality, and social and institutional norms (191). In Oliver's crime fiction, the female detective is also always on the border between detective and victim. According to Walton and Jones, writers of female crime fiction have unlocked "a site of discursive power," and as Oliver's series demonstrates, a space for self-exploration and for the reformulation of how the female body is represented and how victimhood is understood in crime fiction has been opened as well (194). I agree with Walton and Jones that through the genre's gendering, a new "code" for crime fiction has been written, making the female writer – and I would add the female detective as well – what they term "generic outlaws" (195). In Oliver's crime fiction, empowerment springs forth from vulnerability and victimization. Employing a female detective who can take on a sexual assault victim's perspective is an empowering move on Oliver's part, a deviant move that rewrites traditional representations of victimization in crime fiction by forcing the detective to examine and recognize herself as a victim. With Oliver's Lònia Guiu series, a liberating discourse, perhaps delinquent in its own right by challenging and subverting the male canon of crime fiction, is born.

Chapter Five

Lesbianizing the Genre

Lesbianizing the Public Space in Isabel Franc's Emma García Stories

Although not the first female detective to appear on the scene – she was first presented to the world in 1999 in *Plumas de doble filo* (*Double-Edged Feathers/Pens*) by Isabel Franc, under the pseudonym Lola Van Guardia – Emma García *was* the first lesbian detective.[1] García, who is absent from the first novel of the Lola Van Guardia trilogy, *Con pedigree* (*With Pedigree*, 1997), is part of a lesbian ensemble cast whose members collaborate with one another to solve cases involving the disappearance of high-profile lesbian women: the case of the missing politician, Laura Mayo, in the second installment of the series, *Plumas de doble filo*, and the disappearance of the feminist lawyer, Nuria Capell, in the final novel of the trilogy, *La mansión de las tríbadas* (*The Mansion of the Tribades*, 2002). With *No me llames cariño* (*Don't Call Me Honey*, 2004), the character of Emma García moves from being a secondary character in the trilogy to the detective protagonist in this novel and in three subsequent short stories, where she becomes a private investigator after opening up her own office in the Poblenou neighbourhood of Barcelona.[2]

Before the creation of Lola Van Guardia's lesbian trilogy, the representation of lesbianism in Spanish fiction remained, for the most part, invisible both within and outside of the fictional framework because "despite lesbian support, the gay and feminist movements in fact did little to represent or foreground lesbian identity and sexuality," according to Nancy Vosburg and Jacky Collins (10). Furthering this point, Collins has previously remarked, "One of the biggest obstacles to the development of a positive lesbian identity has been the invisibility of women's relationships, both heterosexual and homosexual, throughout history" ("Lesbian Identity" 128). Before Vosburg and Collins, Wilfredo

Hernández offered his explanation for why this was so: "The late appearance of the lesbian subject in Spain is a direct consequence of the political and religious repression exercised during the Francoist regime. Book censorship made it extremely difficult for writers to deal openly with sexuality" (29). In its oppression of the homosexual population, in 1954 Franco's government amended the Ley de Vagos y Maleantes (The Law of Vagrants and Miscreants or Vagrancy Act), "in force since 1933" to control and seclude potentially dangerous individuals from the rest of the public, "to include homosexuals." The Ley de Peligrosidad y Rehabilitación Social (Delinquency and Social Rehabilitation Law) of 1970, which replaced the Ley de Vagos y Maleantes, went so far as to punish those suspected of homosexual activities with incarceration (Collins, "Lesbian Identity" 128).

Even with the transition to democracy and the decriminalization of homosexual acts in 1979, the decade of the 1990s in Spain was one in which lesbianism was described by Rosa Montero as "una homosexualidad oculta" ("a hidden homosexuality") in an article in *El País Semanal* (19). Montero explained that now that Spanish society exhibited greater tolerance towards non-normative sexuality, "la invisibilidad se ha convertido en una cárcel. Mientras que los *gay* han normalizado considerablemente su situación y su presencia, las lesbianas continúan de algún modo en la clandestinidad" ("invisibility has become a prison. While gay men have normalized considerably their situation and presence, lesbians continue in some way in secret") (ibid.; italics in original). This underground homosexuality translated to a literary non-presence or invisibility whereby "until the end of the 1990s, it was impossible to speak of a body of Spanish lesbian fiction" according to Collins ("(Un) natural Exposure" 78). With such limited exposure, the lesbian subject had a restricted space marked out for itself in fiction until Isabel Franc created a space for a total reveal of the lesbian experience.

Published by Egales for its *Salir del Armario* (*Coming Out of the Closet*) series, the Van Guardia trilogy and its continuation in *No me llames cariño* present a generalized "coming out" of the lesbian community, and "makes visible and gives voice to a variety of lesbian identities, lifestyles, and looks" as Vosburg demonstrates ("All L" 195–6). Since the unifying message in the novels is to make lesbianism visible, the characters find themselves prompted to embrace and celebrate their lesbian identities and "'out' themselves in public," which oftentimes results in romance (199). According to Phyllis Betz, lesbian detective novels employ lesbian pulp as their base, and so, "the romantic life of the detective moves from the periphery of the narrative to its center, sometimes even disrupting the criminal investigation in favor of the personal one" (52). Indeed, romance plays a central role in Franc's crime fiction, since the sometimes ineffective and blundering Emma García often falls in love with her suspects and ignores their potential involvement in the crime. Mimicking the male generic model where the detective falls for the femme fatale, the investigation repeatedly takes a back seat to the sexual encounters that occur in the novels as part of what Sally Munt calls "a narrative process of 'discovery'" (*Murder* 141). Poking fun at the hard-boiled male convention, Franc's parodic disruption and subversion of the traditional formula reveals social problems as well, such as the inability of lesbian couples to marry and adopt prior to 2005 and the pervasive problem of gender and domestic violence in Spain.[3]

Previously silenced or repressed in Spanish fiction, the role of lesbian desire in Franc's crime literature, beyond the parody it entails, is part of what Munt calls "our rhetoric of resistance" because "resistance to a homophobic culture is a relentless demand for presence, an occupation of space which we have colonized in the name of a configuration of desires we call 'lesbian'" (*Heroic Desire* 6). This portrayal of lesbian desire fits Munt's definition of "that which is productive, excessive, expansive, a pleasure-machine which can open up new spaces in which we can live" (6). The visibility of lesbian desire, then, allows for "an occupation of space" to use Munt's term – in this case, a colonization of the genre that frees the lesbian subject from the prison of invisibility previously described by Montero. With romance becoming so crucial to the plotline of lesbian crime fiction, what this means is that the lesbian body is also now at the centre of the text. From an outsider marginalized status to the insider centre, there is a realignment of what is made visible in the trilogy and *No me llames cariño*, for as the lesbian subject attains greater visibility, men become invisible. According to Gill Plain, "Lesbian detection begins by empowering the disempowered. It confers a degree of agency upon the outsider, who challenges the status quo through a variety of erotic, didactic and parodic interventions" (217). In Franc's series, empowerment hinges on visibility, and the result is the depiction of a "[l]esbian nation ... an imagined space, envisioned as the symbolic rupture of women from men – or more specifically – 'patriarchy'" (Munt, *Heroic Desire* 146). This concept of a lesbian nation draws on radical feminist Jill Johnston's term, which is also the title of her 1973 book *Lesbian Nation: The Feminist Solution*, where she argues in favour of mobilizing women, specifically lesbians, through separatism. Although Munt is critical of both Johnston's vision and the 1970s lesbian separatist movement in the United States, as it was both "class-and race-specific" (145), she posits that the desire for a lesbian nation evolves "from a historical invisibility contingent on a dea(r)th of signification; lesbians wanted to put themselves on the map" while at the same time removing themselves "from the cartography of heteropatriarchy" (156). Beginning with *Plumas de doble filo,* Franc humorously brings this nation to life in her crime fiction, for according to Collins, the novel "can be seen to act as a vehicle for the creation of a lesbian utopia," an all-female zone "reinforced by the author's decision to write only in the feminine singular and plural, rather than using the masculine singular and plural forms to signify collectively both male and female nouns, the current accepted linguistic practice in Castilian Spanish" ("(Un)natural Exposure" 78, 85). As Vosburg points out, "In Van Guardia's utopian universe, the visibility of the lesbian community and the solidarity it inspires are enough to turn the tide" ("All L" 199), a sentiment shared by many of the previously cited scholars who have written about these novels.

In Franc's novels, the performance of this lesbian utopia functions to rewrite the detective role and to disrupt the masculinity of the crime fiction canon because "the gendered mechanics" of this narrative space, to use Marilyn Farwell's term, are explored and problematized (61). Speaking about the study of the lesbian subject in literature, Tamsin Wilton argues that this entails understanding "'[l]esbian' as a space, a position" (7), which draws on Farwell's emphasis that "gender must be analyzed not as a quality but as a positionality" (67). Thus, the notion of "lesbian-as-space" creates an alternate perspective from which to read, for as Wilton suggests regarding "[l]esbian-ness," it permits "a necessary eccentric perspective from which may be 'read' the hegemonic structures and relations of the heteropatriarchy as they impact on and inflect the production and consumption of literary texts" (135). In lesbian crime fiction, visibility relies on a performance of space, whereby performing "lesbian-ness" (re)sexes the traditionally male-dominated genre as lesbian. Here, we are reminded of Judith Butler's study of how "the performativity of gender" functions as a form of visible resistance and as a rewriting of gender itself (*Gender Trouble* xiv–xv; 177). Since we now read from the "lesbian," this disruption and occupation of the generic space leaves no place for men in Franc's novels, debilitating patriarchy to the point where it becomes an external and yet never present or named threat, and so justice is brought about by and for lesbians.[4]

Franc's latest crime fiction, in the form of two short Emma García stories, "El enigma de su voz" (2010, 2013) ("The Enigma of Her Voice,"

2011) and "Sin tratamiento de cortesía" ("Without Common Courtesy," 2014), presents a private eye who, in response to the socioeconomic crisis, serves the interests of lesbian couples, becoming their accomplice so that they do not fall prey to a patriarchal system that targets them.[5] While male characters were a non-factor in the trilogy and were the victims in *No me llames cariño*, in these Emma García stories men actively threaten the lesbian community, in particular the stability of lesbian couples. If we recall, in *No me llames cariño* the crime being investigated is the murder of five men who abused women. García becomes an abettor to the female criminal, Carol Choy, by letting her elude justice because she agrees that the legal system would have been ineffective in punishing these men for the crime of gender violence (see Corbalán). This, in turn, leads her to think that she should leave the police force and take Montse Murals's suggestion to open a detective agency "*only for women*" (*No me llames cariño* 320; italics in original).[6] In the Emma García stories, however, men attempt to invade and disrupt the space for lesbian love and marriage. Responding to this masculine invasion, the sleuth becomes a hybrid of detective and bodyguard, and a discourse of empowerment emerges as a response to an era of crisis in Spain that could once again endanger the lesbian community with invisibility.

A further departure from the trilogy and from *No me llames cariño* is Franc's use of first-person narration in the two short stories.[7] Both stories are the detective's rendition of what occurred, as well as her way of making the threats to the lesbian community evident. Privileging Emma's perspective further serves to give notice from the beginning of "El enigma de su voz" that the sleuth is no longer an outsider, as she was in the previous novels, and the opposition between Madrid and Barcelona is no longer present in the Emma García stories. As we recall, in *Plumas* Emma, who is part of the Cuerpo Nacional de Policía (National Police Corps) in Madrid, comes to Barcelona to work on the case of Laura Mayo in conjunction with the all-female Catalan autonomous police force, the *Mosses d'Esquadra*. According to Collins's "This Town Ain't Big Enough," the geographic and sociopolitical tensions between Madrid as "centre" and Barcelona as "periphery" (118) are "reflected in the experience of detective inspector Emma García" in the last two installments of the Van Guardia trilogy (119). Even in *No me llames cariño*, where Emma is now a member of the *Mosses d'Esquadra* and is learning Catalan, these tensions continue to exist as she "is portrayed as the outsider" ("Isabel Franc's" 70). This, however, changes in the short stories, partly due to the fact that she now works as a private detective and has gotten to know the city quite well, but also because in "Exòtika," she now speaks Catalan fluently.

From the beginning of "El enigma de su voz," Franc situates us in the Poblenou neighbourhood of Barcelona, where Emma both works and lives, as her private detective agency doubles as her home on *la calle Amistat* (67).[8] In fact, she has taken control of the city, making the space her own. We note how she traverses Barcelona with familiarity and ease, a skill that comes in handy upon accepting Diana Gallard as a client, since the case will involve watching and protecting Diana's aunt. "El enigma de su voz," however, does not begin with the case brought to her by Diana Gallard, but with the clerk of La Licorería telling Emma about the embalmed parrot they keep in the store. A popular liquor store in the Poblenou neighbourhood of Barcelona, La Licorería, best known as "El Lloro del 36" ("The Parrot of 36"), opened its doors in 1932 at 91 Carrer del Taulat (see Casino). As recounted in Franc's text, this establishment is best known for the tale of the parrot brought over from Guinea that was given as a gift to the Farreras family in 1957. It would imitate the sound of the inspector's whistle, creating such confusion that streetcar 36, whose route began and ended in front of the store, would take off before the inspector ever signalled for its departure. It is this story of a false signal, of the parrot's imitation, that provides the frame for Emma's first assignment as a solo investigator. Moreover, we learn that her current case is directly connected to La Licorería, since it involves protecting Diana Gallard's aunt from her husband, who is soon to be released from jail. Twenty years ago, in that very store, he had murdered the man he suspected of being his wife's lover. From the start, this investigation is intimately linked to one of Poblenou's iconic establishments, suggesting that the city will also play a crucial role in this case.

Apart from being driven by economic necessity due to the crisis, Emma also accepts this first job because even before she meets Diana in person she is attracted to her sensual voice: "[U]na voz de mujer, de una sensualidad que ponía la piel de gallina, llamó para requerir mis servicios. Una voz, ciertamente, intrigante" (69) ("I received a call from a woman wanting my services; her voice was so sensual, it gave me goose bumps. It was certainly an intriguing voice") (65). As in the previous novels, Emma allows her desires to play a role in how she handles her case, and it will be up to her sidekick Dos Emes, known in the novels as Montse Murals and whom Emma protects with this pseudonym because she still works for the *Mosses d'Esquadra*, to solve the case. The enigma, at least initially and as the title indicates, has more to do with the reason for Diana's involvement, the intrigue that her voice conceals. In fact, Emma is disappointed at first, because it was "una tarea más propia de una guardaespaldas que de una detective. Sin embargo, no podía rechazar mi primer caso y, a decir verdad, me parecía estupendo trabajar para una señora tan fantástica" (70–1) ("more of a case for a bodyguard than a detective. Still, I didn't think I could say no to my first case and, to be honest, I thought it would be stupendous to work for so fantastic a woman") (66–7). Due to her attraction to Diana, she ignores the clues that the tone of her voice gives away: "[N]o quería que controlara al tipo, sino que vigilara a la mujer: 'No la pierda de vista,' me había exigido. Y, de nuevo entonces, su tono de voz había variado, recuerdo que tuve que hacérselo repetir" (71) ("She didn't want me to do anything about the man, just to keep my eye on the woman. 'Don't lose sight of her,' she'd pressed. And her voice was so quiet this time, I had to ask her to repeat it") (67). She first takes note of what happens with the other woman's voice when she asks if her job is only to look after her aunt. Diana's response gives something away: "'Sí, sólo vigilarla,' en un tono de voz bajísimo, que entendí sólo por el gesto afirmativo. Claro que no le di la menor importancia" (71) ("'Yes, just watch her,' she said in a very low voice, so much so that I understood it only because of the body language that went with it. Of course, I didn't give it any importance then") (67). Emma is hired to keep an eye on Diana's aunt, but the other aspect of her investigation has to do with making sense of the signals that her client's voice seems to be giving off. During their last meeting in "El enigma de su voz," Emma and Diana will share a kiss, but nothing more because the detective realizes it would be inappropriate, and so their relationship ends on a somewhat platonic note. The mystery of her voice, however, is directly related to Spain's history of oppression against lesbian couples, as Emma will discover at the end of the story.

Since the job requires watching and protecting Diana's aunt, Emma's first step is to familiarize herself with the older woman and her apartment, and so she enters her dwelling under the pretext of doing an acoustic inspection for the city. As she looks out the apartment window, she reflects upon the changes that Barcelona, particularly the area of the Mar Bella beach, have undergone:

> Durante décadas, la playa se convirtió en un inmenso basurero en el que se combinaban desperdicios y conchas marinas a partes iguales. Un paisaje en blanco y negro en el que destacaban las llamas de las hogueras que

se encendían para quemar residuos. Un lugar propicio para buscadores de metales, mendigos y almas solitarias. El panorama humano y urbano cambió como ha cambiado siempre esta ciudad, con un acontecimiento extraordinario: los Juegos Olímpicos devolvieron el color al barrio. Todo el distrito se transformó ... Enterraron las vías, se limpiaron las playas, se construyó un paseo y el día que abrieron la Rambla al mar, la gente bajó en tropel, como una procesión, como si les hubieran abierto el camino hacia la iluminación. Lo que antaño fuera un nido de barracas, frente a un mar gris y aislado por las vías del tren, se convirtió en una zona privilegiada. (73)

During the next few decades, the beach became a great dump, with equal parts garbage and seashells. It was a black-and-white landscape in which only flames from the burning trash could be distinguished. It was the perfect place for metal scavengers, the homeless, and lonesome souls. The human and urban panorama eventually changed the way it always has in this city: with an extraordinary event. The '92 Olympic Games brought color back to the neighborhood. It was completely transformed ... They buried the tracks, cleaned the beaches, and built a sea walk; the day they opened La Rambla down to the water, people came down in a mad rush, like a procession, as if the way to illumination had been revealed. What had been a nest of shanties facing a gray ocean and isolated by the train tracks became a high-end neighborhood. (69)

This description of the Mar Bella beach area and Poblenou during the dictatorship and up until the Olympic Games of 1992 emphasizes the black-and-white nature of the landscape, a neighbourhood that became isolated and closed off, and a place where the marginalized would gather. The face of the city, as Emma signals, changed with the Olympic Games because Barcelona opened itself up to the world, and this, in turn, gave Mar Bella and Poblenou colour once again. The slogans used to advertise the changes that Barcelona would undergo suggest this idea of a city making itself presentable to the world. Catchphrases such as "ciutat cara al mar" ("a city turned toward the sea") and "Barcelona posa't guapa" ("Barcelona, doll yourself up") remark upon the process of refashioning that the metropolis would experience (*Barcelona's Vocation* 216).[9] Barcelona reinvented itself during the 1980s and 1990s, reclaiming the sea from industrial use, rescuing its beaches and coastline from the train tracks and factories, and funding a significant urban renewal, because the city had suffered the revenge of the Franco regime, which withheld investments (see Preston's *The Politics*).

According to Joan Ramon Resina, "To be again someday, Barcelona had to be, in the long decades of the Franco regime, a remembered city" (*Barcelona's Vocation* 7–8). Here Resina refers to what Barcelona had been and to its potential as a "budding metropolis" prior to the Spanish Civil War. It is this memory of Barcelona that had to be kept alive during the dictatorship (7). This idea of a "remembered city" would play a role in how the Barcelona of the post-dictatorship era would rebuild itself by turning to its own past not only "out of nostalgia," but also for the "release of meaning locked in the past" (8). This story of a transformed city that had previously been discriminated against because it was viewed as threatening by the Franco regime frames our understanding of the relationship between the aunt and the woman Emma sees her with, who we will find out is her lover. The discrimination and oppression of Barcelona mirrors the discrimination suffered by lesbian couples during and even after the regime.

While Emma reflects upon the renovations that Mar Bella has undergone, she discovers that the same cannot be said of the aunt's apartment, which "tenía el aire rancio de los años sesenta; ... como si no hubiera pasado el tiempo. Había también algunas fotos antiguas, pero en ninguna aparecía una figura masculina identificable con el marido encarcelado" (73) ("had the rancid air of the '60s; ... as if time had stood still. There were also several ancient photos, but none showed a masculine presence that might be her jailed husband") (69). Whereas the neighbourhood has moved forward into a new era, the interior of the apartment signals a continued oppression even though the husband's presence, in the form of memories, is nonexistent. Emma's reading of the apartment perhaps leads her to think nothing of the fact that "[a] media mañana el ascensor se detuvo en el ático y una mujer llamó a la puerta de mi protegida ... Entró en el piso y ninguna de las dos salió hasta primera hora de la tarde. Llegué a pensar que iba a resultarme un caso aburrido" (74) ("[m]idmorning, the elevator stopped on the top floor and someone knocked on the door of the woman I was protecting ... She went in and neither of them reemerged until the first hour of evening. I began to think this was going to be a very dull case") (70). Emma merely reads their relationship as older widows whose friendship has transformed into companionship, watching as they stroll through La Rambla arm in arm (74). Suspecting nothing, the sleuth is relieved to find out that she has succeeded as the aunt's protector, and that the person who has perished is the ex-convict, who was thought to have gotten drunk, fallen to the Ronda Litoral freeway from one of the pedestrian bridges, and then run over by a truck.

With no witnesses, Emma believes that her first assignment has come to a close, and though the police initially suspect that Diana's aunt is involved, Emma acts as a witness, confirming the widow's alibi because she had been watching her the whole time. It is, in fact, Dos Emes who informs her that the two widows share an important bond, for "la mujer con la que mi protegida había pasado la tarde anterior a la muerte del exconvicto era la viuda del que éste había matado veinte años atrás en La Licorería" (76) ("the companion of the woman I was protecting, the lady from the afternoon prior to the ex-convict's death, was the widow of the man killed twenty years earlier in La Licorería") (72). While Emma does not suspect any foul play, Dos Emes does so from the beginning, as she tells the private eye: "Si quiere que le diga la verdad, a mí esta muerte me huele fatal" (76) ("To be honest with you, this death smells fishy") (72). As in *No me llames cariño*, Dos Emes acts as the voice of reason, and compels Emma to question Diana, who confesses that the woman the detective has been protecting, the so-called aunt, is her mother, and the ex-convict is her father, and that the two women are merely friends joined together by tragedy. Convinced once more by Diana's version of events, because Emma admits to being attracted to her and thinks that there is the potential for something to occur between them, Emma believes Diana until Dos Emes discovers that the two women have registered to get married. According to Dos Emes's theory, which proves to be correct, the two had been lovers all along, and the ex-convict's release from prison would have indeed put them and their relationship in jeopardy.

Finally making sense of both crimes, Emma comes to understand that Diana's father "había descubierto que su mujer le era infiel y tenía razón, pero lo que no podía imaginar era que no se trataba de 'un,' sino de 'una' amante" (80) ("had suspected that his wife was cheating on him, and he was correct, but what he couldn't imagine was that his wife's lover was not a man but a woman") (76). The murder at La Licorería, the first crime, signified freedom, a liberation for the lesbian couple, allowing the two women to be together even if in secret, which explains the rancid air of stagnation that Emma describes in the apartment. The only remaining obstacle for the couple was "el barrio mismo: la gente, las barreras sociales, el qué dirán" (80) ("the neighborhood itself: the people and what they'd say") (76). When both investigators realize that Diana Gallard must have been responsible for the murder of her father to shield her mother from harm, Emma decides, as she did in *No me llames cariño*, to allow the female delinquent to get away with murder. This time, however, her reasoning is different. She becomes an accomplice to the crime because, as she tells Dos Emes, "Dejemos que pasen tranquilas los últimos coletazos de su relación, ¿no le parece?" (80) ("Let's let those two enjoy the last years of their relationship in peace, don't you think?") (77). Franc's sleuth takes on this accomplice role to safeguard the lesbian couple, in defence of their visibility and the legitimization of their union.

As she did with the story of Mar Bella and Poblenou, and while she looks out onto the sea, she writes the history of these two women:

> Intenté imaginar también cómo había sido la vida de aquellas dos mujeres en la dictadura, en el posfranquismo y en la transición. Un secreto mantenido en el fondo del armario hasta el momento en que no hubo más trabas. Su existencia había cambiado como su propio barrio, sólo habían tardado unos cuantos años más. Reabrir el caso, interrogar a Diana Gallard y completar el puzzle habría sido devolver el blanco y negro a la vida de las tres. (81)

> I also tried to imagine the lives of those two women during the dictatorship, and in the Post-Franco era, and through the transition. A secret kept in the deepest closet until there were no more obstacles. Their lives had changed just like their neighborhood, except that they were forty years too late. To reopen the case, interrogate Diana Gallard, and complete the puzzle would be to reimpose a black-and-white existence on the three of them. (77)

Once more, the use of black and white, which was earlier used to describe Mar Bella prior to its transformation as "[u]n paisaje en blanco y negro" (73) ("a black-and-white landscape") (69), is employed here to refer to the oppression suffered by homosexuals in Spain before the changes in legislation. This black-and-white existence refers to the lesbian subjects' place in a society that did not accept them and where they were rendered invisible and discriminated against. While oppression is represented in black and white, Emma has previously described how the Olympic Games "devolvieron el color al barrio" (73) ("brought color back to the neighborhood") (69). What is more, "El enigma de su voz" ends with the sleuth imagining what tourists see out of airplane windows: "¿Cuántos de esos ojos – me pregunté– sabían que, tiempo atrás, el barrio no era en technicolor [*sic*]?" (82) ("I wondered how many of those eyes realized that not so long ago, the neighborhood didn't exist in Technicolor") (78). Again, the opposition of black and white versus colour is brought up to highlight the change from an era of repression during and even after Franco to a neighbourhood now in technicolour. This colour or rainbow of acceptance, this visibility, is precisely what Franc's private eye aims to protect, as patriarchal forces now pose a danger to the lesbian community.

Though gender struggles were mostly absent from the trilogy and *No me llames cariño* with Franc's creation of a lesbian nation, "El enigma de su voz" suggests that this utopia is no longer secure and that the lesbian visibility attained after years of struggle is now in danger. The conservative Partido Popular's (People's Party) rise to power in the 2011 general elections in Spain represented just such a threat to lesbian couples, as they ousted the reigning Partido Socialista Obrero Español (Spanish Socialist Workers' Party). This latter party had championed the legalization of same-sex marriage and the right of adoption by same-sex couples that led to the passing of the 2005 law and reform of the Civil Code during José Luis Rodríguez Zapatero's tenure as prime minister. Led by Mariano Rajoy, who became prime minister of Spain in 2011, some members of the Partido Popular appealed the same-sex marriage law only three months after Congress approved it, making claims that marriage is and always will be a legal institution between a man and a woman, and that same-sex marriage denaturalized heterosexual unions (see Marcos). Although the appeal was ultimately rejected in 2012, the Partido Popular continued to be steadfast in its opposition to the law.

"El enigma de su voz," as well as the later "Sin tratamiento de cortesía," reacts not only to an economic crisis, but even more to a social crisis that could endanger the union of same-sex couples. Collins has remarked that Franc/Van Guardia uses her crime fiction to mobilize the lesbian community, as in *Plumas de doble filo*, which "appeared at a time when Spain's conservative party, el Partido Popular, had been working to prevent the introduction of same-sex partnership laws that would seek to secure equal citizenship rights for gays and lesbians. Van Guardia's novel presented an ironic view of this discussion and could be viewed as a rallying cry to the lesbian community to take up the political struggle" ("Sisters" 180). Franc responds to the changing political scene by reactivating what Ana Corbalán has called her active revolutionary agenda, which promotes lesbian visibility (161). The fight, in these two short stories, against the threat of lesbian invisibility through a private investigator who becomes the protector of lesbian couples illustrates what Barbara Wilson understands as the function of lesbian crime fiction: to bring visibility to the lesbian experience, but also to upset generic conventions and "explore what justice means in an unjust world" (223). Justice in this first short story signifies becoming an accomplice to murder to defend the lesbian community against a return to a black-and-white, oppressive, patriarchal existence. By silencing the male threat, the opening that the lesbian community has attained, like the opening of La Rambla to the sea, can continue without new obstacles to freedom.

Like "El enigma de su voz," male characters reappear in "Sin tratamiento de cortesía," and once again, are viewed negatively, as threatening to the lesbian community.[10] Interestingly enough, in "Sin tratamiento de cortesía," Emma's client is a man who hires her to spy on his female business partner, Paola Sergueti, to ascertain whether she is being unfaithful to her wife, Estela Reyes, the principal shareholder in their company. Emma, who opened her detective agency on Montse Murals's suggestion to start an agency only for women, explains that she accepted a male client because of the economic crisis: "Crisis, crisis. No paro de oír esa palabra, de vivirla en carne propia. ¿Qué quería que hiciera? No aceptar aquel caso habría sido un suicidio profesional" ("Crisis, crisis. I can't stop hearing that word, living it in the flesh. What did she want me to do? It would have been professional suicide not to take that case") (111).[11] Here, the crisis takes on an even more prominent role, since it drives Emma to accept a case brought to her by a man whom she dislikes and distrusts from the very beginning. For a private eye during the crisis, she clarifies, "no están los tiempos como para rechazar nada y menos aún un trabajo corto, rápido, en apariencia sencillo y por el que me pagaba el triple de lo que cobro habitualmente ... significaba unos meses de tranquilidad, de pagar facturas sin que ello me provocara gastroenteritis" ("the way things are going, it's not really a good time to turn down anything, much less a small, fast, apparently simple job for which I was getting paid triple the usual amount ... it meant a few months of calm, of being able to pay the bills without getting gastroenteritis") (111–12).

From the beginning of the story, "Sin tratamiento de cortesía" creates an opposition between Emma's male client and Paola, to whom she is already attracted upon seeing a picture of her, as she recounts in her first-person narration: "Se inicia con la foto de Paola Sergueti y unos ojos verde oliva fulminantes. Mirándolos, creí en Dios; semejante criatura solo podía ser producto de la divinidad. Sin embargo, quien me la estaba mostrando nada tenía que ver con lo celestial y sí mucho con las bajezas humanas" ("It all began with the photo of Paola Sergueti and a pair of intense olive-green eyes. Seeing them, I believed in God; such a creature could only be a product of the divine. However, the person showing it to me had nothing to do with anything celestial, and everything to do with human baseness") (111). A further contrast that accentuates this opposition takes place when Emma describes how her client stares at her: "Gélida y punzante, así era aquella mirada de ojos líquidos, carentes de bondad, tramposos ... Creo que la conjuntivitis que sufrí los días posteriores se gestó justo en aquel momento" ("Cold and piercing: that was the look of his liquid eyes, devoid of kindness, scheming ... I think the conjunctivitis that I suffered in the following days was brought on right at that moment") (112). The first paragraphs of the text depict *lo masculino* (the masculine) as threatening, dishonest, and associated with disease, because Emma gets sick with a cold, gastritis, and a bout of conjunctivitis after this encounter. Taking on a male client for the money to pay her bills, her body turns against her because he quite literally sickens her, provoking the same ailments that she thinks his money will ward off (112).

Another clue to discovering that this job will entail more than she initially suspects comes from the fact that he is the husband of her former client, Laura Magri. What she finds interesting is that she cannot remember how Laura became her client: "[C]ómo obtuvo mi contacto, quién me había recomendado. Parecerá un detalle sin importancia, pero no lo es, porque la publicidad de Detectives E&G solo está en centros, locales, asociaciones y servicios LGBTQ. Y esta señora no parecía ni L ni G ni B ni T ni mucho menos Q" ("How she got ahold of me, who had recommended me. It might seem like a minor detail, but it's not, because Detectives E & G only advertises in LGBTQ centers, spaces, associations and service providers. And this lady didn't look like she was L, G, B, or T, much less Q") (113). Initially perturbed by this, Emma is further perplexed by what Magri says next:

> – Mi mujer me dijo que es usted especialista en ese tipo de casos – soltó, y yo me pregunté qué entendían el uno y la otra por "ese tipo de casos," pero el comentario siguiente me desconcertó todavía más – : Sospecho que tiene "unamante."
>
> Imposible deducir si se trataba de un hombre o de una mujer. Tampoco me quedó claro, en un principio, si se refería a su esposa o a Paola Sergueti. (113)

> – My wife told me you are a specialist in these kinds of cases – he said, and I wondered what he or his wife meant by "these kinds of cases," but the comment that followed unsettled me even more – : I suspect she has "a lover."
>
> It was impossible for me to deduce if he meant a man or a woman. Nor was it clear to me, at first, if he was referring to his wife or Paola Sergueti.

Due to the ambiguity of Senõr Magri's words, there is some linguistic confusion regarding the lover's gender, and whether it is Paola or his wife who has taken a lover. Since Magri does not have the courtesy to clarify, this initial confusion foreshadows and makes Emma's discovery that the two women, Laura and Paola, are the ones having an affair all the more comical. And, similar to what occurred during her first solo case, she becomes their bodyguard, the protector of their relationship.

While Emma tries to gather more information about this assignment, her exchange with Senõr Magri makes clear his opinion of women as he tells the sleuth that he has tried to find out who Paola's lover is himself:

> – Le he preguntado a mi mujer – continuó – ella y Paola son amigas, van de compras juntas, al cine, esas cosas ...
>
> El tono desdeñoso hacía intuir el final de la frase: "esas cosas de mujeres." Seguí obviando sus insolencias ...
>
> – ¿Cree que podría estar encubriéndola?
>
> – Imposible. Mi mujer, si supiera algo, ya me lo habría dicho, y si no, pobre de ella. (115)

> – I've asked my wife – he continued – she and Paola are friends, they go shopping together, to the movies, those kind of things ...
>
> The disdainful tone made me guess the end of his phrase: "those things that women do." I ignored his insolence ...
>
> – Do you think she could be covering for her?
>
> – That's impossible. If my wife knew anything she would have told me, and if she didn't, she'd be sorry.

Emma describes feeling ill because this exchange tells her exactly the kind of man she is dealing with: "un tirano, adinerado, corrupto y, a poco que mi cuestionada astucia me traicionara, maltratador" ("a wealthy and corrupt tyrant and unless my dubious qualities of divination betray me, an abuser") (115). Accepting the assignment, she pictures

Laura Magri, who "había sido generosa conmigo y que, a pesar de vivir como una marquesa, su rostro reflejaba una remota amargura" ("had been generous with me and, despite her living like a queen, her face reflected a remote bitterness") (115–16). Emma sympathizes with Laura, feels some sort of connection with her, and this feeling is strengthened when she realizes that she might be dealing with an abuser as well. Her dislike for Senõr Magri versus her sympathy for Laura Magri and her attraction to Paola set the stage for the story's denouement.

Without needing Dos Emes's assistance this time, Emma is able to solve the case quite easily as she follows Paola, who is picked up "a la altura de Palau Reial" ("up by the Palau Reial") and driven to a house "en una urbanización situada entre Llançà y el Port de la Selva" ("in an urbanization located between Llançà and el Port de la Selva") by another woman, whom the sleuth believes she recognizes as Laura Magri (116). She decides to confirm her suspicions not only to solve the case, but also because she decides that she needs to warn her: "No pensé, no valoré las consecuencias. Me dejé llevar por un impulso, por la intuición, un sexto sentido, la rabia, no sé" ("I didn't think. I didn't weigh the consequences. I got carried away by impulse, by intuition, by my sixth sense, by anger, by I don't know what") (118). As in the previous story, Emma decides that justice is better served by safeguarding the lesbian couple. What further convinces the sleuth to aid the two women is Paola's statement regarding Senõr Magri's ignorance of the fact that she has been divorced for months: "Es un tema tabú, para ese energúmeno el matrimonio entre dos mujeres es algo abominable" ("It's a taboo subject. For that nutcase marriage between two women is abominable") (118). Magri's stance on same-sex marriage reaffirms what Emma has come to think of the man, which is further emphasized by his wife's response to Paola's comment, "'Pero le encantaría veros por un agujero,' apuntó Laura Magri con una mezcla de amargura y repugnancia. 'Me lo imagino babeando como un bulldog en celo'" ("'But he'd love to see you through a hole,' signalled Laura Magri, equally embittered and disgusted. 'I can imagine him drooling like a dog in heat'") (118). While the women are not criminals like Diana Gallard, Emma makes herself their accomplice, and thus jeopardizes her client's interests, when she tells them that Laura Magri's husband has hired her and that he has threatened to sell his shares of the company upon finding out that Paola is having an affair. Once again, Franc "presents a dynamic that destabilizes the traditional generic boundaries between investigator and criminal by blurring of [*sic*] the hero/villain paradigm," as Collins has suggested in her reading of *No me llames cariño* ("Isabel Franc's" 71).

When Emma puts together the report that she will hand to Senõr Magri, all her symptoms disappear: "Ni gastritis ni resfriado ni conjuntivitis" ("Neither gastritis nor a cold nor conjunctivitis") (119). Aligning herself with the lesbian couple, a now healthy Emma allows the two women to get a head start and embark on a trip while she informs Senõr Magri that Paola "se fue con su mujer a su casa de la costa" ("went with her/your wife to her/your house on the coast") (120). Emma reveals, "Lo que ni ella [Dos Emes] ni yo ni Paola ni Laura podíamos imaginar era que el azar o, mejor dicho, una veleidad gramatical nos tenía reservada la guinda de tan jugoso caso. A fin de cuentas, ¿por qué usar la cortesía con quien no la merece?" ("What neither she [Dos Emes] nor I nor Paola nor Laura could imagine was that chance or, rather, a vagary of grammar had saved for us the sweet finale of such a delicious case. After all, why use courtesy with someone who doesn't deserve it?") (119). What Emma is referring to is the grammatical fickleness of the formal mode of address. Since she is using the formal "usted" to address Senõr Magri, he misunderstands what she is telling him, thinking that Paola has left with her wife, "su mujer," and not his. It is for this reason that "a mi comentario, resopló aliviado, ... 'Bueno, al menos por ese lado puedo estar tranquilo, era lo que más me preocupaba. Me tranquiliza pensar que sigue con su mujer'" ("He huffed, relieved after hearing my comment, ... 'Well, at least I can rest easy. It was what worried me the most. I'm relieved to know that she's still with her wife'") (120).[12] Realizing what has caused the error, "[m]i estupefacción inicial pasó a convertirse en una malévola sensación de gozo, cálida, acogedora incluso" ("my initial astonishment turned into an evil feeling of joy, it was warm, even comforting") as she imagines what his reaction will be when he comprehends the true meaning of the phrase "su mujer" (120). With this in mind, "Sin tratamiento de cortesía" ends with Emma's final question to Senõr Magri: "¿Me permite tutearle?" ("May I address you informally?") (120). Once she is able to be informal with him and not treat him with the measure of courtesy that he does not deserve anyway, the "su" in "su mujer" will be replaced with "tu," and he will realize that she meant his wife all along. The linguistic ambiguity that confused Emma when Senõr Magri said, "Sospecho que tiene 'unamante'" ("I suspect she has 'a lover'") comes full circle, since he misunderstands that Emma is informing him that Paola's lover is his wife. Because he represents a threat to Paola and Laura, Emma makes sure that if anyone is to be the victim in this scenario, it is Senõr Magri.

While men reappear in both stories, the one in "El enigma de su voz" does not make it out alive, and Senõr Magri finds himself deceived by his wife and his business partner in "Sin tratamiento de cortesía." Regarding Franc's project in *No me llames cariño*, Collins has previously claimed that "she succeeds in disrupting this paradigm that posits the body as female by transforming the traditionally female victim into that of a male. In addition, the author undermines the subsequent detective/ criminal binary by uniquely presenting both of these elements as lesbian, ... thus resulting in this example of crime fiction being written exceptionally on the male body" ("Isabel Franc's" 71). The same, I would suggest, applies to the short stories where the victims are male and, more significantly, are victimized because the private eye makes this possible in order to create safe spaces for these lesbian couples.[13]

In both stories, the masculine threat to lesbian love is countered by lesbianizing the public space, allowing for these couples to make the transition from the private sphere to the public one. Ann Davies notes that in talking about female detectives and the city, "the movement of female detectives through different city spaces allows for the creation of a multi-layered sense of the city unified by the detective's gaze. Women as detectives make city spaces home spaces: the city becomes home, 'our' city, ... through the invocation of active citizenship, a specific allegiance to city space precisely as home space" (119). While in "El enigma de su voz" the focus is on the city as a reflection of the discrimination suffered by lesbian couples, in "Sin tratamiento de cortesía," the detective travels from the city to become a voyeur, an observer of the lesbian domestic space. Thus, both spaces are linked through Emma, and she succeeds in eliminating the divide between the city and the home. Barcelona, both in the private and public arenas, is not merely feminized, but actively lesbianized in Franc's short stories.

As Judith Mayne points out regarding lesbian representation in cinema, "lesbianism is both lure and threat for patriarchal culture as well as for feminism, and it challenges a model of signification in which masculinity and activity, femininity and passivity, are always symmetrically balanced" (125). Here, Franc upsets the so-called balance, creating realignments where *lo masculino* is forced into passivity because there is a rejection of the site of the passive female victim. Moreover, Farwell proposes, "The lesbian subject, however, is a text image that refuses to align itself with the gendered mechanics and instead challenges those mechanics for its own narrative space, a lesbian narrative space" (61). With this (re)occupation of the narrative space – in this case, that of crime fiction – the lesbian community aligns itself with the active in the genre, in a process of evolution as a ""[l]esbian citizenship" that Munt describes as "self-consciously lived as a form of process, of relational movement" (*Heroic Desire* 143). Franc's series, as Plain suggests more generally about lesbian crime literature, "has also succeeded because it represents the highest or furthest point of the genre's possibility. More than any other appropriation or development of the formula, it has followed narrative possibilities to their extreme" (217). In addition to being a hybrid of detective and bodyguard, Emma also becomes an outlaw, a disruptive force that promotes the empowerment of lesbian couples by challenging and disarming the patriarchal forces that now reappear in the short stories. According to Kathleen Klein, "women detectives emphasize their deviancy, their distance from the proper role of Woman. When the female detective is also a lesbian, her transgressive behaviour multiplies exponentially" ("*Habeas Corpus*" 177). A private eye who emerges from the socioeconomic crisis, Emma rebels by giving visibility to the lesbian community that she protects, but also by revealing that there is no such thing as the lesbian utopia that existed in the trilogy and in *No me llames cariño*. Instead, the history of the invisibility and discrimination of lesbian couples in Spain is retold and emphasized so that it will not be repeated, and Emma García, as the lesbian couples' private eye and protector, serves as their bridge from invisibility and repression to visibility and acceptance.

In Pleasure and in Pain: The Visibility of the Female Body in Susana Hernández's Crime Fiction Series

With her first crime fiction novel, *Curvas peligrosas* (*Dangerous Curves*, 2010), Susana Hernández created the first pair of female police detectives to appear in crime literature in Spain. Rebeca Santana, a lesbian investigator and former adolescent psychologist in her twenties, and the veteran police officer Miriam Vázquez, a divorcée and mother in her forties, form part of a fictional police force in the homicide division of Barcelona's Cuerpo Nacional de Policía. In the three novels of the series so far – *Curvas peligrosas, Contra las cuerdas* (*Against the Ropes, 2012*), and *Cuentas pendientes* (*Pending Accounts*, 2015) – the two women solve cases that involve some of society's most vulnerable populations, including the mentally challenged, women who suffer gender and sexual violence, and children who fall victim to sex traffickers.[14] Although Hernández invokes the police-procedural model, the narrative does not detail the inner workings of the police force, but instead focuses on how the policewomen must learn to navigate their professional responsibilities with their personal dilemmas. In her analysis of *Curvas peligrosas,* where the case involves the murder of three mentally challenged women, Eva Paris-Huesca suggests that Hernández, like other contemporary female crime fiction authors, gives visibility and a voice to various female collectives that continue to suffer different forms of violence and marginalization, and uses a female-centred language to investigate women's sexuality (18–19). Paris-Huesca's reading of Hernández's first novel could likewise apply to the second and third installments of the series. Similar to *Curvas peligrosas,* the case in *Contra las cuerdas* involves a serial rapist and a murderer of women whereas in *Cuentas pendientes,* Rebeca and Miriam investigate an international child sex trafficking ring after one of the kidnapped boys escapes and leads the policewomen to uncover the intricacies of this criminal enterprise. Although their cases give prominence to crimes that target women and children, the series also brings visibility to female sexuality, emphasizing lesbian sexual experiences in the erotic sequences that form part of the texts. Borrowing from the way lesbian crime fiction traditionally incorporates the erotic into the genre, I suggest that women's experience of both pleasure and pain are explored throughout the series. This process has been previously described by Plain, who explains that "it is not simply in its deployment of overt eroticism that lesbian crime fiction disorders the pleasurable text; rather it discomforts through its continued, but qualitatively different, investment in the generic staple of violence" (213). Because the professional and the personal lives of the policewomen become intertwined in the novels, I argue that a twofold process takes place in Hernández's fiction, where both the erotic and the victimized body are made visible.

As in Isabel Franc's detective fiction, I propose that Hernández's series also emphasizes bringing visibility to the lesbian experience, signalling that the genre has moved from a de-eroticization of the female body in twentieth-century female crime literature to the body's (re)eroticization in contemporary lesbian and female crime fiction. Plain has previously argued that in lesbian detective literature "the presence of (or search for) a relationship is one of the few genre constants that is easy to identify. This is in sharp contrast to the heterosexual female private eye (as well as to the earlier male paradigm), whose investigations most often proceed at the cost of her intimate relationships ... In lesbian detection, however, the erotic has been an integral component" (206). In Hernández's series, visibility is given to the lesbian experience of love because readers gain entry into Rebeca's private life and bedroom when she meets the seductive lawyer Malena Montero. While an emphasis is placed on Rebeca and Malena's love scenes, we are also privy to Miriam's heterosexual encounters, and though the sequences with Rebeca are considerably more erotic throughout the series' progression, the episodes involving Miriam also constitute narrative pauses, as the text stops to describe the sexual pleasure experienced. And yet Hernández's contribution to the genre involves more than the re-eroticization of the female and the detective body; it also consists of giving visibility to the victimized bodies of women. I am arguing that Hernández emphasizes both ends of the spectrum – bringing visibility and a voice not only to the female body experiencing and offering pleasure, but also to the body that testifies to the pain suffered, whose agony is also legible.

Curvas peligrosas, for example, recounts Rebeca's first case as a new member of Barcelona's police force with her partner Miriam. The case centres on the murder of three mentally challenged women, but during the investigation, we become familiar with the two inspectors, who start out as an odd partnership and yet end up complementing one another perfectly. A former therapist, Rebeca studies the case from a psychological angle whereas Miriam is more interested in following the leads or facts of the case. Because we are also privy to the characters' internal worlds, the reader learns about Rebeca's childhood trauma: at the age of ten she witnessed both her mother Puri's murder of Eli, her neighbour, who was having an affair with Rebeca's father Toni, and Eli's son Víctor, whose birthday happened to be taking place that day. Intertwined with Rebeca's past is her current love affair with Malena Montero, the lawyer she meets while investigating the three murders and who becomes another fixture of the series. Still, the focus on Rebeca's personal life does not detract from the narrative's portrayal of Miriam's private struggles, which include her recent divorce from Marcos, in addition to her daughter Vero's affair with an older married man, and her resulting pregnancy and attempted suicide. To complicate matters further, Miriam also handles the trauma of aging throughout the series, feeling invisible to men even though she has a one-night stand with her ex-husband and begins an affair with her masseur in this novel. At the end, the women investigators discover that the motive for the crime was none other than the murderer's humiliation because his lies were exposed by his girlfriend Rosa, the first of the three victims. To cover his tracks, the murderer, Mario, kills his best friend's handicapped daughter, Gloria. His mother Elvira, in turn, murders Eva, another mentally challenged woman, in hopes of misleading the police. The investigation ends with Mario shooting Rebeca, injuring her and sending her to the hospital, though ultimately he is killed. *Curvas peligrosas*, however, ends on a happier note, with Rebeca and Malena confessing their love to one another.

Contra las cuerdas takes place a year and a half later. The novel opens with Miriam calling Rebeca to tell her the name of the rapist José Ferrandiz's sixth victim, and Rebeca responds by vomiting on the floor. This beginning prepares the reader for what will be a more graphic approach to female victimization because the case consists of the rape and torture of six women, five of whom have been strangled and killed by Ferrandiz's accomplice, Matías Solana. Ferrandiz's sixth victim is Aina, one of Rebeca's closest friends, and through her, we get a more detailed look at the female body in pain because the narrative is focalized via Aina during these sequences. The novel positions the reader to experience the victimization of three women by offering their perspective either during or after their physical and sexual assault – from Mireia prior to her death, through Marina as the only victim to have survived Ferrandiz's assault; and last, through Aina's suffering from the moment she is kidnapped to Rebeca's disturbing discovery of her disfigured and comatose body. Besides detailing the intensity of the case and its effects on the investigators, the narrative emphasizes the unraveling of Rebeca's personal life: her relationship with Malena has ended over a professional disagreement and a former patient, Anaïs, is stalking her. Meanwhile, Miriam puts an end to her affair with the masseur from *Curvas peligrosas*, and finds herself worrying about menopause and aging, a preoccupation that we have already seen in the first novel. The novel ends with Rebeca and Malena reuniting and with Miriam's new love interest. Although the policewomen's intimate lives improve, Aina, however, remains in a coma, and Matías Solana has escaped to France.

In the third installment of the series, *Cuentas pendientes*, the victims are five boys who have been kidnapped to be sold to Eastern European child sex traffickers. Focalized through Guillermo, one of the kidnapped boys, in chapter 1, we witness how he is able to escape, but also how he becomes traumatized when Kike, a fellow kidnapped victim, is killed in front of him. Significantly, Rebeca uses her experience of childhood trauma to empathize with Guillermo, and this ability to identify with victims helps her solve the case. Rebeca's childhood trauma is further revisited in this novel because Puri, released from prison after serving a twenty-year sentence for the two murders, disappears, and it is up to Rebeca, with the help of her former colleague Rafa Navarro, to find her mother. Another parallel storyline focuses on Malena, now a district attorney, and her investigation of an important case involving the Costa brothers, the sons of her father's business partner, who allegedly tortured an employee. Meanwhile, Miriam's personal and professional life become somewhat complicated in this story, since she takes the blame for a shooting involving Rebeca, who, in an attempt to stop one of Costa's men from threatening Malena, is involved in a shootout where an undercover police officer is killed. Considering retirement after getting suspended for the shooting, Miriam's private turmoil continues when she ends her relationship with her boyfriend Alejandro, and later, when she engages in a sexual encounter with Rafa Navarro, her partner before she was reassigned to Rebeca. The end of the novel links the resolution of the sex trafficking case with Puri's rescue, who was kidnapped by Beni, the husband of the neighbour she murdered. Furthermore, Hernández resolves two lingering plotlines from *Contra las cuerdas* by having the reader witness Matías Solana's eventual demise, when Rebeca watches him get dismembered by a train; and later, when Rebeca's friends come together to spread Aina's ashes, who has succumbed to her injuries. Juggling multiple plots, Hernández masterfully combines the personal and professional storylines of Rebeca, Malena, and Miriam in this novel and also brings to a close the unresolved subplots involving Solana and Aina.

From Rebeca and Malena's first night together onwards, the female body, as a body experiencing and offering pleasure, takes centre stage during these scenes. In their first intimate encounter, the narrative zooms in not only to describe bodily pleasures, but also the heightening of emotions:

> El sexo ansioso de sus fantasías, dejó paso a una complicidad inesperada que sabiamente mezclada con el acicate de la novedad las llevó a descubrirse poco a poco, sin reservas ni urgencias. A buscarse con los ojos, con las manos, con los labios y los cuerpos, y encontrar en cada beso, en cada embestida, y en cada mirada, mucho más de lo que habían soñado recibir.

> Fue una experiencia tan intensa como extraña. Hacer el amor con Malena no se parecía a nada que hubiera vivido antes. (*Curvas peligrosas* 132)

> The energetic sex of her fantasies gave way to an unexpected complicity that, mixed with the spur of novelty, led them to discover each other little by little, without reservation or urgency. They sought each other, in their eyes, their hands, their lips and their bodies, and they found much more than they ever dreamed in each kiss, in each advance, and in each glance. It was an experience as intense as it was strange. Making love to Malena was unlike anything she had ever experienced.

Focalized through Rebeca during these sex scenes, Hernández's crime series stages the female body as a site of narrative and lesbian pleasure. This experience of lesbian pleasure is emphasized throughout the novels, providing detailed erotic descriptions of Rebeca's intimate encounters. In a later scene, we witness how Santana pleasures Malena and the resulting sexual satisfaction and enjoyment: "Santana introdujo tres dedos y los movió con maestría, saboreó el licor mezclado con su sudor, ... 'Tu sabor me vuelve loca,' susurró deslizando la lengua por el cuello y la nuca. No quería perderse ni un rincón de su cuerpo. Malena ancló salvajemente las uñas en su espalda y gimió descontrolada, moviendo las caderas a un ritmo incendiario. 'Ya me tienes, nena, ya me tienes'" ("Santana inserted three fingers and moved them around masterfully. She savoured the liquor that was mixed with her sweat, ... 'Your taste drives me crazy,' she whispered, sliding her tongue across her neck and around to the back of her head. She didn't want to miss an inch of her body. Malena savagely dug her nails into her back and moaned, out of control, moving her hips at an incendiary pace. 'Don't stop, baby, I'm so close'") (192). Betz suggests that in more traditional forms of the genre "[s]ome writers will insist on the detective's heterosexuality by references to her femininity; the detective's own body becomes the focal point for asserting her possession of the signs of acceptable sexuality" (102). With Hernández's Rebeca and Malena, however, the body-in-pleasure is represented to assert possession of a lesbian sexuality – a lesbian subject position. Here, we are reminded of Wilton's "'lesbian-as-space'" proposition, where lesbian becomes a spatial term (8). By making lesbianism visible in crime fiction through the inclusion of these erotic moments, an occupation or a lesbianization of the genre occurs. We should further recall Munt's affirmation that "resistance to a homophobic culture" requires "a relentless demand for presence, an occupation of space" for and of lesbian desires (*Heroic Desire* 6).

Although there is a significant erotic component to the series, we must also highlight that a strong amorous element is also present, for what begins like a casual sexual encounter between Rebeca and Malena turns into love shortly thereafter. Already, at the end of the first novel, the love between the two women is accentuated when Malena confesses her love to Rebeca after the woman sleuth has been shot by the suspect in the case: "'Buscaba un buen revolcón y resulta que me he enamorado de ti. Ni lo pretendía ni lo deseaba, te lo aseguro. Esta mañana me he asustado mucho al enterarme de que ... de que te habían disparado.' [L]as lágrimas se deslizaron por el cutis de Malena. Esta vez no hizo nada por disimular. Ya no le quedaban fuerzas" ("'I was looking for a good lay, and it turns out that I've fallen in love with you. I didn't expect or want this, I assure you. This morning I was very scared when I found out that ... that you had been shot.' Tears slid down Malena's face. This time she did nothing to hide it. She had no strength left") (221). Rebeca replies with a similar heartfelt confession in which she explains what she feared after being shot: "Pensaba que si me moría en aquella mierda de casucha no volvería a verte nunca más. No vi mi vida pasar por delante, ni ningún túnel ni luces blancas. Sólo pensaba en volver a verte, hasta que me quedé inconsciente" ("I thought that if I died in that shitty shack I'd never see you again. My life didn't flash before my eyes and I didn't see any tunnel or white lights. I just kept thinking about seeing you again until I passed out") (222). What is noteworthy about Hernández's inclusion of the lesbian couple is that we observe both how their love develops and how their relationship matures from one text to the next. In *Contra las cuerdas*, for example, the two women end their relationship over a professional disagreement because they had to face off in court, and we observe how each one handles the breakup. Malena delves into self-help literature whereas Rebeca turns to other sexual partners to forget the lawyer. At the end of the novel, the two reunite, and the sexual intimacy that ensues demonstrates that the relationship, while still maintaining an erotic component, is more about love and companionship than only sex: "Quería disfrutarla, saborearla lentamente. Rozó su cuello con la punta de los labios, mientras sus manos moldeaban los pechos de Santana. La subinspectora, impaciente, se volvió hacia ella. 'Mi amor, te quiero tanto' ... 'Te quiero'" ("She wanted to enjoy her, savour her slowly. She brushed up against her neck with the tip of her lips, while her hands cupped Santana's breasts. The sub-inspector, impatient, turned to her. 'My love, I love you so much' ... 'I love you'") (*Contra* 217–18). Through Malena, we obtain a different, more emotional facet, of the female investigator because we become witnesses to the love that develops between the two women.

What is significant about Hernández's inclusion of the amatory in her crime fiction is that the body of the woman sleuth is also given erotic visibility. Rebeca gains corporal representation as a female body experiencing sexual pleasure, becoming in this way an erotic or eroticized body. In *Cuentas pendientes*, the sex scenes are still more graphic and detailed, as in the following example:

> Los labios rodaron rumbo al vientre, rodearon el pubis dejando caer suaves lametazos que hicieron enloquecer a Santana. La subinspectora se agarró con fuerza al tapiz árabe que colgaba de la pared. Malena se apartó de ella un instante y la miró con una sonrisa de satisfacción ... Cada embestida arrancaba un gemido más descontrolado, un golpe de cadera más profundo, un beso más largo, un arañazo más intenso, hasta que la pared, Malena y Santana se contrajeron en un espasmo que estremeció las estructuras del piso y los gritos de la subinspectora resonaron por la ventana abierta, eclipsando el rumor de coches y autobuses que circulaban por la calle Numància. (115–16)

> Her lips slid down to her stomach and surrounded her pubis, licking her softly and making Santana go crazy. The sub-inspector clung tightly to the Arab tapestry that hung on the wall. Malena moved away from her for a moment and looked at her with a satisfied smile ... Each advance elicited a wilder moan, a powerful shake emanating from her hips, a longer kiss, a sharper scratch, until the wall, Malena and Santana collapsed in a spasm that shook the foundations of the apartment, and the sub-inspector's screams rang out of the open window, eclipsing the hum of cars and buses circulating on Numància Street.

While they are not visible to the city, their screams, particularly Rebeca's, make their way to Barcelona's streets, drowning out any other noise. Plain has previously argued that "[g]iven the inherent misogyny of the formula that is being appropriated, it is almost impossible for the lesbian text not to adopt at least one of the disruptive strategies" such as inserting erotic material that is clearly not pertinent to the investigative angle of the work (205). According to Plain, "[t]o insert the erotic lesbian body into the appropriated space of the crime narrative in consequence becomes a political statement, both in terms of the 'external' discourse of crime and the 'internal' discourse of feminism" because "the pleasures enjoyed by the detective herself will have repercussions far beyond the bedroom" (207). The eroticism of this scene has the subversive function that Plain describes, as lesbian sex is made visible and audible through the screams that envelop the city. Lesbian sex and love take possession of Barcelona, at least momentarily, just as the women are taking possession of one another.

If we recall, Betz claims that lesbian pulp functions as a template for lesbian crime fiction because it positions "sexual and emotional desires at the forefront of the narrative" (53). The generic conventions of crime fiction are then used "as a vehicle for the development of relationships, and for the exploration of sexuality and sexual practice" (Plain 203). This is true of Hernández's crime fiction, where through both Rebeca and Miriam, regardless of their sexual orientation, we investigate female sexuality and sexual practices. While it is true that Rebeca's body appears more throughout the series, we also catch glimpses of Miriam, though these scenes are less explicit in the second and third novels. Her sexual encounters with her massage therapist are perhaps the most erotic, particularly their first time together:

> Ella alargó el brazo y tocó tímidamente sus labios. Terim tomó las yemas de sus dedos y las besó con delicadeza. Repitió el procedimiento a lo largo del brazo y siguió bajando por la axila hasta el pecho. Vázquez ya no se contenía, los jadeos seguían el ritmo de la música. Había soñado tantas veces con acariciar su piel tostada y recorrer la perfección de sus bíceps fuertes, de líneas hercúleas. El tacto era increíble, aterciopelado, completamente distinto al de Marcos y otros hombres que había conocido fugazmente ... Sea lo que fuese, era una delicia para los sentidos. Terim succionaba sus pezones con mordiscos suaves, mientras sus manos masajeaban la parte interna de los muslos. Se agarró fuerte a su cabello azabache y lo arrastró hacia ella. (180)

> She extended her arm and touched his lips timidly. Terim reached for her fingertips and kissed them delicately. He repeated the technique along her arm and continued down her armpit and to her chest. Vázquez could no longer contain herself. Her gasps followed the rhythm of the music. She had dreamed so many times of caressing his tanned skin and touching his strong, perfect, Herculean biceps. The way he felt was incredible, velvety, completely different from Marcos and other men that she had been with

> ... Whatever it was, it was a delight for all her senses. Terim sucked on her nipples with soft bites, while his hands massaged the inner part of her thighs. She gripped his jet-black hair tightly and dragged him towards her.

Since women's relationships and sexuality have for the most part remained invisible, according to Collins ("Lesbian Identity" 128), Hernández subverts this convention by representing both lesbian and heterosexual relationships, giving prominence to female sexual pleasure. The privileging of women's enjoyment of sex is fundamental to Hernández's project of visibility. According to Paris-Huesca, "Las tres protagonistas [Rebeca, Miriam, Malena] funcionan como figuras clave en la nueva ficción criminal de autoría femenina. Son sujetos complejos y llenos de contradicciones, que privilegian la libertad de la mujer y celebran la satisfacción del placer erótico femenino" ("The three protagonists [Rebeca, Miriam, Malena] function as key figures in this new crime fiction written by women. They are complex subjects, full of contradictions, who privilege women's freedom and celebrate the satisfaction of female erotic pleasure") (22). All three women purposefully take control and possession over their bodies, their sexuality, and their experience of sex. Hernández's representation, therefore, accentuates women as sexual beings.

All three novels depict lesbian sex and love, making it visible, but it is in *Curvas peligrosas* that the lack of lesbian visibility is criticized during a dinner party that Rebeca hosts for her lesbian friends – Virginia, Vicky, Claudia, and Alicia, Vicky's girlfriend at the time. During this dinner, the women debate whether or not Rebeca should "come out" at work to her colleagues. The question of lesbian invisibility frames this gathering, and the one leading the charge is Rebeca's militant friend Vicky:

> Tú, yo, todas nosotras, tenemos que salir del armario una y otra vez durante toda la vida, cariño. Es así y lo sabes. En cada nuevo trabajo, con cada nueva persona. A veces jode, otras veces tiene un pase, depende, pero siempre es lo mismo: chistes, preguntas curiosas, morbo, etc. Es lo que nos toca, pasarnos la puta vida dando explicaciones para no ser invisibles, para que se nos respete y se nos tenga en cuenta ... Si nos escondemos, no podemos esperar nada. (42)

> You, me, all of us, have to come out of the closet again and again throughout life, honey. It's like that and you know it. In each new job, with each new person. Sometimes it sucks, sometimes it's not so terrible. It depends, but it's always the same: the jokes, the morbidly curious questions, etc. It's

> what we have to do, spend our fucking lives explaining ourselves so we aren't invisible, so that we are respected and taken into account ... If we hide, we'll achieve nothing.

Vicky explains to the women present that they need to make their lesbianness visible, to out themselves professionally because they need to claim their visibility to combat their invisibility in the social system. Vicky puts an end to the debate by directing her argument at Virginia, the psychologist, saying that lesbians, whatever their profession might be, need to "[d]ar un paso al frente y decir 'aquí estamos y no nos avergonzamos de nada.' Todas, Virginia, cirujanas, fruteras o presentadoras de televisión. Hasta que eso no suceda, seguiremos siendo invisibles" ("take a step forward and say 'here we are and we're not ashamed of anything.' All of us, Virginia, surgeons, fruit sellers or television hosts. Until that happens, we'll continue to be invisible") (43). Here, Vicky's arguments remind us of Rosa Montero's metaphor of the prison of lesbian invisibility (19), but also of Lee Edelman's claims that heterosexuality's authority is based, in large part, on protecting "the straight body against the 'threat' of an 'unnatural' homosexuality – a 'threat' the more effectively mobilized by generating concern about homosexuality's unnerving (and strategically manipulable) capacity to 'pass,' to remain invisible," a heterosexual authority paradoxically used with the goal of maintaining homosexuality in the realm of the invisible (4). Edelman proposes that "while the cultural enterprise of reading homosexuality must affirm that the homosexual is distinctively and *legibly* marked, it must also recognize that those markings have been, can be, or can pass as, unremarked and unremarkable" (7; italics in original). The problem, then, is one of what is made visible, for Edelman clarifies that while it is dangerous to read the homosexual body, being unable to read the homosexual body also poses a threat.

In *Curvas peligrosas*, however, Rebeca does not have the opportunity to come out to her colleagues because her mother, Puri, has outed her during a television interview in an attempt to hurt her. Before this episode, Rebeca has visited Puri in jail, where we witness Puri's cruelty towards Rebeca: "'Esto está lleno de tortilleras asquerosas. Dime, ¿no te da asco hacerlo con otra mujer?' 'Tú me das asco, mama,' repuso sin alterarse ... 'Estoy orgullosa de ser lo que soy, y si volviera a nacer, pediría ser igual. Bueno, no, pediría no ser hija tuya'" ("'This is full of disgusting dykes. Tell me, isn't it gross doing it with another woman?' 'You're gross, mom,' she answered, unperturbed ... 'I'm proud of what

I am, and if I were born again, I'd ask to be the same way. Well, not exactly, I'd ask to not be your daughter'") (67–8). Thus, it is through the reporter who interviews Rebeca at work that her sexual orientation becomes known to her colleagues. When the interview airs, the narrative once again describes Puri's cruelty towards her daughter because "[t]uvo palabras poco amables para su hija. La retrató como una persona problemática, con dificultades para relacionarse normalmente y profundamente traumatizada por lo acontecido. Dijo que no le cabía en la cabeza que el Cuerpo Nacional de Policía hubiese admitido a una persona tan desequilibrada como su hija bollera" ("she had some unkind things to say about her daughter. She portrayed her as a problematic person, who had a hard time interacting normally with others and who was deeply traumatized by what happened. She said that she couldn't believe that the National Police Corps had admitted a person as mentally unstable as her dyke daughter") (172). Puri has not allowed Rebeca the opportunity to disclose her sexuality on her own terms. She has taken away Rebeca's opportunity to claim her lesbian visibility, precisely the same visibility that Vicky referred to previously.

Although unexpected, Miriam comes to Rebeca's defence, and though there is a humorous component to how Miriam comes to terms with Rebeca's lesbianism, she demonstrates both empathy and solidarity towards her partner during this moment: "'Por eso había una tortilla en tu mesa esta mañana.' '¡Qué originales! Mañana toca bollo. ¿Qué te apuestas?' 'Nos la comeremos. ¿Cómo es que soy la última en enterarme? Soy tu compañera. Eso debería valerme un trato preferencial en materia de cotilleos'" ("'That's why there was an omelet on your table this morning.' 'Very original! I bet tomorrow they'll leave a bun.' 'We'll eat it. How come I'm the last to know? I'm your partner. I should be given preferential treatment when it comes to gossip'") (139).[15] The episode solidifies the relationship between the two policewomen, and while Puri has attempted to alienate Rebeca from her colleagues, this sequence has the opposite effect since it strengthens the solidarity, the friendship, and love that exists between Rebeca and Miriam.

The visibility of female eroticism and of women's sexuality in Hernández's crime fiction is fundamental to demonstrating that a woman's personal life is indeed sexual. Because female sexuality has been couched in mystery, especially during the Franco regime even until well into the Transition, Hernández's series brings female pleasure into the visible realm. Without giving visibility to this intimacy, her (re)presentation of the three women would have been incomplete, and so it becomes necessary to develop the sexual portion of their lives. According to Betz, "lesbian experience is normalized within the pages of lesbian detective fiction. In other words, the mystery genre is performing the transformative function of all popular literature: making the unknown knowable, and turning the dangerous into the ordinary" (5). Betz's claims about lesbian crime fiction could also apply to the use of the female erotic. By giving visibility to female sexuality, both the lesbian and the heterosexual experience, Hernández normalizes it, making it knowable and ordinary, as Betz has previously argued regarding the lesbian experience. And yet, while there is a privileging of the erotic, of the female body in pleasure, as we have seen in these examples, the narrative also focuses attention on the victimized body.

Nina Molinaro accurately proposes in a recent article that Hernández's crime fiction involves "reimagining victims and victimization as much more than the production of silent female bodies that motivate detection and the reassertion of social control. In so doing she deploys a range of strategies to radicalize the 'woman as victim' trope on which so much past and present crime fiction depends" (30).[16] I agree with Molinaro that the victims in the series "consistently resist silencing and invisibility. In each installment, they are allowed to think, speak, and/or see, and the reader witnesses some measure, however small, of their agency" (32). Unlike what Sarah Dunant has argued about masculine crime fiction, the female victim's body, though made visible in the first two novels, is not graphically depicted or (over)sexualized. And yet, the pain and suffering of the victim is emphasized, as in this description of Rosa, the first victim in *Curvas peligrosas*: "Rosa no era Rosa, no era nadie, tan sólo un amasijo de carne sanguinolenta retorcida en una postura impúdica, con las piernas abiertas en un ángulo extraño, las bragas a la altura de los tobillos" ("Rosa wasn't Rosa, she was nobody, just a jumble of bloody flesh twisted into an immodest posture, with her legs spread open at a strange angle, her panties around her ankles") (25). Though the descriptions of the dead victims are not graphic, they function to describe the horror that they experienced because their cadavers testify to this. This becomes still more apparent in *Contra las cuerdas* where we become witnesses to the abduction and kidnapping of Mireia Lozano until we re-encounter her dead body: "Mireia Lozano, la segunda mujer violada y asesinada en el transcurso de un mes, fue hallada en la cuneta de una carretera comarcal, estrangulada y vejada de un modo salvaje ... Había sufrido múltiples desgarros tanto anales como vaginales al ser penetrada en repetidas ocasiones con un objeto punzante, probablemente un cuchillo jamonero. La muerte le sobrevino por estrangulamiento" ("Mireia Lozano, the second woman raped and murdered in the course of a month, was found in a ditch along the side of a county road, savagely strangled and brutalized ... She had suffered multiple anal and vaginal lacerations; she was penetrated repeatedly with a sharp object, probably a butcher knife. She died of strangulation") (20–1). In her reading of this episode, Molinaro draws attention to how "[t]he event of her death, and the production of her disfigured corpse, are preceded by her quotidian existence, and she registers both the assault and its effects before she is deprived of life and sentience" (40). Molinaro underlines that we not only witness how these women are physically and sexually abused, but we also get snippets of their daily lives, making them more than unrecognizable victims used to advance the story. Here, Molinaro references Shelley Godsland's claim that female crime fiction attempts to restore the victim's voice by affording the abused or assaulted a real narrative presence (*Killing Carmens* 88). Hernández employs this technique, reincorporating the victim by providing a narrative space where her background can be detailed while simultaneously underscoring her victimization.

For example, in chapter 1 we gain Mireia's perspective as the narrative zooms in on the moment that she regains consciousness after having been kidnapped by José Ferrandiz:

> Del exterior llegaba un silencio impenetrable y Mireia supo con toda certeza que estaba lejos de la ciudad, en algún paraje perdido donde nadie la encontraría jamás. Tembló de la cabeza a los pies sin ningún control. Los dientes castañeteaban aprisionados por la mordaza mojada y manchada de sangre. Sintió ganas de vomitar. De pronto, la puerta se entreabrió con un estruendoso crujido de la madera.
>
> – Me alegro de que estés despierta, Mireia.
>
> La penumbra le impedía adivinar los rasgos de su captor, sin embargo aquella voz le pareció vagamente familiar.
>
> – Quiero que lo disfrutes plenamente.
>
> Se acercó despacio, sus pasos estremecían alguna tabla suelta. La sombra avanzó hacia ella, y entonces la reconoció. (15–16)
>
> An impenetrable silence came from outside and Mireia knew with complete certainty that she was far from the city, in some unknown location where no one would ever find her. She shivered uncontrollably from head to toe. Her teeth chattered, imprisoned by the gag, wet and stained with

> blood. She felt like vomiting. Suddenly, the door opened with a thunderous wooden creak.
>
> – I'm glad you're awake, Mireia.
>
> The darkness prevented her from perceiving the features of her captor, however that voice seemed vaguely familiar to her.
>
> – I want you to fully enjoy it.
>
> He approached her slowly. His steps creaked on some loose boards. The shadow advanced towards her, and then she recognized him.

The sequence leads us through the physical reactions that Mireia experiences, but the intensity of the scene heightens as her tormentor enters the room. Struggling to recognize her victimizer, the narrative functions like a camera lens in this moment, playing with the shadows and the sound of his voice when he forewarns her of what is to come – his pleasure of making her feel the pain of rape. Although the narrative does not illustrate the violence that Mireia will endure, it exemplifies how "[v]ictims of human-inflicted trauma are reduced to mere objects by their tormenters: their subjectivity is rendered useless and viewed as worthless" according to Susan J. Brison (40). When the shadow of her victimizer reaches her and a moment of recognition ensues, the scene ends with a narrative cut that leaves us in the dark. Instead, we are positioned to imagine the horrors that Mireia will undergo. Our suspicions are confirmed when the police discover her cadaver, which testifies to the rape, torture, and murder that she has suffered. By witnessing what Mireia is experiencing not only physically, but mentally, the narrative forces the reader to undergo the horror and trauma of victimization alongside the victim. Graphic or gory details of the crime are not given, for the narrative instead underscores Mireia's feelings of helplessness and extreme fear because she knows, and so too does the reader, that her life is in grave danger.

We also observe the trauma that the victims who survive the attacks continue to undergo, in the episode with Marina. Here, Marina, one of Ferrandiz's rape victims, is asked to recount the violation to the two investigators. Upon noting her hesitation, Miriam informs Marina how lucky she is because the rapists' current victims have also been murdered. Providing them with her rape narrative, Marina explains how:

> – Olía a colonia masculina, a ... a sangre, a sudor. Me dolía todo el cuerpo y no podía moverme. Levanté un poco la cabeza, pero me mareaba. Me golpeó otra vez y me su ... su ... sujetó del cabello muy fuerte. Luego me penetró con el cuchillo, y perdí el sentido ...

> – A veces, tengo envidia de esas mujeres, de las que han asesinado.
>
> Sostuvo la mirada de Vázquez, pero no hubo un aire retador, solo un dolor inmenso. (44–5)

> – He smelled like cologne, like ... blood, sweat. My whole body hurt and I couldn't move. I raised my head a little, but it made me dizzy. He hit me again and he he ... he ... held me by the hair really hard. Then he penetrated me with the knife, and I passed out ...
>
> – Sometimes I'm jealous of those women, of the ones who were murdered.
>
> She looked Vázquez in the eye, but it was not a challenging look. In it there was only immense pain.

Marina's testimony of her rape also functions as a trauma narrative, given that she details not only the violence of the event, but also the effects that the rape has had on her life. Brison clarifies that the task of the survivor becomes "coming up with a coherent trauma narrative and integrating it into one's life story" (103). Marina conveys to the detectives that the trauma of the violation does not allow her to sleep or work and that fear keeps her from wanting to leave the house or remain alone (45). According to Cathy Caruth's definition, "trauma is not locatable in the simple violent or original event in an individual's past, but rather in the way its very unassimilated nature – the way it was precisely *not known* in the first instance – returns to haunt the survivor later on" (4; italics in original). Marina continues to be haunted by her rape, and it is for this reason she affirms that at times she thinks the victims who have been killed are the lucky ones since they do not have to live with this trauma. Her trauma testimony functions to demonstrate that while a survivor, Marina continues to be a victim of this rapist, not only because he remains free, but also because she was unable to see him so he could be anyone.

This episode is critical of the way victims tend to be treated and forgotten. Even within a genre like crime fiction, Brison highlights:

> We are not taught to empathize with victims. In crime novels and detective films, it is the villain, or the one who solves the murder mystery, who attracts our attention; the victim, a merely passive pretext for our entertainment is conveniently disposed of – and forgotten – early on. We identify with the agents' strength and skill, for good or evil, and join the victim, if at all, only in our nightmares ... This may explain why there is, in our criminal

> justice system, so little concern for justice for victims – especially rape victims. They have no constitutionally protected rights *qua* victims. (10)

Like Brison, Sarah Dunant has also suggested how "within crime fiction women have been particularly targeted for mutilation and depersonalization" (17). In Hernández's series, however, the portrayal of these victims is different because they do not form part of "a catalogue of faceless defiled corpses" to use Dunant's expression (19). The victims are given a name, a face, and a backstory according to what we have witnessed in the previous episodes, and while their pain is made visible, the narrative cuts out before detailing these crimes, leaving us to imagine what will happen next. Here, the story of crime and detection is not simply written on the victim, as Kathleen Klein has previously claimed regarding traditional male crime fiction ("*Habeas Corpus*" 173). Instead, the reader enters the victim's world, able to experience and observe the suffering from the inside.

Some of the most powerful and gut-wrenching scenes in *Contra las cuerdas* are the ones that feature Aina because the narrative is focalized through her during these sequences. For example, we find ourselves in the room with Aina when she wakes up to her kidnapper asking her to choose the knife that she will be raped with: *"'Que conste que te he dado a elegir.' Empuñó el cuchillo de hoja larga y afilada. 'Este me gusta. Te va a encantar'"* (*"'For the record, I've let you choose.' He grabbed the knife with the long, sharp blade. 'I like this one. You'll love it'"*) (99; italics in orginal). To this she responds by begging him not to hurt her: *"'Haré lo que quieras, pero no me hagas daño,' sollozó, 'por favor'"* (*"'I'll do whatever you want, but don't hurt me,' she sobbed, 'please'"*) (99; italics in orginal). Similar to the episode with Mireia, the scene ends with the rapist's threat of how causing her pain will bring him pleasure, *"'No lo entiendes,' habló muy cerca de su oído, 'de eso se trata, furcia. De hacerte daño, mucho daño'"* (*"'You don't understand,' he spoke very close to her ear, 'that's what it's about, you whore. I'm here to hurt you, to hurt you a lot'"*) (99; italics in original). Again, as the narrative zooms out, we are left to imagine what has happened to Aina until we are privy to her devastating reflection in a later chapter: *"El infierno era esto. Ahora lo sabía. La vejación, el dolor infinito, el asco, la sangre y la orina contaminando el aire, el terror, la certeza de una muerta segura. El cielo no existía. Su madre la había engañado. Los curas llevaban siglos engañando a la humanidad. El infierno está en la Tierra, y el cielo, en ninguna parte"* (*"This was hell. Now she knew. The humiliation, the infinite pain, the disgust, the blood and urine contaminating the air, the terror, the inevitability of certain death. Heaven isn't real.*

Her mother had lied to her. Priests had been deceiving humanity for centuries. Hell is on Earth, and heaven, is nowhere to be found") (157; italics in original). Beyond acknowledging Aina's physical suffering, the body in pain, the episode's impact also comes from how the narrative allows us to experience the victim's internal world, comprehending her mental anguish.

Discovering Aina's mutilated body, Rebeca is profoundly disturbed by the sight of her friend, since the narrative illustrates how "Aina colgaba boca abajo, desnuda y torturada del modo más salvaje" ("Aina hung upside down, naked and was tortured in the most savage way") (189). While Aina's body testifies to the abuse and horrors that have taken place, the impact of the scene also stems from the narrative's description of Rebeca's reactions:

> Lo que vio en aquella cámara blindada se grabaría a fuego en su retina para siempre. Aina estaba irreconocible. Las suaves facciones de su amiga eran un *collage* de golpes amoratados y sanguinolentos. La sangre descendía desde las nalgas hasta los tobillos.
>
> – ¡ No, no, no! ¡No, por favor! ¡Noooooo! – Cayó de rodillas sobre el suelo mojado, sollozando enloquecida, zarandeándola. (189–90)

> What she saw in that locked room would be burned in her retina forever. Aina was unrecognizable. The soft features of her friend were a collage of bruised and bloody blows. Blood ran down from her buttocks to her ankles.
>
> – No, no, no! No, please! Noooooo! – She dropped to her knees on the wet floor, sobbing madly, shaking her.

Rebeca becomes a witness to Aina's victimization, and as readers, we experience the pain that she feels at seeing her friend's disfigured body. Thus, it is not only Aina's trauma that we experience, but Rebeca's because we witness the agony that she undergoes in this novel and the guilt that continues to haunt her in *Cuentas pendientes*. Caruth has previously drawn attention to how "[w]hat returns to haunt the victim, these stories [trauma narratives] tell us, is not only the reality of the violent event but also the reality of the way that its violence has not yet been fully known" (6). Even though Rebeca is not the one in physical pain, she is traumatized not only by the image of her friend's tortured body, but also by her inability to save Aina, who slips into a coma and eventually succumbs to her injuries. The sequence with Aina forces us to become more than mere spectators to these scenes because they involve an act of witnessing. The narrative transforms us from spectators into witnesses because, as E. Ann Kaplan proposes, "witnessing leads to a broader understanding of the meaning of what has been done to victims, of the politics of trauma being possible" (*Trauma Culture* 123).

These sequences give a visibility to trauma, and, according to Kelly Oliver, "Witnessing works to ameliorate the trauma particular to othered subjectivity. This is because witnessing is the essential dynamic of all subjectivity, its constitutive event and process. While trauma undermines subjectivity and witnessing restores it, the process of witnessing is not reduced to the testimony to trauma" (7). If we recall, Brison has previously explained how victims are objectified by their abusers and how "their subjectivity is rendered useless and viewed as worthless" (40). Although these sequences of victimization convey physical pain, emotional anguish, and the resulting trauma that remains after the event, they also restore the victim's subjectivity by converting readers into witnesses. The reader recognizes the victims as individuals and not just as part of a larger storyline to move the main plot forward. This is the fundamental change that female crime fiction has brought about according to Godsland (*Killing Carmens* 88).

While neither Rebeca nor Miriam are physical victims during these novels, Rebeca is a victim of Puri's double homicide because she was there to witness it when she was ten years old. Dubbed the "asesina del cumpleaños" ("birthday killer") since she carried out this killing during a three-year-old's birthday party, Puri has never been particularly fond of Rebeca, disregarding that traumatizing experience and even displaying cruelty towards her daughter throughout the first two novels. In Hernández's series, the maternal is continually problematized through the character of Puri. Paris-Huesca draws attention to how "[e]ste comportamiento violento del pasado, junto con el desprecio con el que trata constantemente a su hija, por ser policía y lesbiana, deconstruyen la imagen materna tradicional. Las escasas visitas que Rebeca le hace a su madre en la cárcel terminan siempre en agresiones verbales propiciadas por esta última" ("this past violent behavior, together with the disdain with which she constantly treats her daughter, for being a policewoman and a lesbian, work to deconstruct the traditional maternal image. The few times that Rebeca visits her mother in jail always end in verbal aggressions caused by the latter") (21). Significantly, Rebeca constantly worries about being like her mother, whom she thinks of as a monster: "Había intentado por todos los medios ser la otra cara de la moneda, el reverso del espejo; ser, por sistema, todo lo que ella no era. Por eso eligió entrar en el cuerpo. Para estar en el lado opuesto. En el bando de los buenos. ¿Bastaría? No estaba tan segura" ("She had tried by all means to be the other side of the coin, the back of the mirror; to be, systematically, everything that she was not. That's why she chose to join the force. To be on the opposite side. On the side of the good guys. Would it be enough? She wasn't so sure") (*Curvas* 71). What has occurred with her mother, however, also empowers Rebeca to a certain extent because she admits that "[s]abía que ninguna otra persona podría hacerle tanto daño, jamás, bajo ninguna circunstancia y esa certeza envenenada lograba que se sintiera más fuerte y poderosa" ("She knew that no other person could hurt her so much, ever again, under any circumstances and that poisoned certainty made her feel stronger and more powerful") (*Curvas* 98).[17] She recognizes that she is able to carry out her job, to confront these horrible crimes and take control over her personal life because she has survived her mother's crime and the resulting trauma.

Rebeca's ideas on motherhood are evidently influenced by this damaging relationship. Conversing with her psychologist in *Contra las cuerdas*, she remarks, "La maternidad está sobrevalorada. Cualquier bicho viviente es capaz de reproducirse y parir" ("Maternity is overrated. Any living animal can reproduce and give birth") (65). In fact, she admits during this episode that she always feared that Puri would hurt her because "[a] veces la sorprendía mirándome ... y me daba escalofríos. Sé que lo pensó, Roberto, que pensó en hacerme daño, en librarse de mí" ("sometimes I caught her looking at me ... and it gave me chills. I know that she thought about it, Roberto, that she thought about hurting me, about getting rid of me") (66). There is, however, a change by the end of the novel, when Rebeca helps facilitate Puri's transfer to another prison, since she was almost killed when her fellow inmates learn that her daughter is a lesbian police officer. Molinaro signals that Rebeca understands her mother as a victim during this novel, and thus, despite Puri's past cruelty towards her daughter, they share a tender moment when "Puri tomó la iniciativa. Dio un paso raudo y, con apenas un roce, besó la mejilla de su hija. 'Me gustaría que vinieras a visitarme alguna vez'" ("Puri took the initiative. She took a swift step forward and quickly, lightly kissed her daughter's cheek. 'I'd like you to come visit me sometime'") (212). This encounter in *Contra las cuerdas* sets the stage for *Cuentas pendientes*, where one of Rebeca's cases will involve the disappearance of the recently liberated Puri, kidnapped by Eli's husband, Beni, whose intention is to kill both Puri and himself, since he is dying from cancer.

In *Cuentas pendientes*, Rebeca starts feeling a certain curiosity about her mother, in particular when she goes to her apartment looking for clues to her disappearance: "Los últimos veinte años, el esporádico contacto que mantuvieron se desarrolló entre los muros del penal. En aquella sala de comunicaciones de la antigua prisión de Wad-Ras desgranó varias capas de la compleja personalidad de Puri, pero era allí, en su recién estrenado pisito de soltera, donde podía ver todo el conjunto" ("Over the last twenty years, the sporadic contact that they had maintained was limited to the walls of the prison. In that visitors' room in the old prison of Wad-Ras, she peeled off several layers of Puri's complex personality, but it was there, in her brand new bachelorette pad, that she could see her whole") (62–3). Rebeca realizes that Puri is attempting to change her life with a new boyfriend, Agustín, by making plans for the future. And so, when she confronts Beni in an attempt to save her mother, Rebeca confesses to him that she no longer hates her: "No, no la odio. Ya no. La he odiado durante demasiado tiempo y ya estoy harta. Estoy muy cansada. No quiero desperdiciar más energía en odiarla ... ¿Cómo se aprende a querer a alguien que te ha hecho tantísimo daño? ... Porque yo no sé cómo se hace, pero sé que no quiero que muera" ("No, I don't hate her. Not anymore. I've hated her for far too long, and I'm fed up. I'm very tired. I don't want to waste any more energy hating her ... How do you learn to love someone who has done you so much harm? ... Because I don't know how to do it, but I know I don't want her to die") (248). Despite her heartfelt confession, Beni tells her that he has already injected both Puri and himself with propofol, a substance that will kill them in the next few hours. And yet, they are able to save Puri at the hospital, whereas Beni dies. An apparently changed woman, Puri tells Rebeca everything that happened with Beni, and in talking about Puri's future with Agustín, Rebeca obtains a new reading of her mother (260). The narrative even gives us the sense that the relationship could perhaps be entering a new phase when Puri suggests that they should go out to eat together with Malena, to which Rebeca responds, "'Ya lo vamos viendo. Ahí viene Agustín. Cuídate.' Se despidió sin un beso. Todavía no estaba preparada para pasar a una segunda fase de intimidad con su madre. Todavía no" ("'We'll see. Agustín is coming. Take care of yourself.' She said goodbye without giving her a kiss. She wasn't ready yet to move into a second, closer type of intimate realtionship with her mother. Not yet") (262). There seems to be hope that this relationship will normalize in the future because a maternal figure that is highly problematic at the beginning of the series becomes somewhat more sympathetic towards the end.[18]

Although her maternal relationship may normalize, Rebeca's identification with the victims of her cases demonstrates that her empathy is rooted in her childhood trauma.[19] For example, in *Cuentas pendientes* the abused victim's current pain and trauma is intermingled with Rebeca's childhood trauma:

> Era la única manera que se le ocurría de llegar a Guillermo, dejar a un lado la psicología y revivir la niña asustada y traumatizada que fue. Tantos años y tanta terapia para olvidar, y ahora necesitaba imperiosamente recorder ...
>
> – ¿A ti también te cogió un hombre malo?
>
> – No. Mi madre hizo algo horrible y yo estaba delante.
>
> – ¿Te asustaste?
>
> – Mucho, Guille, me asusté mucho. Estuve asustada mucho tiempo. A veces, todavía tengo miedo. (18–19)

> It was the only way she could think of to reach Guillermo, by setting aside psychology and bringing back to life the scared and traumatized little girl that she once was. So many years and so much therapy to forget, and now she urgently needed to remember ...
>
> – Did a bad man get you too?
>
> – No. My mother did something horrible and I was there when she did it.
>
> – Were you scared?
>
> – Very scared, Guille, I got really scared. I was scared for a long time. Sometimes, I'm still afraid.

Rebeca identifies with Guillermo as a child who has been the victim of trauma, and her ability to empathize with Guillermo allows him to be able to trust her. Using this trust, she gathers the evidence required to solve the case, making sure that a man who has been wrongfully accused is also set free. The case involving these child victims and her relationship with Guillermo also forces her to reflect on how trauma has affected her life. When she thinks about what to tell Guillermo about the fear that he will continue to face, the narrative exposes the female sleuth's emotional vulnerability: "Obvió decirle que las pesadillas vivían con ella, que los monstruos a veces vienen para quedarse para siempre en el mundo de los sueños, agazapados, esperando su oportunidad de hincar los colmillos" ("She decided not to tell him that the nightmares still lived with her, that monsters sometimes come to stay forever in the world of dreams, crouching, waiting for their chance to sink their fangs into her") (61). This reflection on fear and the effects of trauma reaffirms the multidimensional character that Hernández has created with Rebeca Santana. Hernández's Rebeca is far more complex than the typical investigator because she has experienced life as a victim.

This doubling of the detective-as-victim contributes to Rebeca's ability to identify with the victims in her cases, a characteristic accentuated in Maria-Antònia Oliver's Lònia Guiu series, where the female sleuth empathizes with sexual assault victims because she has been beaten and almost raped herself. Whereas in Oliver's Lònia Guiu novels this vulnerability and victimization is manifested physically because the female detective's body suffers this abuse firsthand, in Hernández's crime literature this vulnerability is more emotional, the after-effects of Rebeca's childhood trauma. Molinaro is correct in highlighting that Rebeca is the only police officer in the series to get seriously injured, perhaps as a way of showcasing her bravery and emotional endurance, but her empathy and emotional susceptibility, I would suggest, stems from witnessing Puri's murder of a mother and her son. Either way, this vulnerability does not weaken these investigators, but empowers them to fight for victims and seek justice. In *Curvas peligrosas*, Rebeca's friend and colleague, Rafa Navarro, remarks that what makes her a great detective is precisely the empathy that she feels because "[e]s bueno que te importen las víctimas, que te maree el olor a descomposición, que se te salten las lágrimas al ver desmoronarse a los familiares de una chica muerta. No permitas que te cambien" ("it's good that you care about the victims, that you get dizzy from the smell of rotting flesh, that tears come to your eyes when you see the relatives of a dead girl break down. Don't let them change you") (230). Instead of becoming more seasoned to the crimes of rape and murder, Rebeca continues to empathize with the victims of her cases, especially in *Cuentas pendientes,* where the child victim reminds her of the fear and trauma that she experienced after her mother's crime. Rebeca never loses sight of the fact that she too was once a victim, and although the sleuth is represented erotically as a body in pleasure, we are also reminded of the emotional pain that continues to form a part of her life.

Crime literature, according to Dunant, "has an intimate relationship with the dead body," usually the victim's silent dead body, and it is from this body that the investigation and the plot unravels (11). The body's legibility is essential to solving the case because the investigator must be able to read the body to untangle the mystery at hand. After the victim's body, especially when it is female, has fulfilled its function in the narrative, it undergoes a process of erasure from the narrative as the criminal body takes the spotlight. In Hernández's series, however, this does not occur – the criminal body never takes over and the victim's body does not undergo erasure. Molinaro correctly asserts that by presenting victims, including the female investigator, in this way, the narrative is able "to overturn the trope of 'woman as silent victim' on which so much past and present crime fiction depends" (37). In fact, Molinaro concludes that "Susana Hernández's police procedural series revises and renews the formula by affording her victims voice, vision, and visibility" (46). Though I agree with Molinaro that Hernandez's revision of the victim in crime fiction is noteworthy, this revision goes hand-in-hand with her reformulation of crime fiction's traditional portrayal of female sexuality, which is no longer in service to a male detective. The eroticized body is now the female detective body – they can be one and the same. More than just an eroticization of women's bodies, it is the female sleuth's body that Hernández presents as an erotic body, which deviates from the genre's conventions. Being able to read the female detective's body in its eroticized form without subtracting her subjectivity and agency constitutes a new phase for the genre. In sum, this subversion of the traditional male model is noteworthy not only because Hernández gives voice to the female body-in-pain, as Oliver does in her Lònia Guiu series, but also because she does the same for women's experience of sexual pleasure, emphasized in the scenes between Rebeca and Malena. Their pleasure transcends the walls of their apartment, taking possession of the city in a moment of total reveal. Consequently, Hernández has reversed the position of women's sexual and erotic invisibility by creating a space for the complete exposure of the lesbian and heterosexual female sexual experience. The politics of visibility are twofold in Hernández's series. Although victim visibility is still fundamental, as it is in the Lònia Guiu series, the re-eroticization of the female body signals a new subversive and empowering direction in women-centred crime fiction. What is more, the politics of visibility function in such a way that, whether in pleasure or in pain, there is no room for the invisibility of the female body and experience, as evidenced both in Franc's Emma García stories and in Susana Hernández's trilogy. First with Franc and now with Hernández, the lesbianization of crime fiction has allowed new models of visibility to proliferate in contemporary crime literature in Spain.

Exploring an Alternative Crime Fiction Genealogy

The 2008 financial crisis in Spain not only jolted the economy, it also provided the space for social movements such as 15-M to inspire artistic renovation, which has led to the creation of new cultural material in the form of films, music, art, and literature. These collective movements also spurred demonstrations that continue to bring visibility to issues plaguing Spanish society, such as gender violence and femicide, protests that have also been stimulated by global feminist movements such as *Ni una menos* (*Not One Less*).[1] In the literary domain, one of the most popular responses to the crisis has been in the form of crime literature with the formulation of an alternate crime fiction model, a subgenre that breaks with the *novela negra* – the *gris asfalto* novel. As discussed in the introduction, the *gris asfalto* narratives chronicle the delinquency of ordinary citizens, everyday people who undergo a process of criminalization as a result of the crisis or crises that they continue to suffer (see Fernández's "Lejos"). Rooted in the grey asphalt of Spanish neighbourhoods that are still experiencing the repercussions of the economic collapse, the *gris asfalto* authors give visibility to the peripheral spaces where these crises continue to unfold. Spatiality and visibility are intimately linked in this alternative subgenre because the spaces of delinquency are being (re)explored at the same time that what constitutes criminality in an era of crisis is being redefined.

With its adoption of the *gris asfalto* formula, present-day female crime fiction continues to examine and denounce violence against women by emphasizing and reorienting the traditional patriarchal and misogynistic inclinations of the *novela negra* by reconsidering corporal and systematic violence, revenge, and urban spaces in connection to gender and crisis. These new narrative practices succeed in complicating established modes of representation of victimized and criminal women.

As a result, contemporary scholars, such as María Xosé Agra, concentrate on exploring how and why women use violence – what she and other critics have called "salir de la inocencia," leaving behind a state of innocence or naiveté, to problematize the connection between female agency and violence. And yet, while they are fictional renditions of women's use of violence to retaliate against their abusers or the trauma inflicted on those close to them, the underlying message, according to Helena González Fernández's study of criminal women, is that their crimes demonstrate that "los mecanismos que deberían asegurar la promesa de seguridad" ("the mechanisms that should ensure the promise of security") are non-functional and changes to the legal system are therefore required (23). Post-2008 female crime fiction reworks the representation of women as passive victims of gender-based violence and activates them, allowing them to "mobilize vulnerability" into forms of resistance, as Judith Butler claims when discussing how "bodily vulnerability" can be marshalled as a strategy to "direct democracy actions" ("Rethinking Vulnerability" 26). In this regard, women-centred crime fiction produced in Barcelona, for example, is especially thought-provoking because the urban narrative of the city intertwines with women's repositioning as active agents, since the Catalan female population shares a history of vulnerability with Barcelona, a city that suffered from the Francoist regime's "politics of revenge," to use Paul Preston's terminology, and was consequently discriminated against. For this reason, authors like Teresa Solana, Empar Fernández, Anna Maria Villalonga, Isabel Franc, and Susana Hernández, just to name a few, connect their female protagonists with Barcelona, employing crime fiction as a narrative space to mediate and redefine vulnerability, violence, spatial and gender relations, subverting in this way the hegemonic depictions of women in the *novela negra*.

My objective with this book has been to explore an alternative genealogy for the politics of visibility of the female body and perspective in crime fiction. In so doing, I focus on four main types of bodies – the delinquent, the victimized, and the eroticized female body, as well as the detective body – and determine what provokes the instances of their visibility or erasure. What I demonstrate is that with the gendering of crime fiction, which I argue occurs from the genre's beginnings with the centrality of the female criminal, there is a blurring of these categories because these types interact or intersect with one another. As a result, what we encounter is the visibility of hybrid female bodies and roles. Doublings take place throughout this genealogy, beginning with the delinquent/victim in Pedro Antonio de Alarcón's *El clavo* and ending with a pairing that includes the detective-as-victim in both Maria-Antònia Oliver's Lònia Guiu trilogy and in Susana Hernández's series.

Although the genre's feminization appears, at least initially, to be founded upon the act of making the female body visible and legible, what follows is precisely the opposite. There is a resistance towards legibility, and thus, misreadings proliferate as we see with Alarcón's Gabriela Zahara through contemporary female detective protagonists. The female body, in its hybridity and in its trespassing of categories and the law, first challenges the act of reading and eventually becomes a site of resistance. In some measure, there is a consistent rejection of the female body as an object of the gaze. This alternative genealogy traces the development of the different inscriptions of the female body in the four phases of the genre's feminization, beginning with delinquency and ending with detection and the (re)eroticized female body.

In the first models of the genre studied in chapter 1, the focus is on the female delinquent body because she serves as a trope to investigate the nation's moral degeneration and the fears surrounding female sexuality and criminality, themes that were prevalent in nineteenth- and early twentieth-century Spanish literature. According to Jo Labanyi, women were considered "the key to the nation's 'ills,' whether as cause or solution" (74). When the female body is reconfigured as a criminalized body, female corporeality becomes a threatening discourse because we are now confronted with a transgressive, dangerous body, which crosses sociopolitical and moral boundaries. Moreover, the female delinquent body figures prominently because it invites its own scrutiny and stages itself as a text to be read, which David Horn has previously discussed in his analysis of Cesare Lombroso's study on female delinquency. Deviance mimics and shares techniques of watching, of scrutinizing that occurred "[i]n prisons, schools, hospitals, factories and families" by "the careful gaze of experts" (Terry and Urla 10). In much the same way that the nineteenth-century clinical or scientific gaze looked to acquire "scientific mastery over troublesome women," the detective figure looks to control and contain the female criminal by bringing her into the visual realm (11). Social and moral disorder, henceforth, are articulated through female deviance and an emphasis is placed on the visibility given to the female criminal body to mitigate her disruptiveness. We first see this exemplified in Alarcón's *El clavo* and later in Emilia Pardo Bazán's *La gota de sangre*.

Despite the politics of visibility surrounding the female delinquent body in these texts, where evidence of deviance is to be found in the body, both women succeed in authoring misreadings of themselves. Gabriela Zahara is able to play the role of three women convincingly enough to make two men fall in love with her, but in the end, she is condemned for her murderous and adulterous transgressions by patriarchal law and morality. Still, she is given the space to argue for a more just system towards women, explaining that her crime was the result of the oppressive institution of marriage. With a criminal that doubles as a victim, a new inscription of the female body emerges in this first model of the crime fiction formula, in which the beginnings of a protofeminist counterdiscourse that argues for women's equality and just treatment before the law emerges, a theme that will be revisited by Pardo Bazán.

Even though both women play with their legibility, it is with Pardo Bazán's *La gota de sangre* that the masculinization of the genre is interrupted with a targeted and mocking parody of the classic Sherlock Holmes type. Pardo Bazán's intrusion into the male-dominated generic form occurs through parody by staging the unmasking of the male detective myth. Rejecting the notion of the "Great Detective as an icon of Man," to use Sally Munt's phrase, the femme fatale, Chulita Ferna, outwits the amateur male sleuth to the point that he allows her to escape prosecution for her part in Grijalba's murder (*Murder* 204). Failing to live up to the Holmesian model, Selva is transformed into a willing accomplice who finances Chulita's last transgression – her defiance of the law. Chulita ensures his failure to restore a patriarchal order because she will not be condemned for her part in the crime. Since the masculinization of the genre is disturbed with the male sleuth's failure and criminalization, justice is feminized in favour of the woman delinquent.

What becomes apparent is that these early challenges to the male gaze set the scene for the gendered substitution of the male I/eye in later examples of the genre. Like the women delinquents studied in chapter 1, Federico Mediante's female criminals in *Sombras siniestras* and *Fuerzas ocultas* and the first woman sleuth in *La señorita detective* demonstrate how the masculinization of the genre continues to be interrupted by focusing on how the male gaze is used against itself. They are disruptive bodies who remain illegible because they are misread by their male counterparts. And yet, unlike Gabriela Zahara and Chulita Ferna, Mediante's women characters do not present a challenge to the patriarchal structure in the same way because they do not denounce the current system or argue for a more feminized form of justice. Like the female delinquents studied, *La señorita detective*'s Diana Fletcher also plays with her own legibility and causes a series of misreadings that ensure her ability to outsmart her male rivals/readers. These challenges to the male gaze, however, occur only after the female body is first put on display, after textual pauses that position her as a site of narrative pleasure. Although novel in its presentation of a female secret agent who goes undercover and uses how men read her beauty and intelligence to her benefit, *La señorita detective* also paralyzes the character in the second half of the novel, and hands the protagonist role to a male reporter. Hence, it is an advance in the genre because Diana Fletcher functions as a professional investigator, but there is a simultaneous regression with the weakening of the female character when the male love interest appears on scene. Paralyzed and marginalized to a hospital bed, the male reporter, Leslie, fulfills the role of the heroic male sleuth, subtracting agency from the female secret agent.

Mediante's model is significant in its anticipation of certain traits of the modern female sleuth, but this use of the male gaze against itself will be seen most clearly in Manuel de Pedrolo's *Joc brut*, where the female delinquent body takes centre stage once again in its heightened form as a femme fatale. What makes Pedrolo's contribution to crime fiction noteworthy is how the reader witnesses the process of Xavier's criminalization because the narrative is focalized through him. As various scholars have previously signalled, this focalization elicits potential feelings of complicity towards the criminal. In this section, I illustrate, instead, how criminalization occurs through victimization, since the male protagonist is forced to see himself through the femme fatale, Juna, who uses his story and condition as a victim to make him hunger for her to finally emerge victorious. Xavier has always been on the losing side, on the side of the victims of the Civil War, and Juna represents hope and the potential for a brighter future. Furthermore, Xavier's desire for Juna mirrors his desire for Barcelona, his ambition to succeed in the city where he arrived with his mother as one of the defeated. Mistaken as a site of pleasure, the female body victimizes the male onlooker, who can now only see the misery of his situation. Here, the femme fatale's transgression consists of compelling Xavier to transit between being a victim and a murderer, and for this reason, she is punished with disfigurement for her defiance of a male order. In *Joc brut*, while the focus may be on male criminalization, it is made possible through a politics of visibility that aligns the female body with male vulnerability and forces the voyeuristic male eye to turn on itself.

Given that Lourdes Ortiz's hard-boiled female sleuth has been harshly criticized by crime fiction scholars, even though *Picadura mortal* has been signalled as the beginning of the feminization of the genre in Spain, I find it necessary to return to what these critics signal as a mere imitation of the male generic form. In my reading of *Picadura mortal*, I suggest that Ortiz relies on parodic inversion to stage a critical exposition of the *machista* attitudes through which crime fiction traditionally operates. In so doing, both male and especially female stereotypes in the genre are revealed as what they are – performances that represent and strengthen a patriarchal ideology and order. Ridiculing the scenes that we are used to encountering in the male forms of the genre, the female body is staged to elicit and then thwart the reader's expectation of these scenes through what Alison Maginn has called a deformed and self-critical parody. What becomes visible is not the body, as the *novela negra* has conditioned us to expect, but the power dynamics of the gazing episode itself, highlighting the sexism that is the vehicle for this sort of representation. The genre's complicity in reproducing this sexism and its accompanying patriarchal ideology is brought to the fore and made visible with Ortiz's Bárbara Arenas, who performs the male look.

Since Ortiz's incursion into the genre, the management of the female body's visibility has clearly changed with the emergence of contemporary female crime fiction because an emphasis is placed on the de-eroticized and victimized body, as exemplified in Maria-Antònia Oliver's Lònia Guiu trilogy. Oliver's Lònia Guiu series cultivates a "new syntax," to use Mary Ann Doane's terminology, to represent both the female victim and the woman sleuth (176). Doane argues that recent feminist films achieve "a continual displacement of the gaze which 'catches' the woman's body only accidentally, momentarily, refusing to hold or fix her in the frame. The camera consistently transforms its own framing to elide the possibility of a fetishism of the female body" (176). As we see in Oliver's Lònia Guiu series, the tendency in contemporary female crime fiction is for the gaze that falls upon the victimized female body to be deliberate and hold her in the frame to force the reader to recognize the effects of gender violence while avoiding fetishization. Reconfiguring the textual pause that presents the eroticized female body, this mechanism is employed by Oliver to emphasize what the genre had previously repressed – the visibility of the victimized. Whereas the victim was the body upon which the detection narrative was inscribed, according to Kathleen Klein, this victimization, I propose, now marks and mobilizes the body as evidence to tell its story. Consequently, it is a reappropriation of the violated female body's narrative. This new inscription of the body in Oliver's Lònia Guiu series results in the strengthening and prevalence of an alternative feminized and personal form of justice. Here, the masculinity of the canon is disrupted by rewriting the female role in the genre through this inversion of the private eye's perspective, but more significantly, by redefining the politics of visibility surrounding the female body so that it can only become visible through victimization. Moreover, it should be noted that the genre's feminization in this phase also brings to light the question of female intellectual and physical agency – that is, not only the victimization but also the empowerment of women.

With Oliver paving the way, serial female crime fiction has stepped out of the shadow of its male counterpart in the editorial market and produced a number of female detectives that continue to be relevant in popular fiction. Following Oliver was Alicia Giménez Bartlett with her Petra Delicado series, and later, Rosa Ribas's Cornelia Weber-Tejedor. Other novelists of the past decade who continue to introduce new installments of their female detectives' adventures include Carolina Solé with her detective Kate Salas, Cristina Fallarás with Vicky González, Maruja Torres with Diana Dial, Berna González Harbour with María Ruiz, Clara Asunción García with Cate Maynes, Rosa Ribas and Sabine Hofmann with Ana Martí, Dolores Redondo with Amaia Salazar, and Susana Hernández's pair, Rebeca Santana and Miriam Vázquez (see Pertusa Seva, "Prólogo"). During this period, lesbian crime fiction also gained popularity, starting with Isabel Franc's Lola Van Guardia trilogy and her Emma García series and continuing with authors such as Ixtaro Borda, Javier Otaola, and Clara Asunción García, in addition to Susana Hernández, who not only included lesbian police inspector Rebeca Santana in her series but has also created the first pair of policewomen in Spanish crime fiction.

The centrality of the woman character – from delinquent to the modern detective – provokes a gendering of the generic form that works against the objectification of the female body. Instead, the politics of visibility that looked to objectify women in the traditional male-centred models are countered by a liberating discourse that exposes weaknesses not only in the male detective formula, but more generally, in the social order. As women's bodies are de-eroticized in twentieth-century female crime fiction to counter this objectification, they are resexualized in the lesbian variation of the genre – where lesbian love and sex take centre stage. Lesbian crime fiction, as I have emphasized with Isabel Franc's Emma García series and Susana Hernández's police-procedural trilogy, focuses on resisting the invisibility of the lesbian subject by a patriarchal system that continues to threaten it. By redefining what is made visible in crime fiction, beginning with Franc's incursion into the genre, crime fiction has been transformed, allowing for the (re)presentation of what has been traditionally considered a subversive and invisible body – the lesbian body. With Hernández's Rebeca Santana and Miriam Vázquez, however, there is a reversal not only of lesbian invisibility, but also of women's sexual invisibility. The lesbian occupation of the genre, or the lesbianization of the genre, has allowed for the cultivation of new models of visibility, a trend that now continues in the *gris asfalto* formula.

Compelling the reader to read from the feminine and the lesbian has activated the genre in such a way that a new syntax for the politics of visibility has been formulated. This is the result of a genre that is born from the female body, that springs forth from the body of the woman delinquent, beginning with Alarcón's *El clavo* and Pardo Bazán's *La gota de sangre*. With this alternative genealogy, my objective has been to illustrate that contemporary women detectives are part of a simultaneous generic tradition that has developed alongside that of the male detective. The modern female sleuth who appears in Ortiz's *Picadura mortal*, Oliver's Lònia Guiu trilogy, Franc's Emma García stories, and Hernández's crime fiction series is a descendant of the nineteenth- and early twentieth-century female delinquent. In these early examples, we already note a refusal to expose the female body as a mere object of the male gaze by reformulating patriarchal models of visibility. Even in the male-centred detective novels examined in chapter 2, female characters challenge the models at hand by forcing the voyeuristic male look back onto itself and by resisting their legibility. In its different phases, the feminization and lesbianization of the genre signifies a plurality of meanings and hybrid bodies, which in turn signal resistance.

With the boom in female crime fiction in the past decade in Spain, the accompanying scholarship has focused first on understanding the "birth" of the feminized detective and then on comparing and contrasting the male versus the female sleuth. Although this is significant work in terms of analyzing how the female sleuth differentiates herself from her male counterparts, this scholarship seems to position female crime fiction and the lesbian subgenre as addendums to the male canon, as epigones of male crime fiction. Viewing the corpus in this way suggests that the woman detective, regardless of her sexual orientation, is no more than a gendered replica modelled after the classic male figure that springs into being with Ortiz's *Picadura mortal*. This view of women-centred crime fiction, however, dismisses a generic tradition that has its roots in the earliest form of crime fiction in Spain with female delinquents. The alternative genealogy that I have developed here attempts to rescue the female detective's early predecessors, who were never male, and suggests that even the female characters in male-centred crime fiction are a phase in the feminization of the genre, all of which leads us to the contemporary woman detective. By reading crime fiction from the feminine, we arrive at a better and more complete understanding of a tradition that developed alongside the male generic forms and that has succeeded from its beginnings in subverting the masculinity of the crime fiction canon.

Notes

Introduction: Detecting the Female Body in Gendered Mysteries

1 Further motivating the birth of the *gris asfalto* novel, which Fernández characterizes as a new crime fiction type or subgenre, was that those with more traditional views of the genre questioned whether recent novels published by both authors, among others, were perhaps deserving of the *novela negra* label (see "Lejos"). Fernández has published *La mujer que no bajó del avión* (*The Woman Who Did Not Get Off the Plane*, 2014), *La última llamada* (*The Last Call*, 2015), and *Maldita verdad* (*Damned Truth*, 2016), and Villalonga has published *La dona de gris* (*The Woman in Grey*, 2014) and *El somriure de Darwin* (*Darwin's Smile*, 2017).

2 Unless noted otherwise, all translations are my own.

3 When I use the term female crime fiction, I am referring to crime fiction narratives in which crime and violence are explored from a woman-centred perspective, a formula used mostly, though not exclusively, by women writers in the genre. Written with the goal of bringing visibility to gender concerns and using crime fiction as a space to articulate feminist interests, this includes lesbian crime fiction, which scholars, such as Phyllis Betz, Jacky Collins, Sally Munt, Gill Plain, Inmaculada Pertusa Seva, and Nancy Vosburg, have previously argued is a crucial variant of female crime literature.

4 In the prologue to *Fundido en negro* (*Cast in Noir*), a female crime fiction anthology published in 2014, Inmaculada Pertusa Seva suggests that 2011 was the year of the female version of the *novela negra* in Spain as authors such as Carme Riera, Teresa Solana, Rosa Ribas, Cristina Fallarás, Maruja Torres, Rosa Montero, and Clara Asunción García all published works with a female protagonist. The use of the *femicrime* label in Spain has sparked criticism from writers and scholars of crime fiction, such as

Àlex Martín Escribà and Javier Sánchez Zapatero, who clarify that the label is problematic because its defining criteria are based on gender, on the feminine condition, and conceiving of literature based on biological and cultural characteristics and not on the nature of the text itself makes it an inappropriate and ineffective criterion or instrument for categorization (115). Still more critical of the *femicrime* label, Villalonga, the editor and one of the authors of two recent female crime fiction anthologies, *Elles també maten* (*Women Also Kill*, 2013) and *Noves dames del crim* (*New Women Writers of Crime Fiction*, 2015) has also problematized this category, explaining that the label *femicrime* is used as another marketing strategy that reinforces the opinion that the *novela negra* is a mass-produced literature with insignificant literary value ("El *femicrime*" 264). For an analysis of the stories and the female protagonists that form part of Villalonga's anthologies, see her recent article "El relat negre" ("The Noir Story").

5 Frank Egholm Andersen has extensively studied the particularities of the Nordic phenomenon in *Den nordiske femikrimi* (2008). For more on MUNCE, see their webpage: www.ub.edu/munce/ and the volume that was produced as a result of the project, *Tras la pista: narrativa criminal escrita por mujeres* (*On the Trail: Crime Narratives Written by Women*). In the introduction to the volume, the editors detail how the MUNCE project has contributed to understanding the nuances of contemporary female crime fiction. In 2016, the Centre Dona i Literatura was then reconstituted as ADHUC-Research Center for Theory, Gender, Sexuality, and their newest project is VANACEM, which stands for Víctimas y agresoras. Representaciones de la violencia en la narrativa criminal escrita por mujeres (Women Victims and Aggressors: Representations of Violence in Crime Fiction Written by Women).

6 Here, as Stott points out, we should also recall Edward Said's term, "the feminine Orient," as the space, "the Orient," in need of taming and domestication, and thus, regarded as feminine (27).

7 See Stott's discussion on women's position on the frontier as being both inside and outside, using Toril Moi's explanation (38–9).

8 In speaking about the *novela negra* author Juan Madrid, John Macklin explains that he "takes over into the *novela negra* the tradition of *film noir* with its stereotypical treatment of women, a kind of extension of the *femme fatale*. It is an example of genre reinforcing a particular ideology" (60). The characteristic that Macklin points out is not exclusive to Madrid, but is a mechanism utilized by many authors who delved into the Spanish hard-boiled variety.

9 See Daniel Linder's "The Censorship of Sex: A Study of Raymond Chandler's *The Big Sleep* in Franco's Spain" for more on the censorship of crime novels during this period.

10 Josefina de la Torre published one crime fiction work titled, *El enigma de los ojos grises* (*The Mystery of the Grey Eyes*, 1938), and Ballesteros Gaibrois would publish *City Hotel* (1938) and *París-Niza* (*Paris-Nice*, 1939) as part of a series titled *La novela ideal* (*The Ideal Novel*) for the Canary Island's printing press, *Diario de Las Palmas* (*Las Palmas Daily News*) (*Killing Carmens* 2).

11 Rodoreda, whose *La Plaça del Diamant* (*In Diamond Square*, 1962) is considered a canonical Catalan work for which she has received international recognition, renounced *Crim* some years after it was published, according to Godsland (*Killing Carmens* 158). As we will discuss in chapter 2, though it emerges relatively late compared to the British or North American models, scholars, like Godsland and Resina, agree that an authentic form of local crime fiction was produced in Catalonia before the rest of Spain due to its earlier development as a capitalist society, and two female authors, Mercè Rodoreda and Maria Aurèlia Capmany, who experimented with the detective genre, paved the way for contemporary Catalan women writers like Maria-Antònia Oliver.

12 Calvo de Aguilar's works include *Doce sarcófagos de oro* (*Twelve Golden Sarcophagi*, 1951), *El misterio del palacio chino* (*The Mystery of the Chinese Palace*, 1951), *La isla de los siete pecados* (*The Island of the Seven Sins*, 1952), and *La danzarina inmóvil* (*The Immobile Dancer*, 1954).

13 It was later titled *Vés-te'n ianqui! o, si voleu, traduït de l'americà* (*Yankee Go Home! Or, If You Prefer, Translated from the American*, 1980) and later retitled as *Vés-te'n ianqui* (*Yankee Go Home*) in 2005. The novel's original title, *Translated from the American*, signals that, as a translation, which were permitted by the regime, it would prove harmless (see *Killing Carmens*).

14 The criticism against the 2004 legislation is that it only protected women who had some sort of sentimental attachment with the male victimizer, leaving others unprotected under the law. A more complete law would be passed in 2010, the Ley de Salud Sexual y Reproductiva y de la Interrupción Voluntaria del Embarazo (Law on Sexual and Reproductive Health and on the Voluntary Interruption of Pregnancy), which would offer greater protection for victims of rape or those that were unknown to their victimizers. Reforms to the 2004 law were again debated by representatives of the different political parties in Spain during the summer of 2017. Considering the staggering number of women that are victims of femicide

each year, the country's high-ranking officials recognized that the gender violence crisis needed to be addressed.

15 For more on the different theories of rape, see Keith Burgess-Jackson's discussion in *Rape: A Philosophical Investigation.*

1. Reading the Female Delinquent in Early Spanish Crime Fiction

1 Stott signals how the femme fatale's unbridled sexuality poses a danger because it is the "dark continent," a term "significantly employed by Freud to describe the mystery of female psychology" (35).

2 Both de Groot and Gilman base their arguments on Foucault's *The History of Sexuality*, where he emphasizes that the nineteenth century is the period in which sexuality was "constructed," and thus, the sexual discourse that was produced in turn was not so much a discourse about sex but "a multiplicity of discourses produced by a whole series of mechanisms operating in different institutions" (33).

3 Here, I build on Doane as well as Stott's argument that "[w]omen's position on the frontier is a *double* position depending on the type of woman" whether inside or outside of the established order (38; italics in original). There is more porousness to this border and to the figure of the femme fatale, as demonstrated by Julie Grossman who argues for more flexibility in our analysis of this character.

4 See Akiko Tsuchiya's introduction to *Marginal Subjects* for her discussion of how Isabel's delinquency was utilized by her detrators and even supporters (15–16).

5 The first version of *El clavo* appeared in 1853 in *El Eco de Occidente* (*The Echo of the West*). There is no surviving copy, but the story was changed and republished in 1856, and again in 1880, which is the definitive edition (see *La novela policiaca española* 90). The genesis of Alarcón's work continues to be hotly debated. Some, like Ricardo Landeira, suggest that Alarcón modelled his novel after Edgar Allen Poe's "The Murders in the Rue Morgue" published twelve years before because Alarcón was said to have called some of his own work Poesque (62). As a counterpart to this argument, José Colmeiro affirms that it is unlikely that Alarcón would have knowledge of Poe's stories before writing *El clavo*, and instead claims that Alarcón was inspired by the French *cause célèbre* of the first half of the nineteenth century, narratives describing infamous criminal court proceedings (*La novela policiaca española* 91). Meanwhile, other scholars have signalled the similarities with the plot of Hippolyte Lucas's short story, suggestively titled "Le clou" ("The Nail," 1843). Foreshadowing the controversies

surrounding *El clavo*'s origins, Alarcón explains in *Historia de mis libros* (*History of My Books*) that "*El clavo* es, por lo tocante al fondo del asunto, una verdadera *causa célebre*, que me refirió cierto magistrado granadino cuando yo era muy muchacho. Como algunas otras novelillas mías, primero la escribí y publiqué muy sucintamente, y la desarrollé después en ediciones sucesivas" ("*The Nail* is, as far as the substance of the matter is concerned, a true *cause célèbre*, which was referred to me by a certain magistrate from Granada when I was very young. Like some of my other novels, I first wrote and published it very succinctly, and later developed it in successive editions") (209).

6 All translations of *El clavo* are from Robert M. Fedorchek's *"The Nail" and Other Stories*.

7 Felipe first meets the young widow in the fall of 1844. Two months pass and 1 November of that same year he visits Zarco and learns about his love affair with Blanca. That same day they discover Alfonso's skull with the nail sticking out of it. Three months go by without Gabriela being captured, so Felipe leaves, promising Zarco that he will return next year, though he actually comes back earlier. Felipe is in Granada during the winter of 1845, presumably February of 1845 if the timeline is correct.

8 See Articles 349 through 353 of the *Código penal*. For more on the history of divorce in Spain, see Inés Alberdí's *Historia y sociología del divorcio en España* (*History and Sociology of Divorce in Spain*).

9 Pardo Bazán's columns appeared in the newspaper, *La Ilustración Artística* (*The Artistic Illustration*) from 1895 to 1916.

10 Yet, even before she became a regular contributor she had already written about the topic in 1890 in her short story "Piña" ("Pineapple") where she uses two monkeys to represent the problem of gender violence according to Ruiz Ocaña (179).

11 The columns were first published together in 1928 by Alberto Ghiraldo in a volume titled, *El crimen de la calle de Fuencarral: cronicón de 1888–1889* (*The Crime on Fuencarral Street: Chronicle of 1888–1889*). The case was also the inspiration for two of Galdós's novels, *La incógnita* (*The Unknown*, 1888–1889) and *Realidad* (*Reality*, 1889), and for the play *Realidad* (*Reality*, 1892). More recently, the case was the basis for a 1985 movie directed by Angelino Fons titled *La huella del crimen: el crimen de la calle Fuencarral* (*Crime's Footprint: The Crime on Fuencarral Street*) for Televisión Española (TVE), Spain's national public broadcaster. In more recent editions, *El crimen de la calle Fuencarral* is published together with Galdós's *El crimen del cura Galeote* (*The Crime of the Priest Galeote*). For a detailed study of what

occurred at the real preliminary hearings and then at Higinia's trial, see María Jesús Raimundo Rodríguez's "El crimen de la calle Fuencarral" ("The Crime on Fuencarral Street").

12 In one of his final columns on the Fuencarral murder, Galdós also divides the press into *sensatos and insensatos*, explaining that the *insensatos* admit no more proof than that which suits them (48–9).

13 Donis explains that Pardo Bazán and Pío Baroja would be present at Higinia's execution, which, judging from their writings, affected them both greatly (see also Raimundo Rodríguez 344). Both Baroja and Pardo Bazán give accounts of the execution, but Baroja would later include a version of Higinia's execution in his novels *Mala Hierba* (*Bad Weeds*) and *La sensualidad pervertida* (*The Perverted Sensuality*) (see Donis).

14 Furthermore, a package is later found containing Grijalba's personal effects in Selva's home. Selva's theory is that the package was thrown into his home through an open window from the plot of land where Grijalba was found.

2. Investigating the "Eye" in Twentieth-Century Spanish Crime Novels

1 See Salvador Vázquez de Parga for more on this process and on the popularity of these translations in the 1920s and 1930s and the later inclusion of Spanish crime fiction authors in these sorts of series, in chapter 1 of his book, *La novela policiaca en España* (*The Crime Novel in Spain*).

2 Despite his popularity, Mediante was said to publish under pseudonyms such as Bill O'Hara, Boris King, and H.A. Waytorn. I owe this information on Mediante to Alberto Sánchez's blog dedicated to the *bolsilibro* in Spain: bolsilibrosmemoriablog.wordpress.com.

3 According to Valles Calatrava, he wrote "numerosas historias de tipo enigma como *El abogado que asesinaba* (1943), *El club de los trece asesinos* (1943), *¿Quién robó la 'Lágrima de Budha'?* (1944) o *El robo de 'El Sol de Oriente'* (1944)" ("numerous enigma-like stories such as *The Lawyer Who Killed* (1943), *The Club of the Thirteen Murderers* (1943), *Who Stole the 'Tear of Budha'?* (1944) or *The Theft of 'The Sun of the East'* (1944)") (143). Even before the forties, however, the writer introduced a detective of sorts known as "El Duende de la Colgiata" ("The Elf of Colgiata") (*La novela policiaca* 48), and, using the pseudonym Jack Forbes, he established a recurring amateur detective character, "Gu-Gú" (ibid. 83–4).

4 Lacruz would publish *El inocente (The Innocent Man*) in 1953 to give way to the psychological crime novel, a reformulated generic form that Salvador

would follow with *El charco (The Puddle,* 1953) and *Los atracadores* (*The Robbers,* 1955). For more on these authors, see Vázquez de Parga.

5 Besides *La señorita detective*, Mediante published three other detective novels under his own name, *Pájaros de cuenta*, *Sombras siniestras*, and *Fuerzas ocultas* for the Serie Wallace. I have been unable to determine with certainty the years of publication for some of these novels because they do not appear in the novels themselves (or the years appear between question marks) or in the archives of the Biblioteca Nacional Española.

6 The exceptions to this are Cañada Honda, the train station where Diana Fletcher is thrown off the train, and, in character names, Domingo de Ramos, a black man who works as a train attendant. There are other references, such as the "coñac español" ("Spanish cognac") that they drink in Dubois' office that are also small hints of the Spanish element in the novel (18).

7 For more on the censorship process, see Daniel Linder. According to Linder, "Publishers were required to submit all titles for prior censorship, after which readers were assigned, and a judgment was issued. The censors filled in a Reader's Report designed to help them screen out any offensive references to the dogma of the Regime, the Regime itself, its allies, the Church, Church ministers, and morality in general. Readers were encouraged to state in the Report whether they felt the book should be authorized or not, but the final decision about any particular work resided with a superior or the minister himself ... The outcome of the censorship process could be authorization, authorization with omissions, or non-authorization" (158–9).

8 While this description specifies that she has very dark hair and dark-coloured eyes, the illustration on the cover page of *La señorita detective* portrays a woman with lighter coloured hair, a light brown colour, and with blue eyes, thus a more anglicized type. The rest of the illustrations in the book are of the male characters of the novel, but Leslie is not one of them, and they are all in black and white.

9 Dubois happens to be a friend of the lady who has been robbed, and is told about Diana's bravery in this matter. Another interesting coincidence is that Lewis Maulette is one of the men responsible for stealing the valuable formula to make the fake diamonds. Lewis is also the one who pushes the secret agent off the train after injecting her with a potion that causes the paralysis. He later reappears at the hospital to try to kill her, but Leslie is sent there by the Secret Service to protect her and ends up killing Lewis by accident when Lewis's gun goes off.

10 Before Tasis published his novels, however, Catalan novelists Antoni i Careta i Vidal and C.A. Jordana had also attempted to emerge on the scene with their detective works (see Hart's "From Knight Errant" 74). Tasis's three best-known works in this genre are *La Bíblia valenciana* (*The Valencian Bible*, 1955), *És hora de plegar* (*Quitting Time*, 1956), and *Un crim al Paralelo* (*Crime on Paralelo Avenue*, 1960).

11 *Es vessa una sang fàcil* (*Easy Blood Is Spilled*), written in 1952 and published in 1954 by Albertí in Barcelona, is his first incursion into the crime fiction genre, according to Resina's *El cadáver*.

12 For more on Pedrolo's work as a translator, see Francesc Parcerisas' article on Manuel de Pedrolo in addition to Jordi Canal i Artigas and Àlex Martín Escribà's *La Cua de Palla: retrat en groc i negre* (*The Straw Tail: Portrait in Yellow and Black*) for more on the history of the series.

13 Pujol clarifies that the other, more ambitious aim of La Cua de Palla was "to create Catalan literature in the crime fiction genre, something which hardly existed except for five novels," which included Pedrolo's first two crime fiction novels, *Es vessa una sang fàcil* (1954) and *L'inspector fa tard* (1960), and Rafael Tasis' *La Bíblia valenciana* (1955), *És hora de plegar* (1956), and *Un crim al Paralelo* (1960) (175). Furthermore, Pujol demonstrates that "the output of crime fiction written originally in Catalan in the period 1963–70 is literally nil, with the two aforementioned exceptions by Pedrolo. The period 1972–9 produced a meagre catalogue: Maria Aurèlia Capmany's *El jaqué de la democràcia* (*The Morning Coat of Democracy*) (1972); Jaume Fuster's *De mica en mica s'omple la pica* (*Little by Little, the Basin Fills*) (1972); Ramon Planes' *Crim al carrer Tuset* (*Crime on Tuset Street*) (1973); Núria Mínguez's *Una casa a les tres torres* (*A House in the Three Towers*) (1974); Lluís Utrilla's *Una llosa de marbre negre* (*A Black Marble Slab*) (1974); Jaume Fuster's *Tarda, sessió contínua, 3.45* (*3.45 Afternoon Session*) (1976); and Jordi Carbonell's *Un home qualsevol* (*Any Man*) (1979)" (177). For a history of crime fiction originally written in Catalan, see Piquer Vidal and Martín Escribà.

3. Parodying the Male Gaze in Lourdes Ortiz's *Picadura mortal*

1 Jésica, better known as Yes, appears twice in the Carvalho novels, first in *Los mares del Sur* (*Southern Seas*, 1979) and again in *El hombre de mi vida* (*The Man of My Life*, 2000). It is for this reason that Charo and Carvalho do not get back together when Charo returns in *El hombre de mi vida*, because he falls in love with Yes in this novel. In fact, Carvalho plans to spend the rest of his life with Yes until she is murdered by the men that he is

investigating. Teresa Marsé, who is also introduced for the first time in *Tatuaje* (*Tattoo*), reappears in *Los mares del Sur* (1979) and *Los pájaros de Bangkok* (*The Birds of Bangkok*, 1983). There are, then, female characters that reappear in the Carvalho series, but Charo is the most prominent one.

2 For more on Ortiz's biography, see the entry for her in *The Feminist Encyclopedia: N–Z*. After the publication of *Picadura mortal* in 1979, Ortiz would also publish *En días como éstos* (*At Times Like This*, 1981), *Urraca* (1982), *Arcángeles* (*Archangels*, 1986), *Los motivos de Circe* (*Circe's Reasons*, 1991), *Antes de la batalla* (*Before the Battle*, 1992), *La fuente de la vida* (*The Fountain of Life*, 1995), *Fátima de los naufragios* (*Fátima of Shipwrecks*, 1998), *La libertad* (*Freedom*, 1999), and *Cara de niño* (*Child's Face*, 2002), among others.

3 For more information on the significance of the year 1979 for the genre, see Resina's *El cadáver en la cocina*.

4 For more on this group, see de Grado's discussion as well as the Coordinadora Feminista's webpage for details on the group and on the 1979 Jornadas Feministas: www.feministas.org/Presentacion.html. Regarding the condition of women in Spain during the Transition and the strengthening of the feminist movement during this transition to democracy, see *Españolas en la Transición* (*Spanish Women During the Transition*).

5 For more on equality and difference feminisms, see Roberta Johnson's chapter, "Equality and Difference Feminisms in the Castilian and Catalan Areas of Spain," in *A New History of Iberian Feminisms*.

6 Brooksbank Jones discusses these changes in consciousness with women's entry into the workforce more thoroughly in her book, *Women in Contemporary Spain*.

7 The 1996 Alfaguara edition of the book has a colourful cover page with a caricature of Bárbara's face on the cover, and the 2011 e-book edition has condominiums and a beach as its cover page backdrop.

8 For more on this idea of the silencing of the female body, especially when talking about pornography and the fetishization of women's bodies, see Susan Griffin's *Pornography and Silence*.

4. A New Politics of Visibility in the Lònia Guiu Series

1 According to Isidor Cònsul, the group, first known as DRACS (using the first letter of the authors' last names), started out with Miquel Desclot, Carles Reig, Pep Albanell, Jaume Cabré, and Joaquim Soler (31). After their first joint publication failed, Desclot and Reig left the group, and new members, such as Maria-Antònia Oliver, Jaume Fuster, Josep Maria Illa, Joaquim Carbó, Xavier Romeu, Quim Monzó, and Joan Rendé joined,

followed by the later incorporation of other writers such as Isidre Grau, Margarida Aritzeta, Assumpció Cantalozella, Antoni Serra, Josep L. Seguí, and Joana Escobedo, all of which would also come to form part of Ofèlia Dracs (31). The purpose was to create texts that would appeal aesthetically to the public and to make, as Patricia Hart has previously noted, "publishing in Catalan viable and to encourage the new generation to read in their native tongue" by "producing works of fiction in popular as well as 'high' literary forms" ("Catalan Culure" 302).

2 The group Ofèlia Dracs published *Deu pometes té el pomer* (*Ten Little Apples Has the Apple Tree*, 1980), *Lovecraft, Lovecraft* (1981), *Negra i consentida* (*Hardboiled and Spoiled*, 1983), *Essa efa* (*That Ef*, 1985), *Boccato di cardinali* (*Cardinal Boccato*, 1985), and *Misteri de reina* (*Mystery of Queen*, 1994).

3 See Carles Cortés and Dari Escandell's *Maria-Antònia Oliver* for the series *Retrats* (*Portraits*) for information on Oliver's literary career. Fuster began his career as a detective fiction writer in 1972 with the introduction of his first detective protagonist Enric Vidal in *De mica en mica s'omple la pica* (*Little by Little, the Basin Fills*). The couple met in Palma, Majorca in 1968 and decided to move to Barcelona and get married there the next year.

4 While her first publications were in her native Catalan, her first literary undertakings were in Castilian until she took a college course with Aina Moll Marquès, a renowned linguist, who, in the 1980s, would influence the linguistic policies and politics of the Generalitat de Catalunya, the Catalan Government (Cortés and Escandell 17). As she would later comment, it was during this time that she read her first book in Catalan, *Balanç fins a la matinada* (*Balance until Dawn*) by Manuel de Pedrolo, and it was from that time forward that she decided that she would write only in her native tongue (17). According to Cortés and Escandell, the traditional oral folktales of Majorca, the *rondalles mallorquines*, that she heard as a child growing up in Manacor provided the initial foundation for her storytelling in the 1960s and 1970s, and allowed her to interweave themes such as the destruction of the land and the victimization caused by a patriarchal and totalitarian system, topics she continues to revisit in her later fiction (21–4).

5 It was not until 28 December 2004 that all parliamentary groups unanimously approved integrated protective measures under law against gender violence in Spain.

6 Arquer is the protagonist in Jaume Fuster's crime fiction series. We will return to this connection later in the chapter.

7 Still, it must be noted, as María Antonia García de León does in her study of Spanish women during the Transition, that "[n]o hubo un *modelo*

femenino claro de ciudadana democrática en la Transición, por el contrario (y tal vez por causa de ello) sí hubo un tratamiento muy ambivalente del feminismo y de las feministas en el discurso de la Transición" ("there was no clear *female model* of democratic citizenship during the Transition, on the contrary (and perhaps because of that) there was a very ambivalent treatment of feminism and feminists in the Transition's rhetoric") (24; italics in original). During Franco's regime, however, there was a clear female model to follow, "el rol del *ama de casa*, que desde la esfera privada ejercía su ciudadanía, en una muy curiosa relación (de separación) de las esferas privada y pública de la vida social" ("the role of *housewife*, who exercised her citizenship from the private sphere, in a very curious relationship (of separation) between the private and public spheres of social life") (24–5; italics in original).

8 Similar to what occurs with Lònia's male detective counterparts, I would suggest that the redefinition of her function as a detective is also intimately linked with the *desencanto* (disillusionment) phenomenon in Spanish crime fiction, which Joan Ramon Resina discusses in "Desencanto y fórmula literaria" ("Disillusionment and Literary Formula").

9 A study of the representation of the female body in Oliver's crime fiction also leads us to a discussion of passivity versus action. The female detective protagonist in Oliver's short story and trilogy does not subscribe or reproduce the patriarchal ideology that she too is a victim of, but the critique of this passivity, of women reproducing or reenacting traditional roles is still present in Oliver's crime fiction since Lònia's feminist education is one of the major themes that structure the series, as critics like Vosburg and Godsland have previously noted.

10 The translation of the short story is by Kathleen McNerney, which was published in 1991 in *A Woman's Eye*, a collection of female crime fiction stories edited by Sara Paretsky.

11 Vosburg also mentions this link between male aggression against women and against nature in relation to Cristina's rape in *Antípodes* and in "On ets, Mònica?" ("Genre Bending" 66–7).

12 For more on the phenomenon of balearization in Majorca, see Biel Horrach Estarellas' article, "La balearización: Mallorca, el laboratorio de experimentación del turismo y su manifestación en el litoral" ("Balearization: Majorca, the Laboratory of Experimentation of Tourism and Its Effect on the Coastline").

13 For example, Vázquez Montalbán's Pepe Carvalho has a gastronomic obsession, whereas Eduardo Mendoza's detective's fetish is drinking Pepsi.

14 Translations of all three novels are from Kathleen McNerney's editions.

15 According to Godsland and White, "Oliver's novels force us to rethink the logistics of the fetishistic violence which is one of the hallmarks of the hard-boiled genre, by confronting readers with the results of aggression" (224). By seeing "the attack[s] through her eyes," this confirms that "there can be no glorification of the frightening experience" (224).

16 As we will discuss in a later section, the example of Maria Goretti is also used in *Estudi en lila* when talking to Sebastiana to point out that rape is never consensual regardless of whether the victim fights back or not.

17 In 1985, abortion was depenalized under three circumstances in Spain: if the woman had been raped, if the pregnancy put the woman in some sort of physical or mental danger, or in the case of malformation of the fetus.

18 A contrast to this description would be the portrayal of women's bodies in Manuel Vázquez Montalbán's Pepe Carvalho series. One such example is the portrayal of Pedrell's widow and Yes in Vázquez Montalbán's *Los mares del Sur* (*The Southern Seas*), where the narrative pauses to draw attention to their body parts in piecemeal fashion. There is, therefore, a clear departure between the depiction of the female body in female, versus male, crime fiction. In *Estudi en lila*, Quim, however, focuses in on Gaudí's body parts and oversexualizes his description of her. This is done in an effort to assuage his guilt over not recognizing her and letting her escape because of the way that she was dressed.

19 Fuster's Arquer is a play on Ross Macdonald's Lew Archer, and he too refers to Oliver's protagonist in one of the novels of the series. Fuster's detective series, in which Arquer is the detective protagonist, is made up by the following novels: *Les claus de vidre* (*The Glass Keys*, 1984), *Sota el signe de sagitari* (*Under the Sign of Sagittarius*, 1986), and *Vida de gos i altres claus de vidre* (*A Dog's Life and Other Glass Keys*, 1989). Fuster, as previously mentioned, was a member of Ofèlia Dracs and Oliver's husband.

20 For more on these protests, see María Ángeles Larumbe's *Las que dijeron que no* (*Those Who Said No*) (107–53).

21 These include: *El blau pàl·lid de la rosa de paper* (*The Pale Blue of the Paper Rose*, 1985), *L'arqueòloga va somriure abans de morir* (*The Archaeologist Smiled before She Died*, 1986), *Espurnes de sang* (*Drops of Blood*, 1987), *RIP, senyor Mosqueiro* (*RIP, Mr Mosqueiro*, 1989), and *Cita a Belgrad* (*Date in Belgrade*, 1992).

22 A very clear distinction between Mosqueiro and Oliver is the portrayal of female characters, for Mosqueiro's *al·lotes*, the female characters in the series, are either femmes fatales or damsels in distress, which of course is the exact opposite of what we find in Oliver's trilogy. More often than not, women in the Mosqueiro series are responsible for the crimes committed

or at least are the provocateurs according to Hart (see "From Knight Errant" and "Catalan Culture and Identity" 312–13).

23 We are also reminded of an earlier scene with Senyora Cros, who, upon forgetting Lònia's name, refers to her as a *daixonses*, an expression meaning "what's her name" or "what's her face" (40). Lònia comments on how insulting it is to be called this, for what Senyora Cros has done to Lònia in the beginning of *El sol que fa l'ànec* by calling her a *daixonses* is what Oliver essentially does to her by making her into a character, erasing her identity outside of Oliver's fiction.

24 It would appear that Oliver was, in fact, friends with this couple.

25 Oliver also uses the character of the seer, Madame Tasi, to invoke the traditional oral folktales of Majorca, the *rondalles mallorquines*. Madame Tasi's visions would remind readers of these oral stories passed on from generation to generation. Moreover, this character is the one who teaches Catalina's mother the verses of the song that she keeps repeating. The mystery of the case all circles back to Madame Tasi, who has also conned Lònia into getting involved in the case, so that she can be Catalina's mother's caretaker and inherit the estate. There is a connection drawn between the character of the seer, the *rondalles mallorquines*, and the popular song.

5. Lesbianizing the Genre

1 Readers were introduced to the first gay detective in the 1970s with Jose (P. García) García Martínez's Gay Flower detective series. Interestingly, the first lesbian investigator protagonist to appear on the scene is Blanca Álvarez's Bárbara (Baby) Villalta in 1992. Baby is a criminal in the first half of the novel, *La soledad del monstruo* (*The Loneliness of the Monster*), as she kills Carmen Fajares, who she suspects is responsible for the death of her lover, Pamela. It is in the second part of the novel that Baby takes on the role of an amateur investigator by looking into the murder of Juanma, a regular at her bar.

2 While I will only be focusing on the first two Emma García stories, Franc has written another story featuring the detective, "Exòtika" ("Exotic Women"), this one in Catalan, which appears in Anna Maria Villalonga's female crime fiction anthology, *Noves dames del crim* (*New Women Writers of Crime Fiction*, 2015). This story focuses on the problem of female sex trafficking. In a personal interview with the author, Franc indicated that we can expect another Emma García novel.

3 The parodic nature of the trilogy and of *No me llames cariño* has been thoroughly discussed by Vosburg ("All L," "Barcelona"), Collins ("Isabel

Franc's," "Sisters," "This Town," "(Un)natural Exposure"), Pertusa Seva ("Entrevista," "Nuevas detectives"), Ana Corbalán, and Ivonne Cuadra.

4 For more on how this lesbian form of justice functions in the trilogy, see Vosburg's "All L Breaks Loose."

5 "El enigma de su voz" first appeared in the journal *Letras femeninas* in 2010, and was later translated into English and published as part of *Barcelona Noir* in 2011. The Spanish version of the text was included in *Barcelona negra* in 2013, which is the edition I quote from here. I concentrate on "El enigma de su voz" and "Sin tratamiento de cortesía," both narrated in the first person, because both stories present Emma as a hybrid private eye/ protector of lesbian couples following the sociofinancial crisis. The plot of "Exòtika," on the other hand, centres on the problem of adolescent and teenage female sex trafficking and their sexual exploitation in Spain. No longer a first-person narrative, "Exòtika" is a departure from the earlier Emma García stories, as it does not focus on threats to the lesbian community. The main victim is a seventeen-year-old Gambian girl who has been stabbed, and who we later find out is a sex slave at a club on the outskirts of Barcelona. Still, some elements in this story are repeated, such as the reappearance of Emma's sidekick, Dos Emes ("Two Ems"), now "Doble Ema" in Catalan, and Emma's immediate attraction to women who are involved in her cases in some way.

6 For more on this novel, see Collins's "Isabel Franc's *No me llames cariño*" and both Cuadra's and Corbalán's articles.

7 As Franc told Pertusa Seva in an interview, Emma's voice started getting closer to her own authorial voice, and thus, "García pedía tener un espacio propio" ("García asked to have her own space") (Pertusa Seva, "Entrevista").

8 The translation of "El enigma de su voz" ("The Enigma of Her Voice") can be found in *Barcelona noir* (pages 63–78).

9 This positive vision of the urban renewal brought about, at least in part, by the preparations for the Olympic Games of 1992, is not shared by all. Resina, for example, criticizes the privileging of Barcelona over other areas of Catalonia (*Barcelona's Vocation* 209–15).

10 As previously mentioned, men also appear in *No me llames cariño*, and, according to Corbalán, they are all characterized as "abusivos, inútiles e incluso estorbos para el apacible desarrollo de la comunidad femenina" ("abusive, useless and even hindrances to the peaceful development of the female community") (169). Furthermore, heterosexual marriage is seen as subjugation, since all married women are victims in the novel (169).

11 Unless noted otherwise, all translations are my own.

12 Here, Franc takes advantage of the grammatical nuance whereby the same possessive adjective, "su," is used both for the formal "usted" and the "él/ella" forms. Like the possessive adjective "tu," "su" can also mean "your," but what differentiates the two is the degree of formality being employed. Thus, when Emma asks if she can "tutear" Senõr Magri, she wants to drop the formal "usted" form so that this distinction of whose wife she is talking about can become clear. The possessive adjective "su," like "mi" and "tu," does not have masculine or feminine forms and remains unchanged regardless of the noun modified. This contributes to Magri's misunderstanding in thinking that she is talking about "su/her [Paola's] mujer" and not his.

13 I take this idea of a safe space for visibility from Jill Robbins, who, in describing Chueca as a "gay village," explains that Chueca "created a safe space that allowed lesbians to become more visible with fewer risks" (117). In the fictional realm, Margaret Frohlich emphasizes how "lesbian fiction hones in on the binaries equal/oppressed and visible/invisible, encouraging us to understand the role that visibility plays in sociopolitical constructions of the lesbian subject" (39). Literary or fictional visibility also translates spatially, supporting the establishment or creation of alternate spaces for the lesbian subject in literature.

14 In a recent conversation with Susana Hernández, on 21 July 2016, the author mentioned that we can expect another installment of the series.

15 *Tortillera* is slang for lesbian, so leaving a *tortilla* (omelet) on her desk is a reference to Rebeca's homosexuality. *Bollo*, on the other hand, is a slang term for female genitalia, which again would be a way of signalling Rebeca as a lesbian.

16 Molinaro's article recently appeared in *Violence and Victimhood in Hispanic Crime Fiction*. The author was kind enough to share it with me prior to publication.

17 Interestingly enough, *Curvas* ends with another criminal mother, Elvira, but this mother kills a mentally challenged girl to protect her son Mario from getting caught, thinking that this third murder will confuse the police.

18 Regarding how the maternal is represented in the novel, Hernández explained during a recent conversation, "Me interesaba representar diferentes tipos de mujeres y de madres" ("I was interested in representing different types of women and mothers").

19 Regarding Rebeca's identification with the victims in her cases, Molinaro gives the example of Rosa, one of the victims in *Curvas peligrosas*, to illustrate that "the detective-protagonist explicitly links herself to Rosa because

they are both viewed as negatively different by their shared society" (36). In addition to Molinaro's assertion, I would argue that Rebeca's identification, beyond feeling like a marginalized figure because of her homosexuality, also has to do with the fact that she has felt like an outsider because she is the daughter of a killer.

Conclusion: Exploring an Alternative Crime Fiction Genealogy

1 Between 2003 and 2017, 885 women were murdered in Spain by their partners or ex-partners (see Clemente). According to the site *Separadas y Divorciadas*, 92 women were victims of femicide in 2017.

Works Cited

Agra Romero, María Xosé. "Violencia(s): hacer correr la sangre." *Tras la pista: narrativa criminal escrita por mujeres*, edited by Elena Losada Soler and Katarzyna Paszkiewicz, Icaria, 2015, pp. 19–40.

Alarcón, Pedro Antonio de. *El capitán veneno: historia de mis libros*. 12th ed., Sucesores de Rivadeneyra, 1922. *HathiTrust*, https://babel.hathitrust.org/cgi/pt?id=njp.32101067488062;view=1up;seq=9. Accessed 16 May 2015.

– *El clavo y otros relatos de misterio y crimen*. Edited by Joan Estruch Tobella, Editorial Fontamara, 1982.

– *"The Nail" and Other Stories by Pedro Antonio de Alarcón*. Translated by Robert M. Fedorchek, Introduction by Cyrus C. DeCoster, Bucknell UP, 1997.

Alberdi, Inés. *Historia y sociología del divorcio en España*. Centro de Investigaciones Sociológicas, 1979.

Alemán, Mateo. *Aventuras y vida de Guzmán de Alfarache*. Edited by José María Micó, Cátedra, 1987.

Allen, Virginia M. *The Femme Fatale: Erotic Icon*. Whitston Pub. Co., 1983.

Álvarez, Blanca. *La soledad del monstruo*. Grupo Libro 88, 1992.

Andersen, Frank Egholm. *Den nordiske femikrimi: læbestiftslitteratur eller fornyelse af en genre*. Her & Nu, 2008.

Asociación "Mujeres en la Transición Democrática." *Españolas en la Transición: de excluidas a protagonistas (1973–1982)*. Biblioteca Nueva, 1999.

Bayó Belenguer, Susana. "Montalbán's Carvalho Series as Social Critique." *Crime Scenes: Detective Narratives in European Culture since 1945*, edited by Anne Mullen and Emer O'Beirne, Rodopi, 2000, pp. 300–11.

– *Theory, Genre, and Memory in the Carvalho Series of Manuel Vázquez Montalbán*. The Edwin Mellen Press, 2001.

Berglund, Birgitta. "Desires and Devices: On Women Detectives in Fiction." *The Art of Detective Fiction*, edited by Warren Chernaik, Martin Swales, and Robert Vilain, St Martin's Press, 2000, pp. 138–52.

Betz, Phyllis M. *Lesbian Detective Fiction: Woman as Author, Subject and Reader*. McFarland, 2006.

Bieder, Maryellen. "Contesting the Body: Gender, Language, and Sexuality. The Modern Woman at the Turn of the Century." *Women's Narrative and Film in Twentieth-Century Spain*, edited by Ofelia Ferran and Kathleen M. Glenn, Routledge, 2002, pp. 3–18.

Bordo, Susan. *Unbearable Weight: Feminism, Western Culture, and the Body*. 10th anniversary ed., U of California P, 2003.

Brison, Susan J. *Aftermath: Violence and the Remaking of a Self*. Princeton UP, 2002.

Brooks, Peter. *Body Work: Objects of Desire in Modern Narrative*. Harvard UP, 1993.

Brooksbank Jones, Anny. *Women in Contemporary Spain*. Manchester UP, 1997.

– "Work, Women, and the Family: A Critical Perspective." *Spanish Cultural Studies: An Introduction: The Struggle for Modernity*, edited by Helen Graham and Jo Labanyi, Oxford UP, 1995, pp. 386–93.

Brownmiller, Susan. *Against Our Will: Men, Women, and Rape*. Simon and Schuster, 1975.

Burgess-Jackson, Keith. *Rape: A Philosophical Investigation*. Dartmouth UP, 1996.

Butler, Judith. *Gender Trouble: Feminism and the Subversion of Identity*. 10th anniversary ed., Routledge, 1999.

– "Rethinking Vulnerability in Resistance." *Vulnerability in Resistance*, edited by Judith Butler, Zeynep Gambetti, and Leticia Sabsay, Duke UP, 2016, pp. 12–27.

Canal i Artigas, Jordi, and Àlex Martín Escribà. *La Cua de Palla: retrat en groc i negre*. Alrevés, 2011.

Capmany, Maria Aurèlia. *El jaqué de la democràcia*. Nova Terra, 1972.

– *Traduït de l'americà*. Alberti, 1959.

– *Vés-te'n ianqui! O, si voleu, traduït de l'americà*. Laia, 1980.

Caruth, Cathy. *Unclaimed Experience: Trauma, Narrative, and History*. Johns Hopkins UP, 1996.

Casino, Xavi. "El loro que confundía a los pasajeros del tranvía." *La Vanguardia*, 7 May 2016, www.lavanguardia.com/local/20160504/401554823177/loro-tranvia-poblenou-barcelona-secreta.html. Accessed 20 June 2016.

Casper, Monica J., and Lisa Jean Moore. *Missing Bodies: The Politics of Visibility*. New York UP, 2009.

Chandler, Raymond. *The Long Goodbye*. Ballantine Books, 1982.

Choi, Myung N. *La mujer en la novela policial: evolución de la protagonista femenina en cinco autoras hispanas*. Palibrio, 2012.

Clemente, Yolanda. "Más de 800 mujeres muertas por violencia machista." *El país*, 9 Mar 2017, elpais.com/elpais/2017/03/03/media/1488565128_697938.html. Accessed 20 May 2017.

Close, Glen. "Desnudarse y morir: la erotización del cadáver femenino en el género negro." *Narrativas del crimen en América Latina: transformaciones y transculturaciones del policial*, edited by Brigitte Adriansen and Valeria Grinberg Pla, LIT Verlag, 2012, pp. 89–107.

Código Penal De España. Edición official reformada, Madrid: Imprenta Nacional, 1850. *Biblioteca Virtual del Patrimonio Bibliográfico*, bvpb.mcu.es/es/consulta/registro.cmd?id=404113. Accessed 2 May 2016.

Collins, Jacky. "Isabel Franc's *No me llames carinõ*: Contesting Patriarchy in Spanish Lesbian Feminist Crime Fiction." *CLUES: A Journal of Detection*, vol. 27, no. 2, 2009, pp. 66–73, https://doi.org/10.3172/CLU.27.2.66. Accessed 28 Sept. 2014.

– "Lesbian Identity in Contemporary Spain: 'One of the Greatest Taboos Ever.'" *Women in Contemporary Culture: Roles and Identities in France and Spain*, edited by Lesley K. Twomey, Intellect, 2003, pp. 127–38.

– "'Sisters Are Doing It for Themselves': Lesbian Identities in Contemporary Spanish Literature." *Lesbian Realities/Lesbian Fictions in Contemporary Spain*, edited by Nancy Vosburg and Jacky Collins, Bucknell UP, 2011, pp. 175–92.

– "'This Town Ain't Big Enough for the Both of Us(?)': Regional and Social Tensions in Two Novels by Lola Van Guardia/Isabel Franc." *Crime Scene Spain: Essays on Post-Franco Crime Fiction*, edited by Renée W. Craig-Odders and Jacky Collins, McFarland, 2009, pp. 118–32.

– "(Un)natural Exposure: Lola van Guardia's *Plumas de doble filo*. Creating a Real and Imagined Lesbian Space." *Mujeres Malas: Women's Detective Fiction from Spain*, edited by Jacky Collins and Shelley Godsland, Manchester Metropolitan UP, 2005, pp. 78–90.

Colmeiro, José F. *La novela policiaca española: teoría e historia crítica*. Anthropos, 1994.

– "The Spanish Detective as Cultural Other." *The Post-Colonial Detective*, edited by Ed Christian, Palgrave, 2001, pp. 176–92.

– "Stretching the Limits: Pedrolo's Detective Fiction." *Catalan Review*, vol. 3, no. 2, 1989, pp. 59–70.

Cònsul, Isidor. *Llegir i escriure: papers de crítica literària*. Edicions de la Magrana, 1995.

Corbalán, Ana. "Abajo el patriarcado: utopia lésbica en *No me llames carino*, de Isabel Franc." *Letras Femeninas*, vol. 36, no. 1, 2010, pp. 161–78, *JSTOR*, www.jstor.org/stable/23022341. Accessed 28 Sep. 2014.

Cortés, Carles, and Dari Escandell. *Maria-Antònia Oliver: retrats*. Associació d'Escriptors en Llengua Catalana, 2006.

Coundouriotis, Eleni. *Claiming History: Colonialism, Ethnography, and the Novel*. Columbia UP, 1999.

Cruz, Anne J. *Discourses of Poverty: Social Reform and the Picaresque Novel in Early Modern Spain.* U of Toronto P, 1999.

Cuadra, Ivonne. "*No me llames cariño* de Isabel Franc: la novela detectivesca lesbiana en España." *Confluencia*, vol. 22, no. 2, 2007, pp. 29–41, *JSTOR*, www.jstor.org/stable/27923222. Accessed 28 Sep. 2014.

Davies, Ann. *Spanish Spaces: Landscape, Space and Place in Contemporary Spanish Culture.* Liverpool UP, 2012.

Dilley, Kimberly J. *Busybodies, Meddlers, and Snoops: The Female Hero in Contemporary Women's Mysteries.* Greenwood Press, 1998.

Doane, Mary Ann. *Femmes Fatales: Feminism, Film Theory, Psychoanalysis.* Routledge, 1991.

Donis Serrano, Marisol. *Sirvientas asesinas: trece historias reales de sirvientas que mataron a sus amos: violencia de género, crimen pasional, "delitos de estatus."* Nowtilus, 2011.

Dopico Black, Georgina. *Perfect Wives, Other Women: Adultery and Inquisition in Early Modern Spain.* Duke UP, 2001.

Doyle, Arthur Conan. "A Scandal in Bohemia." *Adventures of Sherlock Holmes.* New York and London: Harper & Bros., 1892, pp. 3–28.

– *A Study in Scarlet.* Cosimo Classics, 2011.

Dunant, Sarah. "Body Language: A Study of Death and Gender in Crime Fiction." *The Art of Detective Fiction*, edited by Warren Chernaik, Martin Swales, and Robert Vilain. St Martin's Press, 2000, pp. 10–20.

Ebert, Teresa L. "Detecting the Phallus: Authority, Ideology, and the Production of Patriarchal Agents in Detective Fiction." *Rethinking Marxism*, vol. 5, no. 3, 1992, pp. 6–28. http://doi.org/10.1080/08935699208658021.

Edelman, Lee. *Homographesis: Essays in Gay Literary and Cultural Theory.* Routledge, 1994.

El Saffar, Ruth S. *Rapture Encaged: The Suppression of the Feminine in Western Culture.* Routledge, 1994.

Falcón, Lidia. "Spain: Women Are the Conscience of Our Country." Translated by Gloria Feiman Waldman, *Sisterhood Is Global: The International Women's Movement Anthology*, edited by Robin Morgan, Anchor Press/Doubleday, 1984, pp. 626–31.

– *Violencia contra la mujer.* Vindicación Feminista, 1991.

Farwell, Marilyn R. *Heterosexual Plots and Lesbian Narratives.* New York UP, 1996.

Federación de Asociaciones de Mujeres Separadas y Divorciadas. "Estadísticas del terrorismo machista en gráficos." *Separadas y divorciadas*, 14 Feb. 2018, www.separadasydivorciadas.org/wordpress/graficos-en-2017/. Accessed 28 Feb. 2018.

Fernández, Empar. "Lejos del negro absoluto." *Editanet, Espacio literario y artístico* 34, January/March 2016, archivos.editanet.org/34/en-blanco-y-negro/index.html. Accessed 22 May 2017.

Foucault, Michel. *The History of Sexuality. Volume I: An Introduction*. Translated by Robert Hurley, Pantheon Books, 1978.

Franc, Isabel. "El enigma de su voz." *Barcelona negra*, edited by Adriana V. López and Carmen Ospina, Edhasa, 2013, pp. 67–82.

– "The Enigma of Her Voice." *Barcelona Noir*, edited by Adriana V. López and Carmen Ospina, translated by Achy Obejas, Akashic Books, 2011, pp. 63–78.

– "Exòtika." *Noves dames del crim*, edited by Anna Maria Villalonga, Llibres del Delicte, 2015, pp. 65–88.

– *No me llames cariño*. Egales, 2004.

– *Plumas de doble filo*. Egales, 1999.

– "Sin tratamiento de cortesía." *Fundido en negro: antología de relatos del mejor calibre criminal femenino*, edited by Inmaculada Pertusa Seva, Alrevés, 2014, pp. 111–20.

Frohlich, Margaret. "Representation and the Politics of Visibility." *Lesbian Realities/Lesbian Fictions in Contemporary Spain*, edited by Nancy Vosburg and Jacky Collins, Bucknell UP, 2011, pp. 31–59.

García de León Álvarez, María Antonia. *Rebeldes ilustradas (La otra Transición)*. Anthropos, 2008.

Gentry, Caron E, and Laura Sjoberg. *Beyond Mothers, Monsters, Whores: Thinking about Women's Violence in Global Politics*, Zed Books, 2015.

Gilman, Sander L. "Black Bodies, White Bodies: Toward an Iconography of Female Sexuality in Late Nineteenth-Century Art, Medicine, and Literature." *Critical Inquiry*, vol. 12, no. 1, Autumn 1985, pp. 204–42. http://doi.org/10.1086/448327.

– *Difference and Pathology: Stereotypes of Sexuality, Race, and Madness*. Cornell UP, 1985.

Giralt, Alicia. "La detective Bárbara Arenas, a la búsqueda de modelos." *Mujeres Malas: Women's Detective Fiction from Spain*, edited by Jacky Collins and Shelley Godsland, Manchester Metropolitan UP, 2005, pp. 91–107.

Godsland, Shelley. *Killing Carmens: Women's Crime Fiction from Spain*. U of Wales P, 2007.

Godsland, Shelley, and Anne M. White. "Investigating Fictions of Identity: Contemporary Catalan Crime Fiction by Women." *Crime Scenes: Detective Narratives in European Culture since 1945*, edited by Anne Mullen and Emer O' Beirne, Rodopi, 2000, pp. 219–27.

González Fernández, Helena. "Homicidas, asesinas y terroristas: violencia, comunidad y vínculo." *Violencia y discurso en el mundo hispánico: género, cotidianidad y poder*, edited by Miguel Carrera Garrido and Mariola Pietrak, Universidad Maria Curie-Skłodowska / Padilla Libros, 2015, pp. 15–36.

Grado, Mercedes de. "Encrucijada del feminismo español: disyuntiva entre igualdad y diferencia." *La mujer en la España actual: ¿evolución o involución?*, edited by Jacqueline Cruz and Bárbara Zecchi, Icaria, 2004, pp. 25–58.

Grella, George. "Murder and the Mean Streets: The Hard-Boiled Detective Novel." *Detective Fiction: Crime and Compromise*, edited by Dick Allan and David Chacko, Harcourt Brace Jovanovich, 1974, pp. 411–28.

Griffin, Susan. *Pornography and Silence: Culture's Revenge against Nature.* Harper & Row, 1981.

– "Rape: The All-American Crime." *Ramparts*, vol. 10, no. 3, 1971, pp. 26–35, www.unz.org/Pub/Ramparts-1971sep-00026.

Groot, Joanna de. "'Sex' and 'Race': The Construction of Language and Image in the Nineteenth Century." *Sexuality and Subordination: Interdisciplinary Studies of Gender in the Nineteenth Century*, edited by Susan Mendus and Jane Rendall, Routledge, 1989, pp. 89–130.

Grossman, Julie. *Rethinking the Femme Fatale in Film Noir: Ready for Her Close-Up.* Palgrave Macmillan, 2009.

Gurrea, Ana. Introduction. *La gota de sangre* by Emilia Pardo Bazán, Ediciones Internacionales Universitarias, 1998.

Hanson, Helen, and Catherine O. Rawe, editors. "Introduction: 'Cherchez la *femme*,'" *The Femme Fatale: Images, Histories, Contexts*, Palgrave Macmillan, 2010, pp. 1–8.

Hart, Patricia. "Catalan Culture and Identity Through Popular Forms: The Collaborative Efforts of the Ofèlia Dracs Group in *Negra i consentida (Hardboiled and Spoiled)*." *Imagination, Emblems, and Expressions: Essays on Latin American, Caribbean, and Continental Culture and Identity*, edited by Helen L. Ryan, Bowling Green State UP, 1993, pp. 301–14.

– "From Knight Errant to Ethical Hero to Flatfoot: The Development of the Detective in Catalan Fiction." *Catalan Review*, vol. 3, no. 2, 1989, pp. 71–95.

– *The Spanish Sleuth: The Detective in Spanish Fiction*. Fairleigh Dickinson UP, 1987.

Hartman, Saidiya V. *Scenes of Subjection: Terror, Slavery, and Self-Making in Nineteenth-Century America*. Oxford UP, 1997.

Hedgecock, Jennifer. *The Femme Fatale in Victorian Literature: The Danger and the Sexual Threat*. Cambria Press, 2008.

Hernández, Susana. *Contra las cuerdas*. Alrevés, 2012.

– *Cuentas pendientes*. Alrevés, 2015.

– *Curvas peligrosas*. Odisea Editorial, 2010.

Hernández, Wilfredo. "From the Margins to the Mainstream: Lesbian Characters in Spanish Fiction (1964–1979)." *Tortilleras: Hispanic and U.S. Latina Lesbian Expression*, edited by Lourdes Torres and Inmaculada Pertusa, Temple UP, 2003, pp. 19–34.

Hirsch, Marianne. *The Generation of Postmemory: Writing and Visual Culture after the Holocaust*. Columbia UP, 2012.

Horn, David. *The Criminal Body: Lombroso and the Anatomy of Deviance*. Routledge, 2003.

– "This Norm Which Is Not One: Reading the Female Body in Lombroso's Anthropology." *Deviant Bodies: Critical Perspectives on Difference in Science and Popular Culture*, edited by Jennifer Terry and Jacqueline Urla, Indiana UP, 1995, pp.109–28.

Horrach Estarellas, Biel. "La balearización: Mallorca, el laboratorio de experimentación del turismo y su manifestación en el litoral." *Revista Iberoamericana de Urbanismo*, vol. 2, 2009, pp. 17–33. http://hdl.handle.net/2099/12259.

Hutcheon, Linda. *A Theory of Parody: The Teachings of Twentieth-Century Art Forms*. U of Illinois P, 2000.

James, P.D. *An Unsuitable Job for a Woman*. Faber, 2010.

Jameson, Fredric. "On Raymond Chandler." *The Poetics of Murder: Detective Fiction and Literary Theory*, edited by Glenn W. Most and William W. Stowe, Harcourt Brace Jovanovich, 1983, pp. 122–48.

Johnson, Patricia. "Sex and Betrayal in the Detective Fiction of Sue Grafton and Sara Paretsky." *Journal of Popular Culture*, vol. 27, no. 4, 1994, pp. 97–106, http://doi.org/10.1111/j.0022-3840.1994.2704_97.x.

Johnson, Roberta. "Equality and Difference Feminisms in the Castilian and Catalan Areas of Spain." *A New History of Iberian Feminisms*, edited by Silvia Bermúdez and Roberta Johnson, U of Toronto P, 2018, pp. 317–27.

Johnston, Jill. *Lesbian Nation: The Feminist Solution*. Simon and Schuster, 1973.

Jones, Margaret E.W. "*Vindicación Feminista* and the Feminist Community in Post-Franco Spain." *Recovering Spain's Feminist Tradition*, edited by Lisa Vollendorf, MLA, 2001, pp. 311–36.

Kaplan, E. Ann. "Introduction to New Edition." *Women in Film Noir*. Rev. and expanded ed., edited by E. Ann Kaplan, British Film Institute, 1998, pp. 1–19.

– *Trauma Culture: The Politics of Terror and Loss in Media and Literature*. Rutgers UP, 2005.

Keen, Suzanne. *Empathy and the Novel*. Oxford UP, 2007.

Kermode, Frank. *The Sense of an Ending: Studies in the Theory of Fiction with a New Epilogue*. Oxford UP, 2000.

Klein, Kathleen Gregory. "*Habeas Corpus*: Feminism and Detective Fiction." *Feminism in Women's Detective Fiction*, edited by Glennwood H. Irons, U of Toronto P, 1995, pp. 171–89.

– "Women Times Women Times Women." *Women Times Three: Writers, Detectives, Readers*, edited by Kathleen Gregory Klein, Bowling Green State UP, 1995, pp. 3–14.

Kuhn, Annette. *The Power of the Image: Essays on Representation and Sexuality*. Routledge, 1994.

– *Women's Pictures: Feminism and Cinema*. 2nd ed., Verso, 1994.

Labanyi, Jo. *Gender and Modernization in the Spanish Realist Novel*. Oxford UP, 2000.

Landeira, Ricardo. *El género policiaco en la literatura española del siglo XIX*. Universidad de Alicante, 2001.

Larumbe, María Ángeles. *Una inmensa minoría: influencia y feminismo en la Transición*. Prensas Universitarias de Zaragoza, 2002.

– *Las que dijeron no: palabra y acción del feminismo en la Transición*. Prensas Universitarias de Zaragoza, 2004.

Lauretis, Teresa de. *Alice Doesn't: Feminism, Semiotics, Cinema*. Indiana UP/ Macmillan, 1984.

Levine, Linda Gould. "Feminismo y repercusiones sociales: de la Transición a la actualidad." *La mujer en la España actual: ¿evolución o involución?*, edited by Jacqueline Cruz and Bárbara Zecchi, Icaria, 2004, pp. 59–72.

Linder, Daniel. "The Censorship of Sex: A Study of Raymond Chandler's *The Big Sleep* in Franco's Spain." *TTR: traduction, terminologie, rédaction*, vol. 17, no. 1, 2004, pp. 155–82, www.erudit.org/fr/revues/ttr/ 2004-v17-n1-ttr1014/011977ar/. Accessed 20 Mar. 2016.

Lissorgues, Yvan. "La novela detectivesca española actual: un posibilismo realista." *Actas Irvine 92*, vol. 4, edited by Juan Villegas, U of California P, 1994, 173–82.

Lombroso, Cesare, and Guglielmo Ferrero. *Criminal Man*. Translated and with a new introduction by Mary Gibson and Nicole Hahn Rafter, Duke UP, 2006.

– *Criminal Woman, the Prostitute, and the Normal Woman*. Translated and with a new introduction by Nicole Hahn Rafter and Mary Gibson, Duke UP, 2004.

López de Úbeda, Francisco. *La pícara Justina*. Edited by Bruno Mario Damiani, Porrua-Turanzas, 1982.

Losada Soler, Elena, and Katarzyna Paszkiewicz. "Ellas también escriben sobre el mal." *Tras la pista: narrativa criminal escrita por mujeres*, edited by Elena Losada Soler and Katarzyna Paszkiewicz, Icaria, 2015, pp. 7–18.

Ludmer, Josefina. *El cuerpo del delito. Un manual*. Perfil Libros, 1999.

MacKinnon, Catharine A. *Toward a Feminist Theory of the State*. Harvard UP, 1989.

Macklin, John. "Realism Revisted: Myth, Mimesis, and the *Novela Negra*." *Leeds Papers on Thrillers in the Transition: "Novela Negra" and Political Change in Spain*, edited by Rob Rix, Trinty and All Saints, 1992, pp. 49–73.

Maginn, Alison. "Breaking the Contract in the Female Detective Novel: Lourdes Ortiz's *Picadura Mortal*." *Letras Femeninas*, vol. 28, no. 1, 2002, pp. 45–56, *JSTOR*, www.jstor.org/stable/23021384. Accessed 15 Jan. 2014.

Mandrell, James. "'Experiencing Technical Difficulties': Genre and Gender, Translation and Difference: Lourdes Ortiz, María Antònia Oliver, and Blanca Álvarez." *The Journal of Narrative Technique*, vol. 27, no. 1, 1997, pp. 55–83, *JSTOR*, www.jstor.org/stable/30225456. Accessed 9 Sept. 2014.

Marcos, Pilar. "El PP recurre al Constitucional las bodas gays por 'desnaturalizar' el matrimonio." *El país*, 1 Oct. 2005, elpais.com/diario/2005/10/01/sociedad/1128117603_850215.html. Accessed 26 June 2016.

Martín Escribà, Àlex, and Javier Sánchez Zapatero. "Cuando no existía el 'femicrime': Maria-Antònia Oliver y la novela negra." *Tras la pista: narrativa criminal escrita por mujeres*, edited by Elena Losada Soler y Katarzyna Paszkiewicz, Icaria, 2015, 113–30.

Mayne, Judith. *The Woman at the Keyhole: Feminism and Women's Cinema*. Indiana UP, 1990.

McGovern, Lynn. "'A Private I': The Birth of a Female Sleuth and the Role of Parody in Lourdes Ortiz's *Picadura mortal*." *Journal of Interdisciplinary Literary Studies: Innovative Approaches to Hispanic Literature (JILS)*, vol. 5, no. 2, 1993, pp. 251–79.

Mediante, Federico. *Fuerzas ocultas*. Editorial Cisne, 1944?.

– *La señorita detective*. Editorial Cisne, 1944.

– *Sombras siniestras*. Editorial Cisne, 1944?.

Molinaro, Nina. "Susana Hernández's Crime Fiction and Resolution Through Resistance." *Violence and Victimhood in Hispanic Crime Fiction: Essays on Contemporary Works*, edited by Shalisa M. Collins, Renée W. Craig-Odders, and Marcella L. Paul, McFarland, 2018, pp. 30–49.

– "Writing the Wrong Rites?: Rape and Women's Detective Fiction in Spain." *Letras Femeninas*, vol. 28, no. 1, 2002, pp. 100–17, *JSTOR*, www.jstor.org/stable/23021388. Accessed 24 Apr. 2013.

Montero, Rosa. "El misterio del deseo: así son y así viven las lesbianas en España." *El País Semanal*, 31 Oct. 1993, pp. 16–28.

Mulvey, Laura. "Afterthoughts on 'Visual Pleasure and Narrative Cinema' inspired by King Vidor's Duel in the Sun (1946)." *Visual and Other Pleasures*, Palgrave, 1989, pp. 29–38.

– "Visual Pleasure and Narrative Cinema." *Film Theory and Criticism: Introductory Readings*, edited by Leo Braudy and Marshall Cohen, Oxford UP, 1999, pp. 833–44.

Munt, Sally. *Heroic Desire: Lesbian Identity and Cultural Space*. New York UP, 1998.

– *Murder by the Book? Feminism and the Crime Novel*. Routledge, 1994.

Oliver, Kelly. *Witnessing: Beyond Recognition*. U of Minnesota P, 2001.

Oliver, Maria-Antònia. *Antipodes*. Translated by Kathleen McNerney, Seal Press, 1989.

– *Antípodes*. La Magrana, 1997.

– *Blue Roses for a Dead ... Lady?* Translated by Kathleen McNerney, UP of the South, 1998.

– *Estudi en lila*. La Magrana, 1987.

– "On ets, Mònica?" *Negra i consentida*. Compiled and edited by Ofèlia Dracs, Laia, 1983, pp. 119–47.

– *El sol que fa l'ànec*. La Magrana, 1994.

– *Study in Lilac*. Translated by Kathleen McNerney, Seal Press, 1987.

– "Where Are You, Monica?" Translated by Kathleen McNerney, *A Woman's Eye*, edited by Sara Paretsky, Delacorte Press, 1991, pp. 370–99.

Ortiz, Lourdes. *Picadura mortal*. Sedmay, 1979.

Otero Blanco, Ángel. "Novela negra y existencialismo: Manuel de Pedrolo, Manuel Vázquez Montalbán y Juan Madrid." *Pórtico: Revista de Estudios Hispánicos del Recinto Universitario de Mayagüez*, vol. 2, 2007, pp. 53–72.

Parcerisas, Francesc. "Manuel de Pedrolo, introductor a Catalunya de la narrativa nord americana contemporània." *Quaderns: Revista de traducció*, vol. 14, 2007, pp. 39–48.

Pardo Bazán, Emilia. *Al pie de la Torre Eiffel*, Administración, 1899.

– "Impresiones y sentimientos del día diecinueve." *El Imparcial*, 20 July 1890.

– *La gota de sangre*. Introduction by Ana Gurrea, Ediciones Internacionales Universitarias, 1998.

– "La vida contemporánea:" *La Ilustración artística* 1.416, 15 Feb. 1909, pp. 122.

– "La vida contemporánea." *La Ilustración artística* 1.740, 3 May 1915, pp. 302.

– "La vida contemporánea: Como en las cavernas." *La Ilustración artística* 1.029, 16 Sept. 1901, pp. 602.

– "La vida contemporánea: Ensaladilla." *La Ilustración artística* 1.017, 24 June 1901, pp. 410.

Paris-Huesca, Eva. "*Curvas peligrosas* en el contexto de los feminismos del nuevo milenio." *Polifonía*, vol. 3, no. 1, 2013, pp. 18–28.

Pattison, Walter Thomas. *Emilia Pardo Bazán*. Twayne Publishers, 1971.

Pedrolo, Manuel de. *Joc brut*. Introduction by Carme Ballús Molina, Educaula 62, 2009.

– "Que falla, 'la cua de palla'?" *Serra d'Or*, vol. XIV, no. 149, 1972, pp. 44–6.

Pérez, Janet, and Maureen Ihrie, editors. "Detective Fiction by Spanish Women Writers." *The Feminist Encyclopedia of Spanish Literature: A-M*, Greenwood Press, 2002, pp. 166–71.

– "Ortiz, Lourdes (1943–)." *The Feminist Encyclopedia of Spanish Literature: N–Z*, Greenwood Press, 2002, pp. 449–52.

Pérez Galdós, Benito. *El crimen de la calle de Fuencarral: el crimen del cura Galeote*. Edited by Rafael Reig, Lengua de Trapo Ediciones, 2002.

Pertusa Seva, Inmaculada. "Entrevista: Isabel Franc y la primera agencia de detectives lesbianas en las letras peninsulares." *Grafemas*, Dec. 2009, people.wku.edu/inma.pertusa/encuentros/grafemas/diciembre_09/pertusa.html. Accessed 22 June 2016.

– "Nuevas detectives lesbianas para un nuevo milenio." *Otherness in Hispanic Culture*, edited by Teresa Fernández Ulloa, Cambridge Scholars, 2014, pp. 105–21.

– "Prólogo." *Fundido en negro: antología de relatos del mejor calibre criminal femenino*, edited by Inmaculada Pertusa Seva, Alrevés, 2014, pp. 9–13.

Piquer Vidal, Adolf, and Àlex Martín Escribà. *Catalana i criminal: la novel·la detectivesca del segle XX*. Documenta Balear, 2006.

Plain, Gill. *Twentieth-Century Crime Fiction: Gender, Sexuality and the Body*. Edinburgh UP, 2001.

Preston, Paul. "Materialism and Serie Negra." *Leeds Papers on Thrillers in the Transition: "Novela negra" and Political Change in Spain*, edited by Rob Rix, Trinity and All Saints, 1992, pp. 9–16.

– *The Politics of Revenge: Fascism and the Military in Twentieth-Century Spain*. Routledge, 1995.

Proctor, Tammy M. *Female Intelligence: Women and Espionage in the First World War*. New York UP, 2003.

Pujol, Dídac. "A Catalan Series of Crime Fiction: 'La Cua de Palla' and Its Sequels (1963–2009)." *Journal of Catalan Studies*, vol. 14, 2011, pp. 173–200.

Raimundo Rodíguez, María Jesús. "El crimen de la calle Fuencarral." *Los procesos célebres seguidos ante el Tribunal Supremo en sus doscientos años de historia*, Boletín Oficial del Estado y Tribunal Supremo, 2014, pp. 289–344.

Reddy, Maureen. "The Feminist Counter-Tradition in Crime: Cross, Grafton, Paretsky, and Wilson." *The Cunning Craft: Original Essays on Detective Fiction and Contemporary Literary Theory*, edited by Ronald G. Walker and June M. Frazer, Western Illinois UP, 1990, pp. 174–87.

– "Women Detectives." *The Cambridge Companion to Crime Fiction*, edited by Martin Priestman, Cambridge UP, 2003, pp. 191–207.

Resina, Joan Ramon. *Barcelona's Vocation of Modernity: Rise and Decline of an Urban Image*. Stanford UP, 2008.

– *El cadáver en la cocina: la novela criminal en la cultura de desencanto*. Anthropos, 1997.

– "Desencanto y fórmula literaria en las novelas policiacas de Manuel Vázquez Montalbán." *MLN*, vol. 108, no. 2, Mar. 1993, pp. 254–82, http://doi.org/10.2307/2904635.

– "Detective Formula and Parodic Reflexivity: Crim." *The Garden across the Border: Mercè Rodoreda's Fiction*, edited by Kathleen McNerney and Nancy Vosburg, Susquehanna UP, 1994, pp. 119–34.

Robbins, Jill. *Crossing through Chueca: Lesbian Literary Culture in Queer Madrid*. U of Minnesota P, 2011.

Rodoreda, Mercè. "Crim." *Primeres Novel·les. Volum II*, edited by Roser Porta, Fundació Mercè Rodoreda, Institut d'Estudis Catalans, 2008, pp. 115–292.

Rose, Margaret A. *Parody: Ancient, Modern, and Post-modern*. Cambridge UP, 1993.

Ruiz Ocaña, Eduardo. "Pardo Bazán y los asesinatos de mujeres." *Didáctica (Lengua y Literatura)*, vol. 16, 2004, pp. 177–88, http://revistas.ucm.es/index.php/DIDA/article/view/DIDA0404110177A/19359. Accessed 2 May 2013.

Said, Edward W. *Orientalism*. Vintage Books, 1979.

Sánchez, Alberto. "Federico Mediante Noceda, El Explicador." *La memoria del bolsilibro: un homenaje a los escritores de novela popular*, 8 June 2016, bolsilibrosmemoriablog.wordpress.com. Accessed 12 June 2016.

Sánchez Salas, Daniel. "La figura del explicador en los inicios del cine español." *Tras el sueño: Actas del Centenario. VI Congreso de la Asociación Española de Historiadores del Cine. Cuadernos de la Academia*, vol. 2, 1998, pp. 73–84.

Santana, Mario. "Manuel Vázquez Montalbán's *Los mares del Sur* and the Incrimination of the Spanish Transition." *Revista de Estudios Hispánicos*, vol. 34, 2000, pp. 535–59.

Shipman, Pat. *Femme Fatale: Love, Lies, and the Unknown Life of Mata Hari*. HarperCollins, 2007.

Sieburth, Stephanie. *Inventing High and Low: Literature, Mass Culture, and Uneven Modernity in Spain*. Duke UP, 1994.

Spires, Robert. "Lourdes Ortiz: Mapping the Course of Postfrancoist Fiction." *Women Writers of Contemporary Spain: Exiles in the Homeland*, edited by Joan L. Brown, U of Delaware P, 1991, pp. 198–216.

Stott, Rebecca. *The Fabrication of the Late-Victorian Femme Fatale: The Kiss of Death*. Palgrave Macmillan, 1992.

Sully, Jess. "Challenging the Stereotype: The Femme Fatale in Fin-de-Siècle Art and Early Cinema." *The Femme Fatale: Images, Histories, Contexts*, edited by Helen Hanson and Catherine O'Rawe, Palgrave Macmillan, 2010, pp. 46–59.

Talbot, Lynn K. "The Politics of a Female Detective Novel: Lourdes Ortiz's *Picadura mortal*." *Romance Notes*, vol. 35, no. 2, 1994, pp. 163–9.

Thompson-Casado, Kathleen. "On the Case of the Spanish Female Sleuth." *Reading the Popular in Contemporary Spanish Texts*, edited by Shelley Godsland and Nickianne Moody, U of Delaware P, 2004, pp. 136–49.

Tsuchiya, Akiko. *Marginal Subjects: Gender and Deviance in Fin-de-siècle Spain*. U of Toronto P, 2011.

Urla, Jacqueline, and Jennifer Terry. "Introduction: Mapping Embodied Deviance." *Deviant Bodies: Critical Perspectives on Difference in Science and Popular Culture*, edited by Jennifer Terry and Jacqueline Urla, Indiana UP, 1995, pp. 1–18.

Valles Calatrava, José R. "Los primeros pasos de la novela criminal española (1900–1975)." *Revista Iberoamericana*, vol. 2, no. 7, 2002, pp. 141–9, *JSTOR*, www.jstor.org/stable/41672980. Accessed 2 May 2013.

Vázquez de Parga, Salvador. *La novela policiaca en España*. Ronsel, 1993.

– "La novela policíaca española." *Novela Criminal: Los Cuadernos del Norte*, vol. 19, mayo-junio 1983, pp. 24–37.

Vázquez Montalbán, Manuel. *El hombre de mi vida*. Planeta, 2000.

– *El laberinto griego*. Planeta, 1991.

– *Los mares del Sur*. Planeta, 2008.

– *Los pájaros de Bangkok*. Seix Barral, 1983.

– *Tatuaje*. Plaza & Janes, 1986.

Villalonga, Anna Maria. "El Femicrime, una etiqueta surgida de la nada." *El género negro: de la marginalidad a la normalización*, edited by Àlex Martín Escribà and Javier Sánchez Zapatero, Andavira, 2015, pp. 263–9.

– editor. *Elles també maten*. Llibres del Delicte, 2013.

– *Noves dames del crim*. Llibres del Delicte, 2015.

– "El relat negre femení en català: per què maten les dones? De la dona defensora a la dona botxí." *Violència i identitat*, edited by Francisco Ardolino and Elena Losada, Edicions de la Universitat de Barcelona, 2017, pp. 27–38.

– "Si no pot ser 'negra' ... li direm 'gris asphalt.'" *Núvol*, 12 Jan. 2016, www.nuvol.com/opinio/si-no-pot-ser-negra-li-direm-gris-asfalt/. Accessed 22 May 2017.

Vosburg, Nancy. "'All L Breaks Loose': Lola Van Guardia's Lesbian Trilogy." *Lesbian Realities/Lesbian Fictions in Contemporary Spain*, edited by Nancy Vosburg and Jacky Collins, Bucknell UP, 2011, pp. 193–210.

– "Barcelona in Spanish Women's Detective Fiction: Feminist, Postfeminist, and Lesbian Perspectives." *Mujeres Malas: Women's Detective Fiction from Spain*, edited by Jacky Collins and Shelley Godsland, Manchester Metropolitan UP, 2005, pp. 22–30.

– "Genre Bending: Maria-Antònia Oliver's Catalan Sleuth." *Letras Femeninas*, vol. 28, no. 1, 2002, pp. 57–70, *JSTOR*, www.jstor.org/stable/23021385. Accessed 18 Jan. 2013.

Vosburg, Nancy, and Jacky Collins, editors. "Introduction." *Lesbian Realities/Lesbian Fictions in Contemporary Spain*, Bucknell UP, 2011, pp. 9–27.

Walton, Priscilla L., and Manina Jones. *Detective Agency: Women Rewriting the Hard Boiled Tradition*. U of California P, 1999.

Welles, Marcia L. *Persephone's Girdle: Narratives of Rape in Seventeenth-Century Spanish Literature*. Vanderbilt UP, 2000.

Wells, Caragh. "The Case for Nostalgia and Sentimentality in Manuel Vázquez Montalbán's 'Serie Carvalho.'" *Hispanic Review*, vol. 76, no. 3, 2008, pp. 281–97, *JSTOR*, www.jstor.org/stable/27668848. Accessed 25 Nov. 2015.

White, Rosie. "'You'll Be the Death of Me': Mata Hari and the Myth of the Femme Fatale." *The Femme Fatale: Images, Histories, Contexts*, edited by Helen Hanson and Catherine O'Rawe, Palgrave Macmillan, 2010, pp. 72–88.

White, Sarah L. "Liberty, Honor, Order: Gender and Political Discourse in Nineteenth-Century Spain." *Constructing Spanish Womanhood: Female Identity in Modern Spain*, edited by Victoria Lorée Enders and Pamela Beth Radcliff, State U of New York P, 1999, pp. 233–57.

Wilson, Barbara. "The Outside Edge: Lesbian Mysteries." *Daring to Dissent: Lesbian Culture from Margin to Mainstream*, edited by Liz Gibbs, Cassell, 1994, pp. 217–28.

Wilton, Tamsin. *Lesbian Studies: Setting an Agenda*. Routledge, 1995.

Woodward, Kath. *The Politics of In/visibility: Being There*. Palgrave Macmillan, 2015.

Index

Fictional characters known mainly by their first name are indexed by first name. A parenthetical title after a name indicates that the name is of a fictional character in that work. Because the entire volume is about crime fiction/female crime fiction in Spain, the use of these terms as entry points has been minimized in this index.

Toronto Iberic

1 Anthony J. Cascardi, *Cervantes, Literature, and the Discourse of Politics*
2 Jessica A. Boon, *The Mystical Science of the Soul: Medieval Cognition in Bernardino de Laredo's Recollection Method*
3 Susan Byrne, *Law and History in Cervantes' Don Quixote*
4 Mary E. Barnard and Frederick A. de Armas (eds), *Objects of Culture in the Literature of Imperial Spain*
5 Nil Santiáñez, *Topographies of Fascism: Habitus, Space, and Writing in Twentieth-Century Spain*
6 Nelson R. Orringer, *Lorca in Tune with Falla: Literary and Musical Interludes*
7 Ana M. Gómez-Bravo, *Textual Agency: Writing Culture and Social Networks in Fifteenth-Century Spain*
8 Javier Irigoyen-García, *The Spanish Arcadia: Sheep Herding, Pastoral Discourse, and Ethnicity in Early Modern Spain*
9 Stephanie Sieburth, *Survival Songs: Conchita Piquer's* Coplas *and Franco's Regime of Terror*
10 Christine Arkinstall, *Spanish Female Writers and the Freethinking Press, 1879–1926*
11 Margaret E. Boyle, *Unruly Women: Performance, Penitence, and Punishment in Early Modern Spain*
12 Evelina Gužauskytė, *Christopher Columbus's Naming in the* diarios *of the Four Voyages (1492–1504): A Discourse of Negotiation*
13 Mary E. Barnard, *Garcilaso de la Vega and the Material Culture of Renaissance Europe*
14 William Viestenz, *By the Grace of God: Francoist Spain and the Sacred Roots of Political Imagination*
15 Michael Scham, Lector Ludens: *The Representation of Games and Play in Cervantes*
16 Stephen Rupp, *Heroic Forms: Cervantes and the Literature of War*
17 Enrique Fernandez, *Anxieties of Interiority and Dissection in Early Modern Spain*

18 Susan Byrne, *Ficino in Spain*
19 Patricia M. Keller, *Ghostly Landscapes: Film, Photography, and the Aesthetics of Haunting in Contemporary Spanish Culture*
20 Carolyn A. Nadeau, *Food Matters: Alonso Quijano's Diet and the Discourse of Food in Early Modern Spain*
21 Cristian Berco, *From Body to Community: Venereal Disease and Society in Baroque Spain*
22 Elizabeth R. Wright, *The Epic of Juan Latino: Dilemmas of Race and Religion in Renaissance Spain*
23 Ryan D. Giles, *Inscribed Power: Amulets and Magic in Early Spanish Literature*
24 Jorge Pérez, *Confessional Cinema: Religion, Film, and Modernity in Spain's Development Years, 1960–1975*
25 Joan Ramon Resina, *Josep Pla: Seeing the World in the Form of Articles*
26 Javier Irigoyen-García, *"Moors Dressed as Moors": Clothing, Social Distinction, and Ethnicity in Early Modern Iberia*
27 Jean Dangler, *Edging toward Iberia*
28 Ryan D. Giles and Steven Wagschal (eds), *Beyond Sight: Engaging the Senses in Iberian Literatures and Cultures, 1200–1750*
29 Silvia Bermúdez, *Rocking the Boat: Migration and Race in Contemporary Spanish Music*
30 Hilaire Kallendorf, *Ambiguous Antidotes: Virtue as Vaccine for Vice in Early Modern Spain*
31 Leslie J. Harkema, *Spanish Modernism and the Poetics of Youth: From Miguel de Unamuno to* La Joven Literatura
32 Benjamin Fraser, *Cognitive Disability Aesthetics: Visual Culture, Disability Representations, and the (In)Visibility of Cognitive Difference*
33 Robert Patrick Newcomb, *Iberianism and Crisis: Spain and Portugal at the Turn of the Twentieth Century*
34 Sara J. Brenneis, *Spaniards in Mauthausen: Representations of a Nazi Concentration Camp, 1940–2015*
35 Silvia Bermúdez and Roberta Johnson (eds), *A New History of Iberian Feminisms*
36 Steven Wagschal, *Minding Animals in the Old and New Worlds: A Cognitive Historical Analysis*
37 Heather Bamford, *Cultures of the Fragment: Uses of the Iberian Manuscript, 1100–1600*
38 Enrique García Santo-Tomás (ed.), *Science on Stage in Early Modern Spain*
39 Marina S. Brownlee (ed.), *Cervantes'* Persiles *and the Travails of Romance*

40 Sarah Thomas, *Inhabiting the In-Between: Childhood and Cinema in Spain's Long Transition*

41 David A. Wacks, *Medieval Iberian Crusade Fiction and the Mediterranean World*

42 Rosilie Hernández, *Immaculate Conceptions: The Power of the Religious Imagination in Early Modern Spain*

43 Mary L. Coffey and Margot Versteeg (eds), *Imagined Truths: Realism in Modern Spanish Literature and Culture*

44 Diana Aramburu, *Resisting Invisibility: Detecting the Female Body in Spanish Crime Fiction*

www.ingramcontent.com/pod-product-compliance
Lightning Source LLC
LaVergne TN
LVHW090153080826
844660LV00013B/787/J